A Thousand Farewells

NAHLAH
AYED

A Thousand
Farewells

A Reporter's Journey
from Refugee Camp to the Arab Spring

VIKING

VIKING
an imprint of Penguin Canada

Published by the Penguin Group
Penguin Group (Canada), 90 Eglinton Avenue East, Suite 700, Toronto, Ontario, Canada M4P 2Y3
(a division of Pearson Canada Inc.)

Penguin Group (USA) Inc., 375 Hudson Street, New York, New York 10014, U.S.A.
Penguin Books Ltd, 80 Strand, London WC2R 0RL, England
Penguin Ireland, 25 St Stephen's Green, Dublin 2, Ireland (a division of Penguin Books Ltd)
Penguin Group (Australia), 250 Camberwell Road, Camberwell, Victoria 3124, Australia
(a division of Pearson Australia Group Pty Ltd)
Penguin Books India Pvt Ltd, 11 Community Centre, Panchsheel Park, New Delhi – 110 017, India
Penguin Group (NZ), 67 Apollo Drive, Rosedale, Auckland 0632, New Zealand
(a division of Pearson New Zealand Ltd)
Penguin Books (South Africa) (Pty) Ltd, 24 Sturdee Avenue, Rosebank,
Johannesburg 2196, South Africa

Penguin Books Ltd, Registered Offices: 80 Strand, London WC2R 0RL, England

First published 2012

1 2 3 4 5 6 7 8 9 10 (RRD)

Copyright © Nahlah Ayed, 2012

Manufactured in the U.S.A.

LIBRARY AND ARCHIVES CANADA CATALOGUING IN PUBLICATION

Ayed, Nahlah
A thousand farewells : a reporter's journey from refugee camp to the Arab spring / Nahlah Ayed.

Includes index.
ISBN 978-0-670-06909-5

1. Ayed, Nahlah. 2. Middle East—History—21st century.
3. Journalists—Canada—Biography. 4. Foreign correspondents—Canada—Biography.
5. Palestinian Canadians—Biography. I. Title.

PN4913.N39A3 2012   070.92   C2012-900364-6

Visit the Penguin Canada website at **www.penguin.ca**

Special and corporate bulk purchase rates available; please see
www.penguin.ca/corporatesales or call 1-800-810-3104, ext. 2477.

ALWAYS LEARNING   PEARSON

To my mother,
who taught me more languages than any school.
And to my father,
whose tenacious ambition underwrote our own.

CONTENTS

PROLOGUE

The white-clad, neatly uniformed policemen fanned out around the green lawn of the traffic circle, their eyes narrowed and spines stiffened by the presence of the riot police standing at the ready some distance away. They, in turn, were wrapped in padded black uniforms, their steady gazes already shielded by black helmets, their resolve steeled by their batons and their sheer numbers.

When the protesters finally appeared in Tahrir Square, there seemed to be little cause for concern. There were only a few dozen, though they were seething with accusations. They said security forces had prevented them from gathering in the first place, violently breaking up their gatherings even before the march started. They should have numbered in the thousands, they said. But once again, their best efforts at expressing dissent had been thwarted.

Those who had made it anyway began to round the circle in defiance, heading in the direction of a grotesquely oversized poster of President Hosni Mubarak. There were so few of them police didn't even bother stopping traffic, and cars inched slowly behind the protesters, honking incessantly. It wasn't clear whether the drivers were doing so in support or out of disdain—or simply as Cairenes normally would, even when they aren't stuck behind a bunch of troublemaking dissidents.

The protesters tried hard to make up for their shrunken rebellion: they shouted anti-Mubarak slogans, called for his downfall, and frantically waved their arms and placards in the air. Hordes of journalists with their cameras lined up to capture the scene to see for themselves the kind of crackdown Egyptian riot police had nearly perfected. Residents turned up on their balconies to observe, while a few Mubarak supporters tried to break it all up by waving pictures of their long-time president and trying to out-shout the mavericks with their own clever rhyming slogans.

The anti-Mubarak protesters came from all walks of life—teachers, engineers, stay-at-home mothers in hijabs—and most of them were young. Many of them carried round yellow stickers with their group's slogan emblazoned in red: "*Kefaya.*"

Enough.

The protesters had come to say they'd had enough of Mubarak, who had already been president for nearly a quarter-century, and who by then was seventy-seven years old. Mubarak's Egypt was rotting under the repression of an authoritarian and corrupt regime that stifled dissent and disregarded the people's most basic rights. The Egyptians he presided over were increasingly young, educated, religious, hopeless, and hungry. It was time to let someone else try.

Just then, a beat-up little car covered with pro-Mubarak slogans tried provocatively to make its way through the protesters. The white-clad police ran over and surrounded it, beating on top of the hood with the palms of their hands, at once begging and ordering the driver to make haste before he caused a confrontation. On one of the car's side windows was a neatly inscribed, red-and-white "Yes to Mubarak" poster. As the car passed through the crowd, a contrarian young woman slapped a yellow sticker right on top of it. Hers read "*Kefaya Istibdad.*" Enough tyranny.

Enough with the emergency law, the military trials, the indefinite imprisonment without charge. Enough with the repression of criticism and opposition of any kind.

The anti-Mubarak protesters fought one another for a moment to keep the more eager among them from attacking the bold little car with its confrontational messages. Sweaty young men spread their arms wide to try to contain the angry ones who wanted to pry that driver out of his car and teach him a lesson. "This is a peaceful protest," they yelled. Reason eventually prevailed, but only after a few tussles with the seemingly benign white-clad police.

But in Tahrir Square that day there would be no breaking of heads, no twisting of arms, no ramming of bodies into police trucks—the hallmarks of so many other Egyptian protests, every time anyone dared raise a defiant fist in the face of a despotic and neglectful regime. The world's media were here now, and there were limits to what Mubarak's machine was willing to do before the cameras to muzzle the discontent. That would come later, after the cameras had left and the world stopped paying attention.

It was 2005, and it was election day in Egypt. The first time Hosni Mubarak ever competed with anyone for the title of president.

⚔

In my experience, there are only two occasions when foreign TV crews are allowed to roam relatively free from the usual constraints of a Mideast country ruled by a dictator: wars and elections. The rest of the time, working in this part of the world is an exhausting obstacle course of visas, permits, explanations, minders—"tourist escorts"—policemen, and everything in between. So that fall, I was somewhat relieved when I had the opportunity to visit Egypt on the eve of its first contested presidential election since the 1950s. My cameraman and I escaped the usual maddening visit to the Information Ministry and were largely left alone on the streets.

Mubarak was more accustomed to referendums, in which voters had two choices: yes or no. He could always count on

winning an astounding percentage of the votes, as could Iraq's
Saddam Hussein and other leaders in the region who allowed a
vote of any kind. But those days were now ostensibly over in Egypt,
due in part to Washington and the pressure it applied to its friends
in the region to adopt reforms in the wake of September 11, and
thanks as well to the wake-up call provided by the overthrow of
Saddam. Mubarak now apparently had to work for those votes,
having implemented a controversial and largely cosmetic change
in the constitution earlier that year that allowed multi-party presidential elections. Mubarak the candidate appeared humble in slick
television ads as he explained his vision for the country to his fellow
citizens. His rivals did the same. But there was much to differen-
tiate this election from most other forms of what one might call a
democratic vote.

For one, Mubarak was still in charge of the rules. The consti-
tutional changes—which were put to a referendum that was also
tightly controlled—assured he would ultimately determine who
could form a party and who could run for office.

Once the campaign started, Mubarak, unlike all the other
candidates, had state resources working on his behalf. On election
day, opposition poll observers were harassed and barred from
entering some polling stations. Yet at one we visited, a throng of
Mubarak supporters gathered inside, openly greeting voters and
foreign media alike with pro-Mubarak ditties.

That's not to mention the allegations of vote-rigging and the
harassment of opposition voters, the absence of foreign election
observers, and the pathetic voter turnout. Then there were the
protests that were brutally shut down in the months prior to
the election; the campaign of arrests of opposition figures and
supporters; the detention without trial of so many others. The
Kefaya protesters desperately wanted the world to know all this—
that the vote was a farce, a cynical exercise in pretend democracy

aimed at a foreign audience. They'd gone to the streets to call for a boycott. But their voices were drowned on election day in a parade of fingers made purple by indelible ink and a cacophony of chatter about the dawn of freedom in Egypt.

On the ground, it was clear that the election was a highly imperfect exercise whose outcome was predetermined. But it was lauded by the international community as a step forward, another sign of a fledgling "Arab Spring."

But Mubarak won with nearly 90 percent of the vote, and Egyptian "democracy" suffered an unsurprising early death. The cameras gone, Mubarak's Egypt cracked down once again, then lumbered on as if nothing had happened.

The protesters waited for another day.

Just over five years later, that day came, and I made my way to an Egypt awash with anger. In late January 2011, tens of thousands of Egyptians took to the streets, engaging in running battles with torrential waves of black-clad police who seemed baffled by the protesters' resolve in the face of tear gas, batons and even bullets.

The uprising was not part of some grand design encouraged from the outside, as the authorities would have everyone believe. It was a peaceful people's uprising, unlike anything the modern Arab world had experienced in recent years, and very much the nightmare scenario that had long dogged the region's autocrats and compelled them to brutally discourage dissent and almost any form of political participation.

The protests that began in Tunisia and then spread to Egypt also moved on to Libya, Bahrain, Yemen, Jordan, the Palestinian Territories, Iraq, and even Syria. It was an awakening owned by the people of those countries alone. They willingly called it the Arab Spring.

Revolutions are always messy, no different in the case of the Arab world. The uprisings had mixed success—some brought down dictators, but some languished in a bloody morass that claimed the lives of thousands. Others petered out altogether.

But they all carried the same message: the status quo—the repression, the entrenched gloom—was no longer acceptable. And if you'd lived in the region for any length of time in the years and decades leading up to the Arab Spring, like I did, none of it came as a surprise.

ONE

My Father's Camera

The beautiful swore he wouldn't be perfect.
—ARAB PROVERB

As a child, I knew nothing of refugeehood and displacement; of grimy UN tents, kerosene lamps, and powdered milk; of children who for years refused to go to sleep without a loaf of bread in their clutches. Instead, I knew swaths of wide boulevards, blankets of green grass, and the warmth of central heating. I knew twenty-four-hour electricity and drinkable water that flowed from a tap. I knew bread could be had at Safeway.

I was born in Canada, in a modern hospital, into the hands of a qualified doctor. I lived in a modest but comfortable duplex on the corner of a quiet street in St-Boniface, then a suburb of Winnipeg. My earliest memories include a swing in front of the house on Archibald Street, a sandbox on the side, and a brand new bicycle to ride on the sidewalk around it. We went to a French school, regularly ate WigWags and Popsicles, sang Christmas carols, and did the Irish jig at school concerts.

That's what life looked like in 1975, when I was about five; that's how life was supposed to continue, eternally. In the snapshots of that life, captured by my dad's Kodak camera, my mother—a curvy woman who took care with her looks—figures prominently, flaunting her hair and full lips. She was a brilliant mother and homemaker. Forever she was supposed to pose flawlessly in fashionable outfits, hair and face perfectly made up, along with one or a few of the four of us kids, and often with pride of place given to a tremendous birthday cake she had made and decorated herself. Dad, dashing too, makes cameo appearances in our festive pictures. The hard-working provider is nearly always in a short-sleeved dress shirt, often with pens in his shirt pocket, just in case. In that world of mine at five years old, Dad was always going to be the busy, smiling assistant manager of a Chicken Delight restaurant.

In those years, life for us kids was about being well behaved. It was about sitting up straight, legs together, hands on laps. It was about keeping clothes clean, about speaking only when spoken to and playing only when given permission. That life was methodically chronicled by Dad's Kodak camera—always tucked in its hard brown leather case, but always at the ready for those spontaneous shots of grinning kids. *Say cheese!* Click.

At first it was just me and my sister, Ayeda, only a year apart, who smiled into its lens. Though Ayeda was older, she and I were often mistaken for twins, undoubtedly because Mom insisted on dressing us in matching outfits that she created out of her imagination, designing and sewing them herself. But we looked nothing alike if you inspected us closely: my sister was born nearly bald, while I was born with a substantial tuft of dark hair. Her eyes were almond-shaped, and mine were round. I had pudgy cheeks and paler skin. She had an elegant nose and her skin had a beautiful olive hue. What we did have in common was our birth month, April, which we also shared with our mother and father. We couldn't wait for April. It was full of birthdays and cake and more pictures.

My first brother, Ayed, arrived one March and made his debut in our photo albums. Shortly thereafter, my parents made him sit up and the three of us posed together. It was just the three of us for some years, until our second brother was born, much later.

Abdullah inherited recessive genes and turned out blond and blue-eyed. His hair was so fine and golden my mother cut a ringlet of it and put it away as a keepsake. But then you don't see much of him in our family pictures after he was a toddler—when our lives had dramatically changed, and taking pictures had become a luxury.

Before all that, life was about having the Jolicoeurs as neighbours and waif-like Jeanette as my best friend. It was about singing French children's rhymes with Jeanette and recording them on tape (which still exists somewhere in my mother's vast collection of life's artefacts). It was about snowy, cozy winters and brilliantly wide prairie summer mornings.

It was also about excelling at school—it was *always* about excelling at school, even if school was only kindergarten. It was also about after-school lessons, written neatly on a chalkboard hung on the back of the basement door.

Funny alphabet. Stubbornly curling in the wrong direction, defying what we learned at school. The teacher—my mother—lectured with an apron on, in between her chores in the small white kitchen. She tried to persuade the skeptics before her that their lives depended on learning this language. She was determined: "*Aleph, Baa, Taa* … again." And again. Until we knew the whole Arabic alphabet by heart.

We were blithely unaware of who and what we were, and what our gentle parents had gone through when they were children. We didn't know we were different. Our names were the only giveaway, but few kids of five and six and seven knew enough yet to pick us out of the annual class picture. That would come later.

In that world, it was perfectly natural to us that at home we were spoken to mostly in Arabic and answered in English, and at school we spoke French. Little in our home gave away our heritage, save for the sheen of faintly olive skin and the blazing red *hatta*—better known as a *kaffiyeh*—that my first brother would wear only for the Kodak pictures. Lebanon's Fairouz, one of the Middle East's most revered singers, crooned from Mom's tape player on many afternoons—as did Egyptian singers Mohammed Abd al-Wahab, Abdel Halim Hafez, and Oum Kolthoum, lamenting lost lovers, lost lands, happier times. But so did Tom Jones and, repeatedly, B. J. Thomas, many years after "Raindrops Keep Fallin' on My Head" was number one on the Billboard Hot 100.

We did, however, know that we had a "home" away from home. We had been there on a visit, in 1973, though none of us kids remembered it. The Kodak pictures, cleverly noting the date, created the memory: all of us in Amman and Kuwait with people we knew we were supposed to love, although we didn't know why. People like my grandmother and my uncle and my aunts on my mother's side. People to whom my mother wrote letters and sent pictures, and occasionally strained to hear over the phone. They existed, but only on the margins of our capacious imaginations.

In those Winnipeg days, Eid was a memorable occasion, but so were Christmas and Easter. But we had no church or mosque services to attend, no weddings to which to bring gifts. In Canada, our little family existed alone, a tiny island that had broken off from the mainland and moored far away. We had no relatives to have over for coffee and gossip, no nosy second cousins to hide from. There were, of course, the handful of Arab families with whom my parents occasionally socialized, people who embodied that invisible line dividing the Jolicoeurs and us—the same line that separated me from pigtailed Andrea, my best friend at kinder-garten. One of those family friends was Uncle Bassam, whose oud playing would occasionally transport us to the world from which we hailed. No one was named Andrea or Jeanette there; they were called Fatima and Aysha and Souad. The solemn conversations the adults had during such visits left us perplexed. But soon we would be beckoned by their children and their unfamiliar toys, and drawn back to a place where there were no lines: the secret and mesmerizing world of children.

Those were the best years.

⚮

They were good years for my parents too. But complicated.

They immigrated to Canada in 1966, having given up on a life they started together in Germany because they felt unwelcome there. Both were Palestinian, both had lived as refugees, and both were anomalies in a Western environment then. Canada promised a more comfortable existence, and Hassan and Nariman arrived and soon acquired citizenship. Winnipeg still wasn't exactly the most hospitable place for Arab immigrants either: it was frighteningly cold, and devoid of anything even remotely familiar—never mind other Arabs. When one day they heard a man swearing in their mother tongue on the street, they latched on to him for dear life, and he became one of their closest friends.

My parents rented a small apartment downtown, and they both took jobs: Mom as a seamstress in a sewing factory, and Dad initially as a galvanizer. They worked hard and saved so they could buy their first house. When my sister was born, my mother turned her attention to raising a family, leaving the breadwinning to my father. Shortly afterwards, they bought that house.

Their conversation about how to raise their children started in those early days at the house on Archibald Street. In short, they felt they needed to take some precautions if they were going to raise us in the West. It had nothing to do with religion—neither of my parents was religious—but it did have to do with values and traditions, with ensuring that we did not forget our roots. So they agreed they would move the family "home" one day so the children could learn the values our parents, as Arabs, held dear.

By the end of 1975, with the arrival of Abdullah, there were four of us. And with every month that passed—and with every perfect English word we uttered and every mannerism we affected—they fretted. How were they going to ensure that their children grew up with the values and discipline they expected when they were living among the bell-bottom generation? My parents felt an urgent need to pre-empt rebelliousness. To do that, they believed that more than just their guidance was required. They decided that we needed to be immersed in the culture in which they had grown up.

It was a difficult decision, because my parents enjoyed their life in Canada. They had many Canadian friends and assimilated well with their neighbours, co-workers, and the parents of our schoolmates. But like many immigrants, they couldn't help comparing the Western world to the world they knew. Here, the streets were surely bigger and meaner. School discipline was clearly laxer. There was far more crime, wasn't there? And far too many temptations. The social homogeneity they were accustomed to at home was largely absent. They were also under pressure—from within and from relatives back home—to prove they were still committed to the values with which their own parents raised them, despite their choice of residence.

Those values, in those years, dictated certain practices and prohibited others. Dating, for example, was forbidden. Elderly parents were to be cherished and taken care of, not placed in an old folks' home. Drinking alcohol and using drugs were frowned upon. Moving out at eighteen was unheard of, especially if you were a woman. The long list of rules was all but impossible to enforce in a country like Canada—where, it seemed to many an immigrant, virtually nothing was taboo.

I clearly remember—the way you do as a child when you register a significant moment—my father explaining to a family friend his concerns about our future. "I don't want my girl to grow up thinking that rolling up a package of cigarettes in her stocking is okay," he said. So my parents decided to take the kids "home." Just for a while. Just long enough for us to grow up and be old enough to *understand*.

At the time, we were too young to understand. All I remember is the sudden urgency with which we divested ourselves of all that was ours in that life: the bicycles, the car, the toys, and, eventually, the little house on Archibald Street. All that remained were the pictures.

⚘

My parents knew all about refugee camps, about UN rations, about hunger. They knew what it was to lose a loved one to a mundane disease or everyday violence. They knew tragedy well because, in their early years, it visited often.

My father, Hassan, was one of only three of sixteen children who survived past infancy. My grandmother Abbasah's fertile years were alternating periods of mourning and futile pregnancies. The rest were marked by poverty and dispossession. By the time I met her she had long been a broken woman, blinded by the years and ravaged by illness and displacement. She was largely incapacitated and was forever stowed in a corner of the family's dark Amman home, from which I never once saw her emerge. I also rarely saw her smile; I don't think she remembered how.

My grandfather Abdullah was, by many accounts, a stubborn, wiry man with an impressive capacity for back-breaking labour. By the time I met him, he too was mostly incapacitated, made lean by the years. He had a perfectly shaped bald head, on which he always wore a knitted cap and, on the rare occasions he went out, a white kaffiyeh. He was the first grown man I'd ever seen cry.

Abdullah's family came originally from the suburbs of Jerusalem. A petty feud split the village and sent half its residents packing in an effort to escape an apparent curse levelled at them by a village elder. And so began the first journey in a family history often interrupted by movement.

Abdullah's family settled in Annabah, a tiny farming community just west of modern-day Tel Aviv and its Mediterranean climate, and a stone's throw from the Latrun monastery and its French-inspired underground winery. The town had its own cemetery and a solitary boys' school, one that my father attended until near the end of grade four. The inhabitants spent their days working the land, and their kerosene-lit nights talking, eating, and gathering at the cafe to listen to the one radio the village owned.

Abdullah planted sesame, wheat, barley, corn, and sundry fruits and vegetables. In Annabah all good things came from the land—flour, olive oil, *tahina*, butter, and wine, which my grandfather apparently drank for its health benefits. Annabah's families had Jewish neighbours with whom they got along. Then war came and everything changed.

With two cows and few other belongings, Abdullah and his family walked away on foot to escape the fighting. They reached what would later be called the West Bank, and with some relatives, they moved into a cave on the side of a mountain to wait out the cold and what they still believed was temporary displacement. The cave was cold, dark, and drafty, but it was free and provided shelter from the elements. Making a living was a bigger challenge, and Abdullah was forced to sell his precious cows. My father, Hassan, and his elder brother, Hussein, then resorted to prowling the countryside, digging into hardened soil to find the dry roots of dead trees to sell as firewood. When they had gathered enough, Abdullah's only daughter, Nehmah, set off with a tangle of twisted wood balanced on top of her head to sell in bustling Ramallah. She brought back just enough coins at the end of the day to keep the family fed.

The wait to go home grew longer than anyone expected. The next winter was harsher and the cave became inhospitable, so they rented a home in a nearby village, becoming tenants for the first time in their lives in a culture that valued land ownership above virtually all else. When UN workers passed through months later and invited the displaced to move to a new refugee camp near Jericho, Abdullah and his family gladly took up the offer. It was 1950. They accepted a free ride into the lowest point on earth, and into one of the darkest chapters of their lives.

Ω

Initially, Nueimah was a collection of sorry tents that barely kept out the elements, stretching as far as the eye could see. Mercifully, the winters were mild in the Jericho area, which had long been a haven for affluent Palestinians from the higher and colder regions. But in that first winter, the new residents of the Nueimah refugee camp endured a freak snowstorm, the first in half a century in one of the hottest places on earth, and under the weight of the snow, Abdullah's tent collapsed right on top of them. If they doubted it before, the family was now certain that the curse levelled at their ancestors had followed them even 260 metres below sea level.

In time, Nueimah became a festering mess of disease, marital problems, overcrowding, and wretched poverty. But there were some advantages to living under the auspices of the UN. Each family regularly received food rations, and there was a clinic and a school. In Nueimah, my father alone was finally allowed to return to his studies. He briefly dabbled in the Arab nationalist cause through his best friend, Muhammed. Many a night, Muhammed would invite Hassan to his home to listen to informal lectures given by Muhammed's relative, Abu Oraib, an unapologetic atheist, a prolific writer, and a philosopher who lived in Amman but occasionally visited family in Nueimah. For Hassan, though, it was just a dalliance. He worked feverishly to become, at the age of twenty-one, the first in his family to complete high school, eight years after they'd walked out of their village.

By then, the war had ended under a UN armistice agreement that stopped the bloodshed—but not the animosity between Arab countries and Israel, their new neighbour. Still, there were no signs that the refugees, many of them guarding keys to their homes, would ever be repatriated. The camp adapted to the reality, and eventually tents were replaced by solid structures and alleys became narrow roads. This was simultaneously a blessing and a curse: it gave the refugees some independence and stability, but it also underscored the permanence of their displacement. The savings that had been hidden in the folds of blankets or the bosoms of older women were traded for corrugated zinc and bricks made from sand, and camp residents hired men to mould it all into homes. For the first time in nearly a decade, Abdullah's family had a couple of rooms to call their own.

Money continued to be a problem, however. Hussein, the eldest son, tried working in nearby Jordan (which ruled the West Bank then), as did my father for a time, accepting employment as one of the thousands of coffee boys who, even today, fetch tiny cups of the brew for storeowners and their clientele throughout the Middle East. Later, the family acquired a mule, which the boys put to work as paid transport. Hussein and Nehmah married cousins, also a brother and a sister. Hassan focused instead on finding a way to leave the camp. Other men were finding work abroad—some in job-rich Arab Gulf countries, and others as far away as Australia and the United States. Hassan wanted to do the same.

Eventually, Hassan joined a group of eighteen young men who had been promised passage to Europe by a Lebanese tourism company. They travelled to Beirut, where they were put on a ship— the first time for most of them—that embarked on a meandering journey through a series of Mediterranean ports before landing, finally, at Marseille. The young refugees dispersed without any assistance or knowledge of the local language. My father took a train to the home of friends in Germany, who took him to the immigration authorities to apply for the residency visa he needed to work legally.

At the immigration bureau, the Germans discovered that Hassan didn't have an entry stamp in his passport, meaning he had entered the country illegally and would most likely be deported back to the squalor from which he had come. The eighteen others suffered that very fate, given only temporary visitor visas that would not allow them to work. My father was luckier. The immigration agent interviewed him at length, begging him to reveal just how he managed to get into the country without the requisite entry stamp. The official dangled before him a compelling incentive: if he revealed his secret—no matter how underhanded his ploy—he would be granted the work permit anyway.

As he always did, Hassan told the truth: when the border official walked through the train to stamp passengers' passports, he happened to be in the loo. By doing his business at the wrong time, he had become an illegal immigrant, and he lacked the language skills to correct the situation.

As promised, Hassan got his permit and set about earning a living. He was embarking on a life abroad that spanned the rest of his years, sparing him, and his children, the hopelessness that was the fate of so many others who never managed to either improve their lives, or get out.

⚸

My maternal grandmother, Nazmiyah, was a naturally free spirit, one who wore humour like a favourite sweater. She had a dazzling presence, loved to laugh, and had a gift for making children laugh with her. She loved singing even more and had a brassy voice, sonorous as a church bell. I loved my grandmother. At times she was the lone ambassador of hope in our lives, when most everyone else brought only bitterness.

Underneath her cheerful demeanour, however, Nazmiyah still possessed an inner tumult, her face lined by time and occasionally crestfallen by painful recall. Her grievous loss as a young wife marked the start of a bleak life for my mother and her siblings. But her constant defiance taught her children, and later her grandchildren, the importance of making the most of what you have.

Nazmiyah was born in Wadi Hunayn, a well-to-do village southeast of Tel Aviv. Its residents were city-dwellers, or *madaniyeen*, their dialect and manner more cosmopolitan than that of the farmers, or *falaheen*. Photographs of the women of the family, in elaborate dresses and carefully coiffed hair, suggest a fairly liberal upbringing. But tradition still ruled. So, like her older sisters, Nazmiyah married young to a handsome, much taller man many years her senior, a member of the British Palestine Police Force. Hafez (the son of an anti-British agitator who regularly distributed pamphlets condemning colonial rule) came from the nearby village of Rantiya. Hafez avoided politics, and when the troubles started with the British, he quit his job with the Palestine police.

In 1948, as war advanced in their direction, Hafez and Nazmiyah decided to leave, carrying just a few of their belongings—they were certain they would be back. A pregnant Nazmiyah hustled her girls into Hafez's jeep, and they drove off amid a frenzy of others fleeing on foot. Nazmiyah had no idea that it would be her final journey in that jeep, or that it would be the last time she laid eyes on Hafez. He deposited Nazmiyah and her children in a tiny village away from harm. Then he turned around, apparently to try to locate his own parents. He never returned.

Evidently because of advancing danger, Nazmiyah was forced to walk to another village in the future West Bank. Along the way, she gave birth to a son under the shade of a tree, attended to by strangers. She named her son Rajaee, meaning "my wish," "my hope." She then joined her own displaced family at a refugee camp in Amman, where she started a frantic search for her husband. She was there whenever there was news of a prisoner release. And she was in constant contact with the Red Cross, writing them letter after letter pleading for assistance. But the years passed without a hint to suggest that Hafez was even alive. Barely twenty, Nazmiyah was a single mother of three and already a widow.

After a few years, Nazmiyah was pressured to remarry. A husband was eventually found, a kind older gentleman who had no children of his own. She married, quietly. And just as quietly, she ceded control of her children and started a young family anew.

According to tradition, custody of Hafez's children—Nawzat, Rajaee, and my mother, Nariman—went to his family. It was the second time they lost the most important person in their lives. My mother was only five. Her sister, at nine, was fully aware of the magnitude of the decision, and within minutes of arriving at their uncle's she was at work in what would essentially become a servant's existence.

Nariman's main memories are of a concrete block of a house in Al-Wihdat, a refugee camp in Amman built by the United Nations Relief and Works Agency (UNRWA) to house Palestinian refugees. She knew that she was an orphan, and that the head of the household was her uncle, not her father. She knew that she had a mother: she would occasionally be taken to see Nazmiyah, who was often prosperously attired, always in a light fog of sweet-smelling perfume. The visits always had an end, when Nariman and her siblings were forced to return to their role as burdensome orphans.

Largely for economic reasons, the three children were pulled out of school at the end of their elementary education and put to work—Nariman and Nawzat at home, and Rajaee on the streets selling newspapers. Rajaee grew up and rebelled, eventually running away to live with the mother who had named him. The girls stayed behind, praying for early marriage.

They learned to take care of each other. For comfort, they listened religiously to the radio, and the music it brought gave them access to a happier world. At night they listened to Oum Kolthoum, the Arab world's most revered singer, live from Cairo. Nariman fell hopelessly in love with her songs and memorized the words, many of which were written by Ahmad Rami and Ahmad Shawqi, two of the most prolific Arab poets of modern times. Nariman sang with the same brassy voice her mother possessed, and like her, she was always naturally in tune.

Eventually, Nawzat got married and moved to Jericho— the Nueimah camp—with her new husband, Muhammed. She suffered a series of failed pregnancies. So the next time she became pregnant, Nariman was sent to live with her in the hope her assistance would help her sister carry a baby to term.

Their mother, Nazmiyah, started a new family, then lost the eldest of those children, Naheel, my mother's half-sister, to a piece of shrapnel in one of the sporadic clashes between Palestinian guerrillas and the Jordanian army. In search of a better, quieter life, Nazmiyah's new family, along with her son Rajaee, moved to Kuwait. Nothing more was ever found out about the fate of her first husband, and the subject was rarely discussed. But his disappearance continued to cast a shadow on his children. The damage they suffered strained their relationship with their mother as adults, and left a lifetime of questions for the next generation—my own— who grew up with refugees as parents.

Hafez might have been pleased, many decades later, that the handful of black-and-white snapshots of him that survived the family's displacements have been contemplated by dozens of his descendants. I, like the others, have brooded over them in a vain attempt to breathe life into the almond-eyed man in the police uniform. In one of several cross-generational attempts to learn his fate, I once sent scanned copies of his pictures to the Palestine Police Old Comrades Association. A retired officer from Hereford surmised that Hafez had been a sergeant in the supernumerary police—a group of watchmen who had some police powers and were answerable to the police authority. The English officer helped me place a query in the association's newsletter, asking for any information about my grandfather, but none came.

𝓍

Once in Germany, my father worked in the steel business and for years sent money back home to his family in Nueimah. At the unusually late age of twenty-eight, he decided that it was time to marry and proudly drove his own car all the way from Germany to Jericho to begin his search for a partner. In the end he would choose Nariman—niece to Abu Oraib, whose lectures Hassan had listened to as a young man in Jericho's dimly lit shacks, and sister to Nawzat, who had married his best friend from high school, Muhammed. Within weeks they were wed, and Dad's Kodak camera first captured Mom shyly standing next to the ruins of Hisham's Palace in Jericho. Then they set out by car back to Germany, where their nomadic life together, away from the terrible memories of refugee camps, began.

Refugees by Design

*He who is jinxed, is jinxed—even if you hang a
lantern at his door.*
—ARAB PROVERB

AMMAN, JORDAN, 1976

I remember clearly the first time we entered the refugee camp, in
the dead of night. I was only six, but I remember getting out of
the taxi and briefly hanging on to my father's shoulder while my
mother carried our youngest brother. I was struck by the darkness
that swallowed us. I remember looking down and discovering a
little river that smelled horribly. I remember having to walk a long
way, the taxi driver helping with our many bags, my parents taking
turns sighing. I felt dread for the first time in my life. But more than
anything, I remember noting the evidence of the finality of our
move. We had *sold* things. We had come a long, long way with large
suitcases stuffed with summer *and* winter clothes, and only our best
toys—the rest were now someone else's. I remember Dad knocking
loudly on a metal door dotted with rusted bullet holes, and strange
people opening it with astonishment. Then I remember nothing
as I slipped into a deep, jet-lagged sleep for what seemed like days.

Though none of us kids had ever lived in Jordan—neither had
my father, who immigrated to Germany long before his family was

forced to leave Nueimah during the 1967 war between Israel and its Arab neighbours—this apparently was, for lack of another, our "home." And it was in Sido Abdullah's house that we took our first steps as refugees by design.

It was an uncomfortable welcome to what was an already overcrowded house. Uncle Hussein was firmly in charge and determined the affairs of everyone within it. This included his own large family, as well as my grandparents Sido Abdullah and Sitto Abbasah, who were well into old age. Also living there at the time was Dad's sister, my *amto*, or aunty, Nehmah, who was now a divorcee with two teenage boys. We were offered a small room off the main *hoshe*, or courtyard, where we staked out a corner for ourselves among the bags of rice, dried lentils, and beans that my uncle sold in the market.

The camp was officially known as Amman New Camp, though by the time we got to it, there was nothing new about it. In Arabic it was insipidly named Al-Wihdat, or the Units, and it was administered at the time by UNRWA. Initially built in 1955 in southeast Amman to accommodate only five thousand Palestinian refugees, it already had many times that number when we first set eyes on it in 1976. The original makeshift homes had with time morphed into unsightly concrete structures, many with corrugated zinc roofs and few windows. Some had become even more permanent, sprouting second storeys to accommodate married sons and their many, many children.

Mud figured prominently in Al-Wihdat, especially in the wet, windy winters. The unpaved alleys were simply seas of *wahl*, with suction so strong it was easy to lose a shoe. Garbage was everywhere: paper and plastic bags, wrappers of all kinds, discarded clothing, tattered notebooks, a lone shoe. The edge of the camp opened onto a small field where residents who had them took their goats and cattle to feed. While the few plants served as an appetizer for the thin animals, the vast buffet of refugee garbage deposited there daily offered a substantial main course. We were amazed at the number of animals we came across in Al-Wihdat: goats, pigeons, and lots and lots of chickens that roamed freely. Some of the animals were domesticated, others raised for sale, and still others dragged from house to house to milk on the spot for cash. Then there were the cats: thousands of refugee cats that boldly prowled the neighbourhood—thinking nothing of stealing into your kitchen to fetch some food, or of spending hours howling at each other while you tried to sleep at night. Some days a walk through the camp felt like a visit to the Winnipeg Zoo. But there we could never get this close, or gleefully feed the goats Kleenex without retribution. One of the early Kodak pictures captured my brother standing next to a skinny goat, smiling at the novelty.

Along the main road into the camp were the little *dukkanahs*— corner stores that sold the basics, along with a surprising variety of cheap, colourful unwrapped candy. Alongside the stores were the tiny *fawwal* stalls—which were where you got hummus, falafel, and fava beans for breakfast, and where rumpled boys lined up in the early mornings with empty bowls brought from home. I eventually learned to stand there myself, whiling away time watching falafel balls bob in the searing hot oil.

The camp was dominated by the boys' and girls' schools, as well as the bustling covered souk. That's where Uncle Hussein maintained his *basta*, the stand where he sold grains, flour, and other dry goods, which he shovelled out of large brown sacks and weighed on an old-fashioned scale. The *basta* was an ideal spot from which to watch the refugees walk by and sample every foul smell the market had to offer. The souk was a place where underwear, live chickens, and bell-bottom jeans coexisted, where stall-keepers advertised their wares at the top of their lungs. It was such a busy place, you couldn't fully extend your stride, even as a child. In those early days, when we could still pretend this was only a badly planned vacation, Dad and I, hand in hand, would inch our way towards the *basta* to visit. We walked in the footsteps of broken men in full-length *dishdashas*, towing behind them wives, children, sometimes an animal or two, trodding a path between rolls of gaudy material, piles of straw mats, and the kidneys, innards, and goats' heads on offer for the evening meal.

"Dad, what are those?"

"Intestines. They're very good. Amto Nehmah will stuff some for you one day."

"Ugh."

ௐ

By many accounts, Uncle Hussein had always been difficult. He was deeply suspicious of everyone and had a fiery temper and a will that could never bend. He was born combative, rarely laughing unless to mock. His default mode was antagonistic: towards his siblings and even his own children. He was accusatory and judgmental, and in his home, his word was law. He often yelled at my father in our presence, dressing him down as if he were a wayward son. It was not a happy home. And we all grew to loathe it.

Mom and Dad had come with plans to buy land to build a house on the outskirts of the Jordanian capital. My grandfather talked my father out of it: it was too expensive, too far from the family. Sido Abdullah advised Dad to stay in Amman, and specifically in Al-Wihdat. To our consternation, Hassan obeyed his father's wishes.

Dad repeatedly pointed out that this "repatriation" was for our sake, but even as a child I found that assertion illogical. I could vaguely understand that it was for my own good when my mother forced a spoonful of cough medicine into my mouth. But no matter which way I turned it in my head, I could not fathom how bringing us to a rat-infested, cockroach-ridden, and cramped refugee camp was for our own good. I concluded within days of our arrival that we kids must have done something so terribly wrong that Al-Wihdat was the only suitable punishment.

Other Arabs—and certainly other refugees—would have given anything to have the safe and secure home we had in Canada. Yet Mom and Dad were giving it all up for the sake of a history lesson. One relative was brave enough to point out how far we'd fallen— but there were nods of approval from most of the others, who believed my parents had done "the right thing" for their children. By returning to Jordan, we could appreciate our culture, meet our relatives, and learn our native language. Most important, we could learn about our roots.

My parents were hardly alone in taking such drastic measures. Recent immigrants to North America—among them many Arabs and Muslims—are often driven to reclaim their heritage in just the same way. Parents worry that by raising children in an adopted country, they may have single-handedly undone generations of tradition, religion, and family history. No immigrant, no matter how open-minded, wants to be that person. There are always questions: Was it wrong to deny their children the opportunity to grow up among people who speak their mother tongue? Was it wrong to deny them the reassuring warmth of a large extended family, with all the support that comes with that? Did they let down their own parents by allowing their children to be assimilated into a foreign society—one that may even be despised back "home"?

Panicked, many of them choose to go home, sometimes permanently. Others remain abroad, but try, often in vain, to contain the "damage" by circling their wagons. We knew such families. They would do it as soon as their children began spending more time with other people's children, or came under the influence of "foreign" teachers, coaches, music instructors, and mentors. These parents would react by pulling the shutters closed in the very country that had welcomed them with open doors. Later, I was thankful that—hard as it was—my parents chose to temporarily dislocate us, rather than keep us in Canada and pretend we didn't live there.

My parents were mostly motivated by a sense of responsibility. They did what they thought was right for us, and for them. And though I endlessly questioned their decision and resented it for many years as a child, as an adult I understood the logic behind it—though I still didn't condone it.

𝓍

As the scene of our initiation into camp life, the family house was tense, but for children it was an amusing place to start. It always smelled of the grains and flour that my uncle peddled at his *basta*. And strangely, it had its own primitive bomb shelter underground, although we were never allowed to explore it. The small courtyard, the *hoshe*, was where I first witnessed the slaying of a goat and the fruitless struggle of chickens long after they had been beheaded, heralding the start of preparations for dinner. We were also introduced to the thousands of rules—*adat wa takaleed* (habits and traditions)—that dictate the behaviour of Arabs in our circles. Our immersion among our extended family also taught us how adults fight, and how easily Arab men cry.

In Uncle Hussein's place, we encountered for the first time the ritual of standing before Mecca, bowing and prostrating to Allah. We studied the prayer mats, the ubiquitous portable carpets that Arab Muslims use five times a day. We were as fascinated by the prayer beads that my grandfather and later my uncle would worry as they contemplated the beginning of a new day, muttering prayers under their breath. It was the first time, save for picnics in the park back home, that we'd sat down on the floor to eat, with the only available utensils our own hands. It was also the first time in memory that we came face to face with children of our own bloodline.

We discovered over time that we had not just first cousins but also second and third and tenth cousins, as well as uncles of all manner of dress, education, attitude, and religiosity. Our first cousins were raised on the *basta*, under the lashing force of my uncle's leather belt and petulant tongue. The girls were far meeker than the boys, but could be just as cruel. Except for Fayzah, the eldest. A mysterious ailment early in life left her with the use of only one eye. The other was permanently shut, forever ending any visions of marriage she might have had. But it didn't impede her tireless housework, nor did it limit her kindness. Some of her siblings, though, were ruthless. My nearest contemporary among them was particularly antagonistic, and not long after we arrived, she challenged me to a street fight. To this day, I do not know the reason. (Thankfully it was aborted when a passing young man slapped us both in the face to stop us.) Our other cousins mocked our English conversations and our attachment to our mother. They made fun of our difficulties with the unfamiliar meaty food, and especially with the custom of eating by hand. They clearly despised what must have appeared to them as our haughtiness. The fact that we wouldn't face the hole-in-the-ground bathroom—and its cockroaches—on our own at night was the subject of endless taunting and snickering.

For me and my sister, it was the first time we saw girls of our own age wrapping their heads before going out and inexplicably wearing *pants* under their sundresses. In that house, we learned how traditional Palestinian women like my aunt dressed. We watched with curiosity as she put on a thick-latticed cap laced with old coins, then pulled her light white scarf over it. We learned the difference between an everyday black embroidered dress and the cheery off-white one with the elaborate red stitching, saved only for the most important of occasions. Naturally, those were Eid and weddings.

In that house, we also began to acclimatize to the prevailing mood of brooding, lament, and disappointment. Everyone was so *serious*. Melancholy. Out-loud laughter was frowned upon, even rude. And if you happened to lapse and laugh hard, you'd better pray for god to deliver you from the evil that it could bring.

�

Thankfully, Dad soon found a small house for us to rent a stone's throw from my uncle's hellhole. But like all homes in Al-Wihdat, it was a hellhole in its own right. It had two rooms and a small concrete yard—with no real kitchen. It also had its very own hole-in-the-ground toilet—with its own native cockroaches—for our exclusive use. Still, it was close to our family and close to where my mother grew up, at the home of her own uncle, which she so happily left behind more than a decade earlier. It was also within walking distance of the schools we would soon attend. Most important, it was available and cheap. Sido Abdullah approved. We were making do in the pursuit of what we were told was a greater good.

Learning about our culture somehow meant being punted back into the Dark Ages. We had no furniture, save for a large playpen to which our little blond-haired, blue-eyed brother was often confined. During the day, we sat on the thin mattresses that at the time were so ubiquitous in Palestinian households; these were set upon straw carpets that did little to protect our feet from the cold concrete floors. At night, the mattresses doubled as our beds. Where was our dining table? Our living room set? Most important, why didn't we have real beds like we did back home? There were no answers.

There was, of course, also the matter of the "bathroom"—the word in itself an overstatement for what we had. If we went at night without discovering we were in the company of a cockroach or two, then the gods were smiling upon us. Shortly after we moved in, the hole in the ground also once produced a large rat. My mother chased it out of the house with a broom, a sight that left us terrified and hysterical. I secretly vowed never to go in there again. A short while later, I inevitably had to renege.

I'm sure that if I'd never laid eyes on it, I wouldn't have believed that a place such as Al-Wihdat existed. And if it weren't teeming with people, you would never believe that anyone would willingly live there. It was apparent to me even as a child that Al-Wihdat was horribly overcrowded. Behind virtually every door, it was not unusual to find a household of ten, sometimes more. Children upon children, so many they were essentially raising each other. In such close quarters, privacy was as elusive as the sunshine. It seemed necessary—unavoidable—for everyone to know everyone else's business. The arguments between the husband and wife who lived next door crashed like a waterfall over the thin wall that separated our two houses. Gossip, naturally, was the camp's favourite pastime. Some of our relatives made it their duty to know precisely what we were doing, and they often deployed their hapless children on missions to find out. Now that we were "back," everyone—including Sido Abdullah and Uncle Hussein—had opinions on everything concerning our lives.

We were not allowed to play outside, period. My mother was so adamant about that, she once granted us every child's desire: the permission to write, paint, and scribble on the peeling paint of one of the "living room" walls. There were too many dangers beyond our corroded metal door, including the *wahl*, a maze of alleys in which we could easily get lost, and the many rough kids who could, in one afternoon, undo all my mother's careful rearing. Kids like Abu Khnaneh. That wasn't his real name; it's what my mother called him. *Khnaneh* is a colloquial word for snot. The kid always had dirty clothes on and half an inch of mucus hanging from his nose, no matter the time of day or the weather. It enraged my mother. If she saw him hovering near our door, she would order him to go home and blow his nose. Infuriatingly, Abu Snot would just stand there and stare: dirty clothes, *khnaneh*, and all.

It is remarkable in hindsight how quickly we adapted to a life so alien to us. My sister and I were enrolled at the local school, which was operated by UNRWA. (In defining who was a Palestinian refugee, the organization included the descendants of persons who became refugees in 1948. So we qualified for enrolment.) It was a girls-only school, with an all-female staff in a decaying, frigid building with a bathroom so unsightly you simply waited until you went home. And like all the other refugettes, we lined up in the rain once a week to receive our own share of the generous assistance funnelled to needy Palestinians in the diaspora—a warm glass of milk and a single pungent capsule of fish oil.

There were constant reminders of the events that led to the creation of this hovel we now unluckily called home. No child grew up in Al-Wihdat without knowing their family history, the name of their ancestral village, and how and why the family left. The culture, the very air, was one of remembrance: at weddings, at funerals, especially in the graffiti that often adorned the camp's concrete walls.

Needless to say, Al-Wihdat was a cauldron of discontent, as was every one of the nine other official Palestinian camps in Jordan. Young men seemed restless and forever angry. Older ones were weighed down by the daily toil of earning a living, mostly working odd jobs in construction or, predictably, as my father did for a while, in the taxi business. Many families—most—relied on UN rations, which helped ease the poverty. Medical care was scarce and expensive. The simple task of getting any kind of official paper—a driver's licence, a birth certificate, or heaven forbid, a passport—was a months-long, humiliating process. Hopelessness was a way of life, resignation the only way to cope.

The answer for many was to leave if they could, chasing prosperity in the Gulf nations or beyond, if possible. On top of everything families had to endure living in a place like Al-Wihdat, they also often had to cope with the pain of separation.

The Arab men we encountered seemed a shadow of the sort we studied about in school—the historic figures of the Arab and Muslim renaissance—or those we heard about in family lore, such as my maternal great-grandfather, whom we were told was a writer and an agitator, a critic of British rule who regularly penned unsigned, scathing diatribes that were distributed by hand. His distinctive penmanship became such a liability he apparently learned to write pamphlets using his foot, holding a pen between his toes, to elude recognition. He was eventually captured by the British and exiled to another city, only allowed to return to Rantiya when he was dead.

By contrast, men in Al-Wihdat seemed defeated, depressed, and weak. It seemed that every man had a grievance—had been wronged by the authorities, by his family, simply by fate, or all of the above. Preoccupied with earning a living, they could do little about it but complain.

There was certainly no love lost in the camps for the repressive Jordanian authorities or the reigning King Hussein. The Palestine Liberation Organization, which had based itself in Jordan, had been routed just five years earlier and forced to relocate to Lebanon in an episode of violence that saw thousands killed and left bitterness among Palestinians. And though most refugees were able to acquire Jordanian citizenship—many of them did after Jordan took control of the West Bank—they were still treated as second-class citizens. Their opportunities were limited, whether they were trying to join the army or attain a place at university. Dissent wasn't tolerated, and if you tried anyway, you risked being picked up by the vast network of *mukhabarat*, or intelligence officers. If you were lucky, you'd get sent home with foot welts so painful you couldn't walk for weeks. If you were unlucky, you'd disappear for years, maybe for good. You might even be forced to sneak out of the country, like one of my outspoken cousins was, separated from family and unable to return without a pardon from the king himself.

That didn't stop the occasional protest and march in the camp, often to mark anniversaries such as the founding of Israel or Yawm al-Ard, Land Day, a commemoration of the March 30, 1976, protests against an Israeli decision to seize Palestinian land in the Galilee. No matter the pretext, the protests in Jordan's camps flirted with criticism of the government and the monarchy. Such gatherings attracted the attention of authorities, who would descend on the camp armed with tear gas and batons, chasing the young men down the streets and alleyways to shut them up, breeding more bitterness.

Protest days were always terrifying, and to a child they felt like the end of the world. People seemed to have gone mad, threatening to upset the order of things—such as they were—in a camp where, unsurprisingly, refugees recoiled from anything that resembled sudden change. For days afterwards, girls would be missing from our classes, kept home by parents upset by the unpredictability of anger freely expressed, however briefly. On iffy days, we children were made to carry half an onion with us to class—a supposed antidote to tear gas—just in case a protest broke out. People didn't like to talk about those days, but then they avoided public discussion of anything related to dissent, as if they too might be rounded up just for having an opinion. Predictably, state television—the only television available back then—never acknowledged the protests either. Rarely were the camps ever mentioned at all. It was as if they didn't exist.

We didn't think much of any of this at the time; we were instead encouraged to focus on school. We were true believers in the church of academic superiority, thanks to my mother's inculcation. In grade three (grade *three*!), I was confronted with the calamitous prospect of being labelled second-rate, and my memory of it is disturbingly clear. It was the last day of school, and the teacher read the year-end results out loud. In beauty pageant fashion, the runners-up came first. The girls in third and second place graciously accepted the applause. Then the teacher uttered the name of the girl in first place, and it was not me. I was horrified and humiliated. I was not first, second, or third. After what seemed like forever, the teacher announced that I had tied for first. Both the other girl and I had an average of 98.

My sister and I donned the blue dress uniform worn to this day in Amman's public elementary schools, our hair perfectly tied back with crisp white ribbons, shoes polished to a shine. Neither of us was ever singled out for punishment like the other girls—with loud slaps to the hands usually administered with a large stick—unless a teacher decided to collectively punish an entire class for rowdiness. On those occasions, everyone got two slaps, one on each hand, and my sister and I would be inconsolable, as though we'd been mortally wounded. More often, as model students, we were recruited for the dubious distinction of helping teachers enforce the rules; this meant checking our classmates' hair for lice and even smelling them for body odour (and sending them home if they failed the test).

Along the way, we had started emulating our aunts and cousins, paying attention to the music they loved and the stars they adored. We were, despite ourselves, adapting—just as our parents wanted. My mother tried to adapt too, but it was clear she didn't relish being back in Al-Wihdat, a place she'd happily left as a teenage orphan-bride. Mom looked weird in our uncomfortable house. In the Kodak snapshots of her from that time, her stylish hair, slick lipstick, and carefully coordinated outfits clash with the grubby walls and sparse furnishings. Needless to say, the home stayed and it was the hair, outfits, and lipstick that eventually faded away.

The Kodak pictures also disappeared, our lives seemingly too forgettable for us to want to remember. Occasionally someone took cheap Polaroid shots of important moments, but they failed to measure up to those pictures of us as Winnipeg children. Even my mother's birthday cakes were a poorer version of the Winnipeg ones. She also struggled as we became harder to control. In just a few years, my poor mother turned from movie star (in my eyes) to a prolific punishment machine.

Paradoxically, it was my father, the one most familiar with life in a refugee camp, who adapted the least. His darkest moment came when he was arrested in his taxi for failing to display the company's decal on the side of the car. Like a number of others accused of similarly benign infractions that day, Dad was handed a one-week jail sentence without ever seeing a judge. Once behind bars he complained, but the police threatened to beat him. This experience, on top of several failed attempts at getting and keeping work, soured him. Soon, Dad could no longer stand it and joined the hundreds of thousands of refugee fathers who sought a living in the Gulf. He didn't last long there either, and came back dejected and defeated.

Much of the merriment, the carefree lives to which we had been accustomed, slipped away. Humour had slithered away among the goats' intestines, open sewers, and endless grievances of Al-Wihdat.

Still, there were occasionally some good days in the camp. The best were those during the Eid holidays: one was just after Ramadan, the holy month of fasting (Small Eid), and one was just after the *hajj* season (Big Eid). We received new clothing and coins, and music rang out from the ramshackle homes. We went to the *dukkanahs* to buy candy, firecrackers, and little toys made in China. Out on the main road, someone would temporarily set up rickety, rusting children's rides where we could tumble, whirl, and spin our money away.

Even better were the summers, when my maternal grandmother made the road trip from Kuwait with her husband and children. Sitto Nazmiyah was no longer the unknown relative we'd once visited as toddlers. We came to know and truly love her and her children, especially Uncle Rajaee. During their visits, humour crept back into our lives: Uncle Rajaee brought an endless supply of jokes and would often sing and dance for our entertainment, and Sitto always brought a billowing abaya full of excitement, yards of supple material, dozens of shiny barrettes, stashes of gold bracelets and necklaces, and arms full of the warmest embraces. Joyfully defying the stern and serious image of the adult Arab to which we'd become accustomed, she would break unprompted into song, and my mother would join her. Sitto also had the habit of breaking into fits of uncontrollable teary laughter that my mother is also prone to, in turn bringing all of us to giggles for no reason at all.

But most of the time, especially in those mundane, howling winters, our lives lacked the hope and humour that people— especially children—need to be able to *thrive*. The toughest blow was Dad's decision to return to Canada. He had barely eked out a living in Amman and knew he could do better back home. It was a difficult goodbye; we all desperately wanted to go with him and didn't understand why we couldn't.

Thankfully, Dad decided to move us out of the camp before he left. But after many months and then years of absence, my father eventually became a mythical figure to us, a man whose existence we sometimes secretly doubted. As we were repeatedly told, however, it was to this now-strange fellow that we owed our whole existence: he was the source of our sustenance, the provider of our livelihood, and it was to him that we owed good behaviour and good marks. It was a powerful weapon effectively wielded by Mom.

Moving to a refugee camp had been as traumatic and as dramatic an upheaval as any. Nothing, though, compared to watching your father leave you behind.

☙

Virtually every one of the families we knew was missing someone: fathers and brothers and occasionally sisters, most of whom were forced by poverty to leave and seek work elsewhere. Amto Nehmah tearfully prayed out loud for her youngest, who'd graduated as a nautical engineer and began travelling to work on ships. Whenever a plane flew over, she would curse it for taking her son, and my father, away. Then she would catch herself and remorsefully pray for its passengers to arrive safely at their destinations.

Moving to Hay Nazzal, our new neighbourhood, softened the blow of Dad's departure. It was an area that was still predominately Palestinian—indeed Palestinians formed the majority in Jordan—but it was far more prosperous and liveable than the camp. We attended regular public schools and rented a respectable house far larger than the one we had left behind—two living rooms, two bedrooms, a foyer, and a small alcove that housed the kitchen and bathroom. And it was not in a refugee camp, and that counted for a lot. Yet even though we'd gained more space, the five of us continued to sleep in one room together, lined up on mattresses next to one another. It was partly economics: we couldn't afford five beds or heating the house in its entirety. We had only one *sobba*—a kerosene-fuelled heater—and when nights turned cold, we all huddled next to it in our collective bedroom. We'd fall asleep side by side, our wet laundry hanging nearby. The bathroom unfortunately remained a hole in the ground, and the bold cockroaches were there too, our presence doing nothing to intimidate them. Soon after we had moved, I woke up once in the middle of the night, lifted the covers, and saw one scurrying out from under me onto the cold tiled floor. I wondered where it was going at such a late hour.

One of the living rooms was dedicated to playing and watching television; the other was reserved for visitors, and we were strongly discouraged from going near it. It housed a real couch, coffee tables, a lamp—all for the enjoyment of our occasional serious visitors. It was only in this room that a picture of my father was displayed—the first thing you saw when you drew aside the curtain that separated the living room from the rest of the house. In the photo, he wore a suit and an earnest smile, and I'd occasionally peek at it to remind myself what he looked like.

In those years, I mostly played with my brother, two years my junior and my partner in all things extracurricular, like mapping our neighbourhood into secret routes to escape from or pursue our imaginary foes. Our domain stretched from our garden, with its sickly rose bush, to the long alley that connected our home to the rest of the compound, which we shared with a tiny kindergarten. The large expanse that was the schoolyard beyond was actually forbidden to us. In the daytime, it was reserved as a play area for the dozens of loud children in identical blue uniforms who attended the school. After hours, it was the exclusive playground of our landlord's children and their weird friends.

Still, we would nonchalantly steal into the compound after school to play on the swings and in the sandbox and to pick mulberries from the giant tree, keeping a wary eye on the picture windows of Abu Hisham's home, which was perched proudly above the kindergarten he owned and operated. He or his wife, or sometimes one of his many children, often caught us, reminding us that we were mere tenants' children availing ourselves of what was certainly not ours to use. All it took was a stern gaze for us to get off their turf. We pretended we were just passing through anyway, and in a couple of days, we'd be at it once again.

Like other poor kids of the neighbourhood, my brother and I adored playing with the detritus of the road; we even collaborated once—unsuccessfully—on building a makeshift car out of wooden planks and greasy ball bearings. On some afternoons, we would jump over the crumbling brick wall that separated our garden from another alley behind our house, usually to run over to the home of Uncle Said—the one with the second wife, not the first—to take a long-distance phone call from my father in Canada. That wall was an important gateway in many of our secret escape plans, and we often bragged to each other about the best way to scale it. My sister had more mature things to preoccupy her, like reading and helping Mom in domestic chores I wanted nothing to do with. And our youngest brother was mostly too young to join us on our adventures, real or imaginary. Unless we let him.

If we were lucky, we'd get to play with the children of the occasional visitor who thought to look in on a displaced family making do without a father in the house. Once in a while, especially in the winter, my siblings and I came grudgingly together to play house or some other group game, often at the suggestion of our busy mother. We relied on imagination: the thin mattresses folded over our knees became trucks careening down a highway. Spent batteries became fancy prizes given out at pretend game shows. But our favourite joint activity required no pretending. Most afternoons we assembled in front of the television to watch Tom and Jerry resume their diligent attempts to annihilate each other. We talked about them as if they were old friends. They brought humour back into our home, half an hour at a time.

Every day before the cartoons began, a reader wearing a long robe and an *imamah*, a tight white turban of sorts, would recite a passage from the Koran. We didn't pay much attention to the words, or the choice of sura, unless the reader happened to be

Abdul Baset Abdul Samad, an Egyptian whose soaring voice could make even the most ardent atheist yearn for a deity.

The news usually came next, a turgid rendition of the day's events, almost always focused on the activities of King Hussein. There were always worrisome developments, news of the violence that raged around the region, such as the chaotic Iranian revolution in 1979 and the Iran–Iraq War, which was in full, murderous swing starting in 1980. The Lebanese Civil War, which began a year before we arrived, in 1975, was prolific and each day brought new slaughter. Why were they fighting? But "why" wasn't a popular question in our circles, especially when it came to politics. You just didn't ask. You were actively discouraged from it.

One afternoon, the Koran reader went into overtime, forcing us to contemplate the unthinkable prospect that *Tom and Jerry* had been pre-empted. A grave-looking news anchor appeared, speaking of a calamity, a massacre. But we had stopped listening, transfixed instead by the images. Confused clumps of hands and legs and torn clothing formed what we eventually recognized as human bodies lying on the ground, several of them slumped on top of one another, others arranged side by side in neat rows. Beneath the bodies were dark pools of what could only be blood. I recognized it because I had seen viscous pools just like that at my uncle's place whenever he'd slain a goat for Eid. Something had gone terribly wrong in Lebanon. And hundreds, maybe more, had died. In the days that followed, Sabra and Shatila became *Sabraandshatila*, an appalling condition, an adjective synonymous with murder and fear, rather than the proper nouns for the two neighbouring refugee camps as they had been just days earlier.

I was bewildered. Television was occasionally serious. It did broadcast the Koran and the news. But I thought its reason for being was to bring us cartoons, to make us laugh. Television wasn't supposed to make you sad.

⚸

But sadness was an essential part of modern Middle East living. If you weren't lamenting a catastrophic, violent event—the latest deaths in some war or conflict—you were mourning a loved one. Someone, somewhere in our circle, was always in mourning. Often it was the perpetual wake for better days and lives gone by. There were relatives whose only role in our young lives, it seemed, was to cry at any mention of the past. It often occurred to me that many of them were still *living* in the past. People on both sides of the family grew up on the collective memory of displacement and the sagas of refugeehood. Memories, good and bad, were passed on to children like family heirlooms. So was the melancholy.

If I didn't know better, I'd swear it was Arabs who invented mourning, so practised and dark it seems in this part of the world. Arabs in general have so many reasons to mourn, stacked one on top of another like bodies at a Baghdad morgue. With each fresh death, with each new misfortune, the mountain of bereavement grows. And instead of dulling the impact, each new addition opens up all the old wounds, eliciting the pent-up outrage and grief.

One of my earliest memories of such displays was in Hay Nazzal, when our after-school horseplay was interrupted by a commotion at a neighbour's place. Hysterical people started flocking to the apartment in question, many of them in tears.

The first arrivals were mostly women with eyes so red and soaring wails so guttural you thought they were being buried alive. We children suspended our play and watched awkwardly, bewildered by the sound of calamity. We stared as yet another woman cut a frantic path to the apartment, ripping her exquisitely embroidered dress from the neck, exposing and then pulling at her own hair, and screaming, to join the others in grief. I'd never, ever seen a woman do that before, and the image stuck.

Terrified but compelled by curiosity, some of the more adventurous among us followed her into the apartment. None of the women paid us any mind, and suddenly a clutch of them formed a circle and started jumping in unison, slapping their own faces and shrieking, indifferent to the cries of the toddlers at their feet. At the sight of this, we sprinted out, alarmed and shocked. Later we understood the depth of the loss: five people from one family, including the head of the household, dead in a plane crash. Still it was an extraordinary show of mourning, even by Middle East standards. Morbid curiosity satisfied, we gladly averted our eyes.

Increasingly harder to ignore as I grew older were the more mundane tragedies of everyday life. Almost everyone we knew still lived in refugee camps all over Jordan, their lives a strenuous routine of surviving hand to mouth while enduring humiliation, oppression, and repeatedly dashed hopes. Mothers were forced to fight daily battles to get their children's maladies treated, and fathers toiled hard and yet came home at the end of the day with only enough to pay for that evening's meal. The poverty forced them to choose which, if any, of their children would go on to study, and whether they could afford to get married.

My great-grandfather, Nazmiyah's father, had for decades endured a loud hum in his head and near-deafness on account of a bullet that had lodged itself squarely in the centre of his brow in 1948 and stayed there. My mother's uncle's family lived cut off from their eldest, who had escaped Jordan after being tortured for dissident activity and was unreachable except by a rare telephone call. Untold households we visited displayed pictures of loved ones with a black ribbon adorning one corner, reminding everyone of their premature passing due to conflict or disease. Everyone had endured a tragedy, and everyone had a story.

I wanted to hear them all.

We had our own challenges. Dad worked double shifts at a

convenience store back in Canada to keep us fed, but sometimes it wasn't enough. My mother refused to ask anyone else for help, and she took up sewing to add to our income, though we weren't allowed to tell anyone. Whatever extra money my mother made, she spent on us. Every dime. Even so, there were times when we were penniless. I always knew things were tight when all we had to eat for dinner was cheese melted on bread on the lone *sobba* that heated our collective bedroom.

Dad occasionally visited and brought with him a fleeting whiff of a more prosperous life, the life we'd enjoyed before this nightmare began. He brought us new clothes, toys, and words of encouragement. When he left, there was nothing but school, chores, and the detestable rules that governed our lives in the periods of our fatherlessness.

The rules. *Adat wa takaleed.* Habits and traditions. Many of them were time-honoured reflections of the warmth and hospitality of Arab culture, vestiges of the tribal system that had ruled most of the region in the past; others stemmed from the dominance of Islam; and yet others came from long-standing superstition. At some times, they were a minor inconvenience, and at others, virtual puppet strings that dictated our behaviour. All were—and still are—essential for survival in most of the Middle East, and we ignored them at our peril.

Don't ever comment on how beautiful a child is without saying "*Masha'Allah*" or "*Ism Allah*" to protect her from the evil eye. Don't show people the bottom of your feet, and always take your shoes off when entering a home. Always eat with your right hand, and don't ever eat, even among strangers, without offering some to others. Always insist that people eat at your home, even if they're not hungry. Always say a greeting when you enter any place, and never leave a greeting unanswered, even from a stranger. Do exchange greetings that become ever more elaborate until you've both run out of air. Touch your hand to your chest when you're not sure if a man shakes hands with women or not. And if you're a woman, don't look people straight in the eye when you're talking, since that would be rude. Do, definitely, have an arranged marriage. And do absolutely everything—anything—to save face.

It's true that adherence to these and thousands of other rules varies from Arab country to Arab country, even within strata of society within one country. But they were closely followed in the circles in which we moved in Amman, and in most cases, they were non-negotiable. They were also closely policed by peers, relatives, even neighbours. Many of those rules tended to single out women, and girls in particular. And as my sister and I grew older, we found ourselves irretrievably entangled in their powerful grip.

I don't recall precisely when the decision was made, or by whom. But there is no question that my sister, Ayeda, and I were forced to wear the hijab against our will. We were on the verge of becoming teenagers, and under the "circumstances"—the fact that Dad didn't live with us—it was expected that we cover up, because people would otherwise "talk." My mother, who had never worn a hijab in her life, also started wearing one. I had a difficult time with it, and with everything else that restricted my behaviour. I complained endlessly: I got itchy, I couldn't hear, it obliterated my peripheral vision, and it was unbearable in hot weather. But I was told repeatedly that my family's reputation depended on it. Wearing the hijab did get in the way of my rebelliousness. But it never had the intended effect of subduing my tomboyish ways.

Over time, I grew uncomfortable in the company of Arab women and invented excuses to escape their hushed conversations. Most of the women I met at the time had no choice *but* to conform—there was no question of rebelliousness for them. Family honour was everything, and much of it depended on the behaviour of the family's women. I could not understand then why I was expected to carry the entire weight of our family's honour on my bony teenage shoulders. But in time, I learned.

There were few role models for us. Amto Nehmah's entire life was ruled by habits and traditions, from the archaic marriage "swap" she was part of as a young woman (she married a cousin whose sister married Uncle Hussein), to the divorce forced on her by her brother's decision to leave his own wife. She had no education to fall back on or trade to allow her to live independently, so again, according to tradition, she had no choice but to move back to the home of her immediate family. On that side of the family, many of my cousins eschewed higher education in favour of marriage. They were arranged transactions that often appeared designed to make the consanguineous lines of our family so thick you'd need a chainsaw to cut through them.

Women in Mom's family were significantly more liberated. They were better educated—often with university degrees—and more socially active members of their circles. They liked music, and some of them even dared to fall in love before a traditional marriage was arranged. They were opinionated and expressed themselves in public. Yet there were still limits, and a strict code governed, among other things, their conduct around men. I witnessed the enforcement of this code time and again, with terrifying results.

One of my many aunts once took us out for an afternoon walk while her family was visiting. Along the way a young man, a former neighbour, recognized us and stopped to chat. It was the briefest of conversations. Excited by the encounter, I offhandedly mentioned it when we got home.

All at once, there was a lot of yelling. My aunt was accused of acting inappropriately. How dare she stop in the middle of the street and speak to a single young man? Someone—I don't recall who—slapped her. It was days before we all recovered. And though my aunt was gracious enough not to blame me for opening my mouth, the incident left me deeply shaken.

My mind created a special dossier for such seemingly inexplicable behaviour, and even before I was thirteen, the dossier was filled to capacity. In it, I gathered stories that I heard late at night, while pretending to sleep—stories whispered to my mother by one of the few confidantes she had in Amman. The woman spoke of the terrible beatings she suffered at the hands of her husband. In that dossier, I also tucked away the stories of various female relatives whose fathers and brothers dictated their movements, their choice of education, their entire lives. The story of my still-unmarried cousin, who because of her lame eye was written off as a spinster before she turned twenty, also deserved special mention. Poor husbandless Amto Nehmah, alone through no fault of her own and struggling to raise her two boys, had a particularly thick file. The hushed stories of honour killings we heard about only rarely as children had a dossier all on their own.

My sister and I were slowly excluded from certain gatherings as we grew older; my brothers weren't, and that made me angry. I noted the growing number of visits to other people's homes that required us to sit separately from the men. I recognized very early the advantages of being male in my adoptive society. I recall with as much clarity the first time I heard the old Arab wives' tale that to turn yourself from a girl to a boy, all you had to do was kiss your own elbow.

I occasionally twisted myself into screaming pain trying.

♐

Still, I had learned how to play the role assigned to me by what I had already concluded was an inequitable society. At relatives' homes, I sat meekly, knees tucked together, speaking only when spoken to, obediently helping with the dishes while my brothers played. I finally wore the hijab, the last female in our household to do so. I constantly fussed with my head cover to ensure not a wisp of hair was showing, just as the other girls did. I was so well behaved, in fact, I was often the one chosen to do a recitation from the Koran at school events, covered head to toe in a crisp white hijab that neatly disguised my mischievousness. At school, my best friend was a pious, nearly perfect girl named Omayma. She had milky-white skin and perfect jet-black hair, cut short, with a white ribbon tied around her head. She of course wore the hijab. I tried to emulate her, cutting my hair the same way and subconsciously biting my lower lip in the exact manner that she did. We were inseparable, and despite her seeming perfection, I loved her with all my heart.

Leaving Omayma was the only thing that saddened me on the eve of our departure—at last—for Canada. We had lived for seven crushing years in the Middle East before my parents decided it was enough. I cried when Omayma and I said goodbye for the last time under the shade of a large tree near the school where we'd met. I was taken aback when she extended her hand to shake mine. There was no question of an embrace—that would be inappropriate on the street, even between two schoolgirls. The rules apparently said so.

Still, I wrote her from Canada, only once, footnoting the news that I had gladly given up the hijab the moment I left Jordan. In a terse letter in reply, she said she was disappointed to hear that I had done so—disappointed in me. She said she'd pray that I would find my way back to wearing it again. It was her harsh rebuke that sealed my youthful bitterness with the Arab world and everyone in it.

I never wrote her back.

THREE

The Store

ໍຄ. {

*Your close neighbour is better
than your faraway brother.*
—ARAB PROVERB

AMMAN, JORDAN, 1983

It had taken an infinity for those seven years in the Middle East to pass, a drip-drip of time in painfully slow motion. After some years, we no longer dared dream we would ever go home. Many nights there were no dreams.

We were thrilled and apprehensive all at once at the news of our impending departure. Of course, we had long hoped for the end of our banishment, our premature entombment in Amman. At thirteen, more than anything, I craved constancy, a mundane teenager's life: a father at home, friends I could keep, an existence where planes played a more diminished role and could just be admired from afar. With major change coming, I wanted to be rooted to one place—one containable world—without regret or longing for another. They say that home can be anywhere—that time can make any place home if enough of it passes to smooth out the rough edges—but I really wanted home to be the one we had left behind seven years ago. By the time we prepared to make that journey—a journey that straddled oceans, many capitals, and several time zones—it seemed so far away. Still, I wanted to go home, and stay home. I had no plans of missing the Middle East.

For the second time in our lives, my mother put our paltry possessions up for sale. She arranged them all on display in the front room: personal things, big and small; worn mattresses; kitchenware; sooty pots and pans; yellowing curtains; rickety chairs; and even well-worn faded dresses, shoes, and jeans—even ones we'd bought second-hand. Our prized couches were also now up for grabs. So were the gas oven and the unsightly beige Formica double wardrobe, where Mother used to keep the blue Samsonite case that imprisoned our Kodak pictures, and what remained of her lost glamour. The closet was one of the first items to be sold. Within a few days it was suddenly dismantled and carried out in pieces by men I didn't know.

There are things you simply couldn't and shouldn't sell, no matter how badly you need the cash. I thought this while watching one woman in particular who spent far too long haggling with my mother over the price of a well-used iron. I was especially enraged when Mom seemed close to tears as she politely haggled back. I wished she would just end the sale and give everything away. Thankfully, she eventually did, turning her focus to preparing for departure.

It already felt as though I'd had a thousand farewells in my life, a good number of them before I turned ten. I've always been good at remembering every last detail of the partings: what I wore, who cried, what was said and to whom. And the last-second gifts—like Uncle Rajaee handing me his (and my) favourite tape, yanked at the last minute from his car cassette player before he drove back to Kuwait. Yet I barely remember that final trip to the Amman airport, or the goodbyes that preceded it—I don't even remember who drove us. All I know is that there was little sadness. It was like getting out of prison: a happy occasion—but one spiked with anger over all the time that had been stolen.

I do recall that once we were beyond the immigration counter at the airport, Mom quietly tugged at our head covers. "You don't have to wear that anymore," she said. My mother was always a believer in goodness, in an inherent justness. But not in the hijab. I breathed deeply.

My mother was only thirty-six, and she too had lost seven (more) years of her life to Amman's damp and callous grip. I watched in awe as she methodically planned our departure, keeping calm despite all that could have undone her. After my father left us, she alone had had to contend with the daily challenges of bringing up four children in an inhospitable place, living virtually as a single mother in a society that held single mothers in contempt.

"*Ma'alesh*," she would say when she modestly spoke of her sacrifices. "It's okay. It's all for the kids."

At the end of seven long years, she still had the energy and the wherewithal to drag us across three continents and through several airports all on her own. Once home, she had the tenacity and elasticity to adapt to yet another new life. In that life, she not only cared for us as she always did, but also deftly learned a new line of work and then laboured full time, shoulder to shoulder with my father, until retirement—with barely a word of complaint.

Our trip home was a long one. There were several stopovers, including one in war-ravaged Beirut, less than an hour away by plane from Amman. I remember staring out the window, wondering what gods had wrought such horrendous damage on what we'd heard was such a beautiful place. What could bring anyone to do such terrible things? And how could the airport still be open? I couldn't believe we had landed in the heart of a place from which we'd heard so much terrible news.

The rest of the trip was a blur. But I remember that as soon as we entered the public area of the Winnipeg airport, I spotted Dad's beaming face and burst into tears. I took his hand and refused to let go.

We eventually piled into Dad's brown Monte Carlo for the drive from the airport to our home. I remember the orderliness of the streets, the familiar humid air, and the vast open spaces. I was back where I belonged.

⚘

Home now was a spacious apartment in a once noble mansion a stone's throw from the Manitoba legislature. I was overwhelmed by its beauty and, despite the building's age and condition, by the relative modernity of everything we suddenly had at our disposal: the appliances, the lights, the sliding doors, and the hardwood flooring. We were most delighted by the rediscovery of the flush toilet and the overhead shower, and availed ourselves at every opportunity. The familiar scent of prairie rain wafted through open, impossibly large windows, welcoming us back. The apartment had enough rooms for the boys and girls to sleep separately in stacked bunk beds—and even the lower bunk was much farther above the floor than we'd become accustomed to. The huge television immediately captured our attention. There was no national anthem, no Koran reader—Billy Graham was the only available reasonable facsimile, yet because he was a novelty, he was, at first, eminently watchable. *Spider-Man* was aired in the morning. *The Flintstones*, *Bugs Bunny*, and the wondrous world of WWF wrestling came in the afternoon. *Tom and Jerry* appeared on more than one station, and seemed funnier than ever.

Within days, we had discovered the park a mere block away. It had swings, a sandbox, even a wading pool, and we could use them any time we wanted without enduring stern looks.

My father had chosen well. But ever practical, he had selected our new home for reasons unrelated to the park, the flooring, or the quaint antique elevator. It had more to do with it being right across a tree-lined street from the Store, the source of our sustenance, and soon to be our second home.

The Store had a distinctive sound and smell that to this day are unforgettable: the unnatural aroma of slushes and microwaved hoagies, mixed with Windex and bleach, old mops and newsprint. The shrill sound of the cash register accenting the base hum of the coolers, set against the quiet shuffle of a customer making his way through the aisles. There were three aisles in our store, and Dad gave us a quick tour. Here were the canned goods, over there the Wonder Bread and packaged doughnuts, and then the overpriced toilet paper, Kleenex, paper plates, and napkins. I loved the convex anti-theft mirror at the very back left corner and was enthralled by the newsstand, which occupied half a wall. We got a quick glimpse of the "back," a tiny alcove full of stock and a small lunch table where Dad did his accounts and ate his meals. There we discovered the clever door that took you into the belly of the refrigerators so you could restock. Once we'd tried it, the milk inside smoothly washed away all memories of the gag-inducing powdered variety we knew and loathed.

The store looked nothing like the forlorn *dukkanahs* in Amman. The variety of items was dazzling, a festival of personalities on parade: Campbell's, Chef Boyardee, and Aunt Jemima jostled on the stages of shelves, while Mr. Big and Oh Henry! were elbow to elbow on the bleachers of the chocolate bar stand. The entire store was awash in slogans of yellow and red. Yellow signs, red typeface, yellow uniforms, red for the cheeky cat mascot and Dad's uniform and cap. Dad didn't own the store; he was the manager. But it didn't matter to our small army of cheerleaders. We were ready to claim ownership, thrilled at the prospect of working at the family store. We vowed to make the Store the best Mac's Convenience ever.

My father already ran a frightfully tight ship. As we worked alongside him, we got reacquainted, and I took note of his skills: attention to detail, endurance, and a remarkable capacity for continuous gruelling shift work. He did various mathematical tasks with the deftness of a bleary-eyed man doing his morning ablutions. I watched him for weeks before begging him to let me do the books. In a few months I was counting cash like a casino worker, and happily making the daily trip to the bank to make the day's deposit. We all took turns manning the cash register, cleaning, and restocking. Sometimes we would all show up on the weekly "grocery" days, when a large truck delivered our order of canned and baked goods, cigarettes, and other non-perishables. On those days, we would busy ourselves finding homes for everything on the shelves. On the yearly inventory days, when the store's contents had to be counted, we were all there, excited by joint activity and a common purpose.

There is something wholly inimitable about growing up with a store in the family. Much as there might be, at the other end of the class spectrum, about growing up with a cottage or a summer house: an extension of the family home in which to gather and create novel memories. The Store was like a second living room—but instead of couches and an end table, it was stocked with chips, gum, milk, and canned soup. It acted as family glue, a bonding agent that brought us closer. It felt as though we were part of an exclusive club. Later I would smile in recognition at other club members—the boys and girls who pumped my gas or nimbly added up my purchases at the little grocery down the street, bringing back good memories. Though both our parents worked odd and long hours, we were never latchkey kids. We could always count on a good lunch and company at the Store. It was the focal point of our lives, the hearth around which we gathered, the television that drew us together—open twenty-four hours a day, seven days a week, closed only occasionally on Christmas Eve.

The Store witnessed some of our biggest decisions. At times it was our battlefield, and at others the green line when we declared an armistice. It heard punishments meted out, report cards condemned, congratulations offered, promises made, and vows broken. Despite the constant flow of strangers, it was a place where we could hide, a sanctuary where we could cry, laugh, celebrate, and be utterly disappointed. Many times, it substituted for the role of the kitchen in an average home. Like a kitchen, it was a place to go when you were feeling lost. You could look in the fridge for answers, even if you had no idea what you were looking for. That was the beauty of the Store. It had several fridges.

My parents were as devoted to the Store as they were to us, and they were devoted to it *because* of us. Mom filled in when Dad had errands to run, then Dad would take over so Mom could go home to cook dinner. They were typical hard-working immigrants: running the business with minimal outside help, all the while urging us to put our efforts into school. Later I took pride in what pioneers my parents had been, the model immigrants they were: they worked extremely hard because they had ambitions, mostly for us. But they also took an active interest in their adopted home. They always voted. They obeyed the law and impressed upon us the importance of respecting authority and playing by the rules. They came to our PTA meetings, applauded at our games and concerts, never once went on the dole, and always paid their taxes on time. They were proud of who they were and where they'd come from, but equally proud of the country that had adopted them. They were aware of its current affairs and tried to foster the same interest in us. They naturally embraced Pierre Trudeau's multicultural, bilingual Canada, and Mom dreamed of learning French, if only she had the time. My parents welcomed customers of all walks of life with open arms, acquiring a motley crew of friends, admirers, and idle chatterers, among them Ethiopians, Italians, Portuguese, Aboriginals, Jews, and French Canadians. My parents despised debt: the more they owed, the harder they worked. The Store barely netted enough income for a small family to live comfortably. But because of their zeal and meticulous planning, my parents soon bought a real house and paid it off in record time, despite the astronomical interest rates. They also managed to put most of us through university, all thanks to the Store. But none of it came without a price.

One night, Dad was nearly killed there in a petty scuffle during the graveyard shift. I occasionally stayed late with him, and I saw for myself the rowdy crowd that came in at the wee hours of the Osborne Village morning: drunks, belligerents, aimless teenagers, and other ghosts who prowled the flipside of regular hours. Dad could sometimes have a short fuse, but he had just the right temperament for dealing with those people. He served them quietly, paying no mind to their taunting or eccentric behaviour. When necessary, he had a knack for showing someone the door without incident.

That night, though, my father's subtle ways failed to rid him of a particularly loud drunk and they ended up scuffling. The young man was strong enough to push my father into the door of one of the many tall coolers near the cash register. It shattered into daggers of glass, and the man disappeared. Someone called 911. Dad was bleeding badly and was rushed to Emergency. The police called my mother to break the news.

But we wouldn't get to visit Dad until the next day. It was a shock to see my father lying helpless in a hospital bed, dazed from the after-effects of anaesthesia and the narcotics he was given to ease post-operative pain. The glass had cut a tendon in one of his arms and left a long gash in the other. He spent a week in the hospital recovering. We were suddenly without him again, a sickening reminder of the days when we'd made do with him gone. It fell upon Mom and us kids to keep the Store running, and we all pitched in. It was a jarring reversal of roles that for me, after years of worshipping my absent father, brought on the realization that he was human and mortal. To this day, my father carries a long scar from that night, and a hand whose fingers refuse to straighten.

Still, the Store did us a lot of good. It gave us kids free job training, skills that later helped get our first real jobs. And in those first few weeks and months back in Canada, it was also an ideal place to bring us up to speed with a society we now found alienating. From the safety of my position behind the cash counter, I had ample opportunity to socialize with hundreds of people. It was a stunning cure for the stunted English we were speaking by then. We also had easy and free access to daily newspapers and dozens of magazines, and I spent many afternoons in their company. I grew to love the smell of the sooty sheets of a freshly printed *Winnipeg Free Press*. Inside the magazines, I devoured articles on politics and popular culture; the teen versions offered advice on making friends and dealing with parents in a North American culture.

But no amount of reading could replace the seven years that we had missed out on in Canada.

⚘

Churchill High School sat on a large property next to the murky Red River, a short walk away from the Riverview neighbourhood home where we now resided. It was one long corridor lined with hundreds of lockers painted in the colours of Smarties—long enough for us to run the fifty-metre dash during winter track practice. It had a door at each end where the tough kids gathered at lunchtime to smoke. The back exit opened onto the all-important football field, where in the fall and spring we did physical education classes during the day and cheered the games at night.

At Churchill we were all subject to taunting at one time or another. My sister was singled out as a "Paki" or a "camel jockey." I had a fair amount of jeering to contend with as well, not least on account of my name, which provided hours of entertainment for those of my fellow students with an aptitude for improvising lyrics.

My parents also endured some taunting at the Store. They were speaking in Arabic to each other one day behind the counter when a customer, unprompted, roared at them: "How did *you* get here? How did you get in to Canada?" My mother tried to actually answer the question. "The same way you did, sir," she said. To that, the man shouted, "You're all baby killers! Terrorists!" and walked out. My parents were confused and deeply hurt, even though several other customers apologized to them for the man's appalling behaviour. "We didn't want any trouble," my mother often said when she told the story. "It's how we've always been since we came here. It's what we've learned to do to survive. So we didn't tell anybody. Didn't complain."

As a child I always spoke a lot; my questions were endless and, according to my mother, bordered on harassment. But at Churchill awkwardness initially left me mute. Scribbling complaints on my desk was as close as I ever got to lashing out. I did it once in Arabic and got caught as our English teacher was passing around a surprise test.

"What's that all about?" she asked.

As usual, I had nothing to say.

"She's cheating!"

A boy who had appointed himself my critic answered on my behalf. He wasn't the sort to have a problem with cheating in principle, only perhaps with the idea that I could cheat undetected because I spoke another language. My teacher didn't press the point, but with arms folded over her chest, she easily stared me down and asked me to stop writing on my desk. I think she knew that I wasn't the cheating type. If I were, I would have mustered better than a C in her class.

I confess now that what I had scribbled was my name, along with some statement about how much I hated that class.

My English had waned noticeably, along with my confidence. I obviously knew how to speak, read, and write, but there were undeniable hiccups in my pronunciation, all ascribable to our counter-training in Amman's public schools. To choose a particularly vexing word: "artery." It kept appearing the first time I had to read out loud in biology class. I couldn't say it. My condition elicited sympathy from the rest of the class, and even from the teacher, but not from my critic. He pursued me daily thereafter with frightfully accurate renditions of my linguistic failures:

"SYSTEMIC ATTA-RIE!"

I was the perfect victim. Presented with a choice of either fight or flight, I always opted for the latter.

⚐

I did eventually make friends. Daphne was the first. She was petite, a good foot shorter than me, and when we went shopping, often in the kids' section, I was occasionally mistaken for her mother. To me, Daphne was a cherished friend, the artist, the fellow flutist, the ballerina-in-the-making. To others, she was the kid with the back brace, the one who struggled to keep up with a school full of able-bodied children. She suffered from scoliosis, which left her with a significant limp and predictions she would have neither children nor a normal lifespan. Yet she was the one friend who endured all my complaining, and often worried for me when I fell ill. We spent hours on the phone, occasionally discussing whether I was dying too, and why we had both been so unlucky.

Others followed, each of them a mentor and indispensible in guiding me, gently, out of geekhood. We were a diverse lot,

Canadians whose roots were Filipino, Chinese, Jewish, Indian, Trinidadian, and Ukrainian; none of us gave it a second thought at the time, assuming such multiplicity was Canada's norm. Later, when I realized it wasn't, I was proud of the colour-blind way in which we'd grown up, and of the diversity in a city often unfairly dismissed as one-dimensional.

With time, all of us kids made friends and eventually stopped sticking out so much. My parents encouraged us to participate in extracurricular activities that helped us fit in. These days, Mom was the family photographer, methodically capturing the boys' layups and tae kwon do moves, and the girls' choral and band performances. There was no limit to what we were allowed to get into, so long as it didn't interfere with studies and eventual graduations—momentous events that Mom obsessively covered with her point-and-click. Otherwise our parents embraced our activities and our friends—to a point.

Dad never once interfered in our individual decisions on religion. He was always strictly secular throughout most of his own life. He wasn't into the idea of the hijab, and he condemned the multiple marriages permissible in Islam. He advocated the use of contraception among cousins who never seemed to tire of making babies. He never knowingly treated my sister and me any differently than he did our brothers. He wasn't that kind of father. But he was *traditional*, the kind of man who might quietly threaten to tear up a tiny skirt he once saw me wearing. He was also the kind of father who forbade any of us to date—it was out of the question. He expected us to marry Arabs, as he had, and preferably well-educated moderates who were not prone to overly religious thinking.

As for their past, my parents could never forget it, but they were unencumbered by it—and they didn't attempt to burden us with it. They taught us the value of refusing to hate and the importance of looking forward, not back. They were refugees, yes, but they'd been lucky enough to escape the kind of life some of their relatives endured in host countries that didn't want them. By physically moving away from the Middle East, they managed to move forward. Many of those who stayed behind remained immersed in tragedy, mourning, and bitterness, and passed those emotions on to their children—in places where injustice is delivered in infinite quantities. Hope and ambition in such places are luxuries, whereas for my parents, they were the fuel of life. They were for us, too, now that we were finally home.

Winnipeg—that blotch of flat prairie land transformed by mostly Eastern European immigrants into a great western city, once dubbed Chicago of the North—is where I had spent most of my early life. It's where all our memories coalesced into a whole, where my father made us swear he would be buried. Winnipeg was where we children were born and where my parents were reborn. It was where we got our first degrees and took our first jobs. It was where our hearts and early friendships flourished. Winnipeg was *family*, despite the fact that we had not a single relative there, not even a distant one. In Winnipeg's mean-spirited snow squalls and wicked sub-zero temperatures, we found warmth. We moaned about the snow but felt out of sorts when it came late. We lamented that Winnipeg was small and remote, but delighted in the pristine lakes and beaches nearby. We camped and barbecued, played pickup football, pool, and the guitar, learned to love Gordon Lightfoot and Joni Mitchell, and knew a Sorel from a Cougar. We learned how to ride bikes in the snow, and how to bumpershine (slide on fresh snow while holding on to a vehicle's rear bumper) behind the Morley Avenue bus. We stood for all that Winnipeg was: a frontier town, diverse, remote, infuriating, and chilly, yet unusually friendly, even by Canadian standards, excessively optimistic, and strikingly naive. It now held us again in its frigid embrace, and we held on back, tightly.

☥

A few years in Winnipeg, and the Middle East receded into distant memory for us kids. But my parents tried to keep up with the news in between their shifts. Wars came and went, and came again. In 1987, Palestinians living in Israel, the West Bank, and Gaza erupted into an uprising, an intifada, against Israel, and people around the Middle East protested in solidarity. Iran and Iraq fought a bloody and costly war that ended in a draw in 1988, the year I graduated from high school. Halfway through my first university degree in 1990, the curtain was finally falling on Lebanon's egregious civil war. But we kids paid scant attention to all this, until Iraqi troops invaded Kuwait later that same year.

It had barely been two years since the inconclusive end of the Iran–Iraq War, when Saddam Hussein moved to annex Iraq's smaller, weaker, oil-rich neighbour. The entire world, it seemed, coalesced in condemnation and threats of retaliation for this "naked act of aggression," as President George Bush Sr. called it, and eventually the threats were backed up with smart bombs. Bush led a coalition of thirty countries, including Canada and several Arab nations, intent on driving Iraqi forces out.

It was a turn of events that left us uneasy—and made us a captive audience for the nightly news.

☥

I didn't know quite what to make of the first images of Desert Storm—captured by night-vision camera and released by the Pentagon to be broadcast on television shortly after the offensive started. Modern warfare didn't look the way I thought it would: a dark early morning sky lit up by a thousand green lights, like fireflies dancing in cheerful assent, punctuated from time to time by a sudden orange glow. It looked oddly like a video game I liked to play at the university arcade when there was no one around to shoot a game of pool. That week I did neither. The television commanded my attention.

Bush declared the conflict would be short. Saddam Hussein claimed it would be the "Mother of All Battles." CNN, meanwhile, covered the war live on location. Reporter John Holliman told viewers he'd never covered anything like it before. His colleague, Bernard Shaw, described being in Baghdad as feeling like "the centre of hell." None of those comments was particularly enlightening, but like so many others around the world, I was transfixed.

Before Desert Storm I knew little about Kuwait—or Iraq, for that matter. Only that when I was a toddler, we had, as a family, traversed Iraq's vast western desert by bus from Amman to see my grandmother Nazmiyah and my uncle Rajaee in Kuwait. My parents claim I ruined the visit by contracting typhoid upon arrival. I have no memories and not much else to show for the journey, apart from a few sun-bleached Kodak pictures and the faded typhoid scars on my face, which remain to this day.

I did learn something of the country from my history and geography classes back in Amman. In typical Middle Eastern denial, though, none of our textbooks addressed Iraq's controversial modern history—the ascent of the Ba'ath Party, or Saddam Hussein's murderous consolidation of power when he became president in 1979. Instead, we read about the gloried past: Iraq's fabled reputation as the cradle of civilization and the birthplace of the alphabet. We learned about Baghdad's status as the unrivalled centre for knowledge in the eighth and ninth centuries. We were regaled with the tale of Caliph Harun al-Rashid and the mechanically brilliant water clock he sent from Baghdad as a gift to Charlemagne, whose court thought it had magical qualities. But by 1991, most everything about the land of Dijla and Furat (Arabic for the Tigris and Euphrates rivers) in the twentieth century was a mystery to me.

But suddenly here was Iraq, beamed right to our old television at *The Manitoban*, the student newspaper where I worked part time while studying human genetics. Our motley crew of reporters stopped for a moment and gathered to watch the dancing lights in silence. It was an odd moment. Like previous generations of university students, we were altruistically anti-war, irrespective of how it started. I was as opposed to the U.S.-led battle as I was to Saddam's decision to appropriate Kuwait and then set its oil fields alight when he couldn't have his way. And I would have been just as disturbed had the same events transpired in South America.

Many North American Arabs were opposed to the war, for different reasons. Some were sympathetic to Saddam and some were not, but all were enraged at the West purely because Iraq was an Arab Muslim country under attack. Many of them viewed as hypocrisy the way in which the Western world descended swiftly on Iraq while other Arab dictators basked in Western friendship—and while Israel continued to occupy Arab land. I didn't think such opinions mattered—until Dad told me the story of a strange recent visit he'd had at the new business he now owned and operated, a Mr. Sub restaurant.

"The guy said he was from CSIS," he said casually. I'd only recently learned that the letters stood for the Canadian Security and Intelligence Service. One of its agents had paid my parents a visit shortly after the war started. He came more than once, brimming with questions.

"He wanted to know what we thought of the war," my father explained, "and whether we supported Saddam and [PLO leader] Yasser Arafat. I told him that we didn't like the war, [and that] the Americans had no business being there," he said.

"I also said that didn't mean we wanted to fight the West. It is just an opinion. If we wanted to be fighters, we wouldn't have come here. We came to Canada to find a better life for our family. I said we have nothing to do with it. We just want to work so we can send our children to university. Your mom got angry."

She took over the narrative. "I said, 'We have been paying taxes and working hard ever since we came to this country.'" My mother was furious about the insulting idea implicit in the man's questions—indeed his very presence—that Arab Canadians might pose some kind of security threat because they opposed the war "back home."

Mom brooded for days. I, too, was infuriated at our being singled out. It occurred to me for the first time that it might not be up to us to define "home," that others would ultimately judge whether we were as loyal to it as we claimed. Perhaps the highly attractive notion of a multicultural and tolerant Canada existed only in the colourful brochures put out by the government.

I was also resentful because the latest Middle East crisis had reached across the world and touched us directly. Other Arabs we knew had been touched too. They huddled at their homes to compare notes over endless pots of coffee and mugs of strong tea. Some said they, too, had received visits from strangers asking political questions. Others reported harassment and taunting and receiving racist phone calls.

I wished the war would stop. I combed newspapers looking for any hint of a resolution, and when I found none, I joined my mother in front of the television. It was clear this was a war with a lot of support. Saddam had made a grievous error, and he was being punished for it. Anti-war voices seemed marginal and distant.

Finally, six weeks after Operation Desert Storm began, Iraqi troops had withdrawn from Kuwait and President Bush declared the campaign a triumph for all of mankind. Left in power, Saddam also declared victory—and proclaimed an annual national holiday to celebrate it.

Emboldened by the war and U.S. encouragement, many Iraqis, especially Shia Muslims and Kurds, subsequently rose up to try to overthrow Saddam in 1991. He crushed them mercilessly. Some *two million* people were uprooted. But in spite of the magnitude of the violence and displacement following the war, we wouldn't hear much about that until many, many years later.

⚶

I had originally chosen to study genetics at university, but in my second year I had begun writing for the student newspaper and soon became heavily involved. Given that, along with my parents' heavy interest in the news, it was no surprise that I began seriously contemplating a journalism career. I abandoned a master's degree in genetics for one in journalism, at Carleton University in Ottawa. My first job after graduating was at The Canadian Press newswire on Parliament Hill in 1997.

I led an uneventful urban life in Ottawa for the next four years. In the Middle East, wars big and small continued. Then the attacks of September 11, 2001, shocked the world, and when it became clear the perpetrators were Arab Muslims, attention was refocused on the Middle East. Part of me instantly knew that while I loathed the prospect of returning to the region, it was really just a matter of time before I would be back in the middle of it.

War

*War by binoculars
is easy.*
—ARAB PROVERB

QUETTA, PAKISTAN, NOVEMBER 2001

I grew up knowing what war did to people. I lived among them, contemplating their vacant stares and the arrested lives they led long after the guns fell silent. Later, I read about the two world wars—wars so immense I couldn't imagine how people went on after their end. No one was built to withstand such horrors. Only death could silence the questions, the nightmares that would surely come. I could understand the compulsion of deserters like my paternal great-grandfather, who abandoned the Ottoman army into which he was drafted in the First World War and walked on foot all the way from Turkey to Annabah, just to avoid fighting. Later, on television, I watched the kind of war where lost human lives were called collateral damage, and wondered how the survivors saw it. I knew one thing: once war begins, it rarely ends. It rages on, even when the violence has ceased.

But I'd only witnessed conflicts vicariously and knew nothing of war first-hand. Now I was in the position to see one in person. I'd normally cringe at the sight of two men yelling at each other, and

I wasn't certain I was ready to have a front-row seat to man's most violent expression of a difference of opinion. But the War on Terror had already begun and I was on my way to Afghanistan. It was, first and foremost, a war of revenge for the acts of 9/11. But it was also a war of liberation. Afghanistan was, after all, ruled by Taliban extremists who'd all but suffocated their people, and it played host to the even more extremist al-Qaeda, now known to be behind the September 11 attacks. The U.S.-led war intended to annihilate both, helped along by a so-called coalition of the willing.

Canada, too, was sending troops to Afghanistan, and The Canadian Press sent me—along with war-tested photojournalist Kevin Frayer—to cover Canada's first combat mission since the Korean War. We arrived in Pakistan to find the city of Quetta overflowing with reporters eager to witness the war. Our mission was different: we'd been dispatched solely to document the arrival of Canadian soldiers to Kandahar, northwest and over the border from Quetta. But by the time we'd arrived, their deployment had yet to start. That provided the two of us with an opportunity to turn our attention to the wider story: the overall war, and what it was doing to the region's people.

Quetta was angry, inhospitable to the foreign press, and out-raged by the war next door. There were regular demonstrations in front of the Serena Hotel, where most journalists stayed, by those who loved Osama bin Laden and didn't fear showing it. In dozens of shops there were T-shirts and key chains bearing his likeness, and car decals declaring open devotion. The owner of one shop shared with us a "secret" carpet that, he claimed, few others had seen. He retrieved it from the back room and carefully unfolded it to reveal two airplanes on the verge of hitting the Twin Towers; woven underneath was bin Laden's face wearing an expression of grim satisfaction. It was just weeks after that apocolyptic day. Whoever made that carpet had worked strikingly fast.

"If you'd like to buy it, I'll give you a discount," the shop owner said. We declined and left.

The closest we could get to the fighting from Quetta was the Pakistan–Afghanistan border. We took several hair-raising trips through the twisting mountain roads to Chaman, a grimy border town that was suddenly overflowing with Afghan refugees. The first glimpse of them penned in by barbed wire to keep them out prompted us to forget the Canadians altogether and delve into their stories instead.

In the desert no man's land at the southeast corner of Afghanistan, the three thousand or so refugees waiting for permission to cross into Pakistan had erected an instant village. To shield them against the wind and the insidious dust, they pitched makeshift, multicoloured tents using old turbans, scarves, and faded carpets. Because they were still inside Afghanistan's border—just—they were not yet recognized officially as refugees. So there were no UN tents, no aid workers to distribute food—just well-armed Pakistani guards keeping close watch. The worst was supposed to be over for these people. Some of them had crossed mountains, and most had dodged bombs to get here. But now they were stuck in a camp for the unwanted, forced to make do in an inhospitable desert.

Within view was the camp where the "lucky" ones were registering with the UN. There, ten thousand refugees sheltered in the familiar thick beige UNHCR tents. Basic food supplies came from two warehouses and water from a communal tank, where barefoot children gleefully stamped in the mud near the taps. Other refugees sat on their still-packed belongings—if they had any—waiting to be processed before heading to the Roghani camp down the road. *That* was already home to another fifteen thousand displaced Afghans. I'd never seen so many people out of place.

At the have-not side of the border, men wrapped in brown shawls squatted silently just inches shy of the barbed wire. They watched the recognized refugees with envy, barely moving for what seemed like hours in an impressive feat of stillness. Despite all their misfortunes—or perhaps because of them—Afghans seemed a supremely patient lot. There was no yelling, no overt signs of anger among the squatters. A middle-aged woman who'd already slept in the cold for three days was decidedly resigned. Lal Bibi told me she'd come alone and had nothing to eat. But she was expressionless.

Another man I spoke to had come with seven others in one car all the way from a village near Mazar-e Sharif in northern Afghanistan. He said they travelled nearly a thousand kilometres, surviving treacherous roads made more dangerous by aerial bombardment and the occasional small-arms fire. "There was bombing in the villages, there was no sleep—that's why we came here," said the man, whose dark beard, white turban, and wrinkled face suggested he was fifty years old. He told me he was twenty-eight. "I don't know how they will solve our problem. There has been fighting for twenty-three years," he said. Since he was five.

This conflict was different from most others that Afghanistan had witnessed since Russian troops invaded more than two decades earlier. A large international coalition, led by the U.S., was backing Northern Alliance Afghan fighters on the ground against the Islamist Taliban, who in turn were backed by thousands of their foreign al-Qaeda guests. It was at once an invasion and a civil war, with anti-Taliban Northern Alliance fighters advancing south into the country and cleaning up in the wake of bombs dropped by American fighter jets. In the aftermath of the fighting, thousands of refugees poured into neighbouring Iran and Pakistan.

With a dearth of supplies and crumbling infrastructure, Pakistan was ill equipped to deal with so many refugees, never mind the casualties who were also crossing the border. Many of the wounded in this multi-layered war ended up there anyway, in a small wing of Quetta's derelict main hospital, primitively prepped and earmarked for the Afghan war-wounded. There I found more persuasive evidence of their enduring patience.

Mahmad was lying in the yellowed sheets of bed number 12, staring at the stained ceiling. For our benefit, he cleared his throat and recounted the moment that annihilated the family he'd been nurturing for half his life. A bomb had crashed into his home in Kandahar, killing his five sons and only daughter. His wife was paralyzed, probably for life, the doctors said. She was lying alone in the same hospital's women's wing. "I lost everything," he said, putting the blame squarely on the Americans. "Only the Americans bomb by air."

Mahmad and his wife were simple peasants caught in the crossfire. But at the same hospital a few days later, we also met combatants.

It was startling to hear Arabic in that filthy hospital ward. I alone was able to make sense of the soft mumbling coming from one of three injured men ambulances had brought over the border that morning. Hospital officials who had previously been welcoming didn't want us there that day, nervous we'd want to interview the men. But I was compelled to go over and hear more.

The injured man was in severe pain from a gunshot wound to the leg and barely able to speak. He had light skin, narrow brown eyes, and a feathery beard. He could have easily been Greek or even French. He was not Afghan, but Arab. It was our first encounter with a member of al-Qaeda.

I asked to interview him, while Kevin slyly snapped pictures from his hip. The man laboured to level his own questions first: "Do you believe in god?" He winced with pain. In formal Arabic, he proceeded to lecture me on the concept of Us and Them. I wanted to explain that Us and Them didn't exist in my world, but I knew I wasn't going to change the mind of a man who had risked his life for bin Laden. So I pushed him instead to get on with telling us what had happened. He started again: "In the name of Allah, the Compassionate, the Merciful ..."

His name was Ahmad, and he was a native of the United Arab Emirates and a father. He had been in Afghanistan for six months, he said, one of thousands who had enlisted in bin Laden's poisoned army. He said he was fighting for an Islamic state "ruled by Allah's word." He denounced his opponents as foolish. "If only they would come down to the ground," he said, referring to the pilots of the jets fighting America's war. "If only [U.S. Defence Secretary] Donald Rumsfeld came down to the ground. I challenge the United States to come down and face us. But they are cowards." Ahmad said the bombing had been relentless, and he'd seen what happened when those bombs touched the ground. "Women were being vaporized," he declared.

Before I could ask any more questions, we were led away by the nervous hospital staff. Ahmad kept talking, now with a raised voice: he said he needed help getting home to get treated. He would pay, he said; he claimed he had the means. The last thing I heard him say was a promise to return and exact revenge.

But the Taliban was disintegrating, and al-Qaeda was not faring much better. Their final holdout was Tora Bora, one of the last remaining battles of the war—a battle some at the time believed might yield bin Laden himself. At Kevin's insistence, we left to follow the action all the way to the White Mountains. We were finally on the way to watch the war.

☿

Peshawar's mad streets were retreating behind us just as the sun began its descent. We were leaving for Afghanistan hours later than was advisable. A week earlier, four journalists had been killed at the other end of the road we were embarking on. In this fast-paced conflict a week was a very long time, but there was no telling what we'd come across on the way.

U.S. forces had reason to believe that Osama bin Laden was hiding in a well-known cave complex in the White Mountains, and they were going after him. Northern Alliance forces, who were fighting on the ground, eagerly anticipated imminent victory and hoped the media would be there to record it. Zulmay, the cousin of a key Northern Alliance commander, sat down with us and a Sky News crew to describe the journey ahead and reassure us that it would be safe. To get to Tora Bora, we would take the famous Silk Road through the historic Khyber Pass and the adjoining tribal areas to Jalalabad—just days ago an al-Qaeda stronghold—then on to our destination. Zulmay was fluent in English, with honey-coloured eyes and a determination about him that seemed trustworthy. We—*I*—had safety concerns, of course, and we spent a long time discussing them. Though Kevin had covered the mad war of the Balkans, I had never covered any war—and certainly neither of us had covered anything like *this*. Ultimately, the possibility of witnessing bin Laden's fate trumped all other considerations, and we were on our way.

Our convoy comprised about nine vehicles filled with a dozen foreigners—Canadians, British, Japanese, and two young American war tourists who claimed they were freelancers—along with Zulmay and his men. We were led and trailed by two pickup trucks full of Afghan gunmen armed with Kalashnikovs and an impressive load of ammunition. The guys at the back smiled and waved to us, indifferent to the sand kicked into their faces by the pickup trucks ahead.

It was still light out as we made our way through the Khyber Pass, which connects Pakistan to Afghanistan through the Hindu Kush range. The original road through this treacherous pass was built centuries ago, but still perilously in use today. Weighed down by television equipment and flak jackets, our convoy laboured on the way up and tiptoed on the winding way down, careful to control speed. The ground levelled off and dried up, and soon we passed what we were told had been bin Laden's family house, now quiet and vacant on a barren plot in the desert. Well after dark, we arrived in newly liberated Jalalabad and spent the night there. The next morning, we took the short drive to a cliff facing Tora Bora. From there we could see the White Mountains lying provocatively across the horizon, like a nude posing for a painter. The snowy peaks were nearly the colour of the bright sky. Our perch on the other side of a deep valley gave us a perfect vantage point in an almost empty theatre.

Bin Laden was apparently heard giving instructions to his men on shortwave radio from inside the caves below Tora Bora. The reports were credible enough that a constant rotation of fighter jets circled overhead around the clock. If the coalition was on the verge of capturing him, we were sitting on the biggest story of the war.

The Sky News crew generously allowed us to share their shelter: a lone mud hut that once housed goats on an otherwise barren mountaintop. We slept in rows in the largest room, shivering from the cold, protected by two guards who excelled mostly at smoking weed. We were so close to the mountains that every explosion erupting over Tora Bora sent the air rushing to us, shaking the ground beneath. I spent a long time sitting and watching as the jets dropped their payload and circled back. It was the first time I'd seen plumes of smoke so large and heard explosions so thunderous. This was no edited vignette on the evening news. This was real and I was awestruck.

But there would be little more than that to report if I couldn't talk to *someone*. Both sides were out of reach: the Americans in the sky, and al-Qaeda hiding from view. The few Afghans we saw were largely locally engaged staff providing security for the journalists.

This could get very boring very fast if there was no one to tell us what was happening.

One of the main stars of this particular theatre of destruction was Haji Zaher, the son of Nangarhar province's recently reinstated governor, and the Afghan Northern Alliance commander who was leading part of the ground offensive against the remaining Taliban and al-Qaeda around Tora Bora. He had a personal score to settle: the Taliban had imprisoned and tortured him for four years before he escaped and lived in exile. It explained why he was down at the front line and apparently shooting at the enemy himself. We met him one morning as he returned from the front line. He said his men were engaging al-Qaeda fighters at a distance of little more than three hundred metres.

Though he came from a wealthy family, Zaher had chosen to live a soldier's life. He eschewed the fine silk clothing his governor father wore in favour of the traditional *shalwar kameez* in rough, olive-coloured material and the Pakul hat that another former Northern Alliance commander, the assassinated Ahmad Massoud, had made so famous. His large hands were rough and callused, snaked by wrinkles that were darkened with dirt. He was a mere twenty-seven years old, years younger than his lined face suggested.

That morning, while Zaher updated the Sky team and us on the situation at the front, his cousin Zulmay, who'd arranged our trip to Tora Bora, gestured from the waiting SUV. *Dinner, tonight*, he mouthed to us. It was the final day of Ramadan, and Eid was starting the following morning. Zulmay and his cousin would not entertain taking us to the front line, but we were being invited to break the fast with the commander whose personal battle was making world headlines.

We were picked up later that day by one of Zaher's brothers in a gleaming new SUV that belonged to the Northern Alliance crowd. It was a quick journey to a clutch of derelict homes that, in the darkness, seemed to appear out of nowhere. Once we stepped through the door of one of them, we were inside Zaher's war room.

In short order, heaps of steaming lamb in dishes full of broth and plates of spicy chicken were placed on the plastic sheeting that had been laid on the floor as our dinner table. It looked like many dinner settings I had sat at as a child in Jordan. We sidled up, each with a spot marked by a round, soft naan-like bread. Pepsi cans were handed out, and at first everyone ate in silence. A number of dishevelled men sat along the walls of the large room, watching and listening to the staccato of conversation. I assumed they were Zaher's men, politely waiting their turn to eat after the guests had finished.

Haji Zaher was utterly serious at first, but after he ate, his face occasionally gave in to a faint smile. He told us in service-able English that the number of al-Qaeda men still fighting had dwindled to perhaps three hundred, and that in his estimate the only thing standing between him and their surrender was actually the relentless American bombardment, which he said made it harder for his men to get at their foes. Others had surrendered, he said, and were now in his custody. To my disappointment and rage, I found out long after we left that those men sitting against the walls watching us eat that night were members of al-Qaeda who were now Haji Zaher's prisoners, but he didn't share that with us.

After what we heard, we were certain the battle would soon be over. But days passed, and even as Kevin and I finally packed our pickup truck to leave our perch on the White Mountains (having run out of developments to report), there was still no word on bin Laden's whereabouts. No word either on when the Canadians would show up.

Back in Islamabad, we caught a UN flight and made our way to Kabul, that shadow of a city, where war was already over and optimism was creeping back in. An always malleable Kabul embraced yet another changing of the guard and its markets threw open their doors. There we reported on the first British troops patrolling the streets, on Hamid Karzai getting sworn in to lead an interim government on December 22, 2001. We covered the reopening of the largest girls' school in the capital, and Kevin took a wonderful picture of the students at break time, with me smiling in their midst. Then Kevin had his own picture taken at a sidewalk photo studio with an ancient camera that produced a cool sepia print—impossible just a few short weeks earlier, because under the Taliban, photos were considered un-Islamic. But Kabul without the Taliban was now breaking all the old rules. Restaurants allowed foreign women to dine alongside the men, while stores offered decades-old bottles of Russian vodka for sale to foreigners desperate for something to toast with on the eve of a new year.

While still waiting for word on the Canadian deployment, I wrote story after story about Kabul's past, present, and future. Among its residents we met women with ambition, men with broken dreams, and far too many people—too many children— who'd lost limbs to landmines, which were still planted on the outskirts of the city in fields that lined the road to the airport. We visited the abandoned parts of western Kabul, whose residents had fled long ago during a different war. What remained of the walls of homes were pockmarked and whittled down by shells and bullets. There were only children there—children in tattered, dirty clothing, playing among the relics of a neighbourhood doomed before they were born, asking us for pens and for money. I assumed they knew the story of that place, of a country more familiar with war than peace, but it seemed to exist only for their amusement. A place left for dead, now a playground for the desperately living.

At the former Intercontinental Hotel, just a short climb from an oversized poster of Massoud, dozens of us journalists collectively prepared for the holidays and marked the new year together. Bin Laden had disappeared, but the Taliban had been overthrown and the war was all but over. The Canadians finally announced that they would start arriving in January, and we made plans to head to Kandahar to complete our original task.

☨

The road into Afghanistan from Quetta lived up to its reputation: bumpy, barren, and dotted with as many dodgy checkpoints as there were cavernous potholes. Our driver missed one checkpoint and barrelled through at speed, and if we hadn't stopped at the last second, the guards were poised to shoot.

Kandahar was no Kabul. It was a dusty, dysfunctional, and conservative city, no surprise given that it had been the Taliban's effective capital. But with this war largely over, a hint of the optimism and post-Taliban revelry in Kabul could be detected here, too.

I met women who dared to contemplate the possibility that perhaps they had truly been liberated this time. The opium brokers were so optimistic they welcomed us warmly into their tents at the market and argued over who would get to show us some of the sticky, olive-black paste. The music sellers re-emerged and peddled their once-forbidden wares as if there had been no interruption. The only radio station in Kandahar was back on the air, for two hours a day, under new management—the province's post-Taliban warlord governor, Gul Agha Sherzai. Like Afghanistan itself and many of its people, Radio Mili swiftly switched allegiances after the Taliban's fall, and its new/old operators were adamant it would flourish again, despite the damage successive wars had inflicted on its operations, and the lives they claimed among the staff.

The studio contained a haphazard collection of ancient radio equipment and, on the roof, bullet-riddled satellite dishes that hadn't functioned in years. Javid Wafa, a doctor-cum-announcer on duty that day, had actually worked there under the Taliban, but now his broadcasts included music.

"It's not my job, it's my duty," Wafa explained. "I have to do this thing for my country." While we were there, the music ground to a halt, twice, until a technician intervened, and at one moment the power cut out, shutting down the entire broadcast. The Taliban may have been toppled, but they were just one of Afghanistan's many disorders in need of immediate attention.

The station manager, Abdul Ali, once a Northern Alliance fighter, wanted all of Afghanistan to follow in his footsteps and renounce violence. "We want to provide education. A pen instead of a weapon."

Down the highway, the Kandahar airfield whirred with activity, awash with more weapons than the city has likely ever seen. Once a base for al-Qaeda, it was now home to thousands of foreign soldiers, mostly American, along with their tents, Humvees, transport planes, and portable latrines.

When we arrived, now joined by Broadcast News reporter Dan Dugas, there were already a few scraggly journalists set up in the terminal, one of the few solid structures on the base. Two of them, also Americans, were wearing fatigues and already knew their way around the base. Another journalist approached us that afternoon to introduce himself and immediately asked if he could take our pictures. "I want to have shots of you just in case you're killed," he said. He wasn't joking. I thought if anyone was going to be killed, it would be him—he did after all insist on wearing a giant yellow slicker in what was still a war zone.

The winter winds had set in and it was biting cold, with dust storms often announcing the start of the day and closing out the evenings. The wind howled the length of the terminal, bringing plenty of sand to wreak havoc with our computers and our lungs.

It didn't help that our workspace was right next to several large windows shattered by bombs weeks earlier.

Just about everything else was housed in tents. Ours was within a few hundred metres of the tarmac, where military planes were taking off and landing all night, making sleep all but impossible. A small "cafe" that offered soothing hot cups of soup on the way to the (open-air) latrines was the only respite. That and the guesthouse we frequented in Kandahar City for a shower and a hot meal.

The Canadian commanding officer was already on the ground. Lt.-Col. Patrick Stogran often walked through the terminal in full battle gear, smoking a cigar, and like an apprehensive expectant father, he seemed to be wondering what was taking so long. His battalion finally began arriving in January, and we were there to stick microphones in their tired faces and shadow them to their austere new homes. Many of the soldiers had little time for journalists. But as we all became accustomed to being in one another's faces in difficult conditions, many of them agreed to speak with us both on and off the record.

Over the next few months, I spent several weeks at the Kandahar airfield and in the city—sometimes in the company of colleagues, and at other times on my own. I was already comfortable covering my head and wearing a *shalwar kameez*, eating on the floor with families in their homes, and driving on the wrong side of the road if that was the occasional local custom. But I had now also learned how to put on a flak jacket in seconds, and how to safely board a Chinook helicopter. I even tried rappelling from the Kandahar airport observation tower—where else would you get the chance?—when one enterprising Canadian platoon did it for practice. And I went along when the troops decided to try to pick a fight, the largest yet Canadian-led operation that took us into Zabul Province, bordering Pakistan, to search out remaining Taliban. They travelled in nearly fifty vehicles for nine hours before reaching the compound of the local governor in Qalat, passing along the way through tiny villages whose people ran out to watch us in horror, wondering what war was being fought now. We camped out for a few days at a local fort that had been a base for the Taliban and the Russians before them. The soldiers scoured the area for fighters or weapons but returned mostly empty-handed.

I was allowed to join some of the journeys to the local governor's home, riding on the high back seat of an open jeep next to the Canadian regimental sergeant major, an affable, white-haired man with a significant moustache and a dazzling smile. I also spent a day with a small Canadian reconnaissance unit led by a confident, temporarily bearded soldier going door to door in civilian clothing, delivering aid and gathering intelligence near Shinkay, believed at the time to be an escape route for Taliban and al-Qaeda fleeing to Pakistan. We ended that day settling into a cracked, dry wadi for hours, whiling away time discussing sports, waiting for the signal to leave. Not a single shot was fired—the Canadian commander suspected the remnant fighters they had come to engage had been tipped off about the operation. The caches of weapons the soldiers gathered to destroy were the only payoff.

The rest of the time, it didn't feel like war, and indeed most of the serious fighting was long over. That, of course, would change later. In quiet discussions back on the base at the time, many soldiers told me they were disappointed. Canada's forces, better known for peacekeeping, hadn't seen combat for half a century, and now that they were here, they wanted to be part of history. With time, the fighting—fierce fighting—would come, claiming the lives of 158 Canadian soldiers. In that first tour of duty in 2002, four Canadians would tragically be killed due to U.S. friendly fire. Otherwise Kandahar remained mostly quiet while the Taliban schemed elsewhere, preparing for a violent comeback.

On July 13, 2002, Canadian combat operations were over—for

now. I stayed long enough for the draw-down ceremony five days later, to watch the Canadian flag lowered and an Inukshuk unveiled in memory of the four soldiers who had fallen. I watched one night as the first military plane carrying Canadian soldiers took off into the darkness, heading for home. Eventually I boarded one myself, leaving the desert behind, and the next thing I knew, I was in Frankfurt, disoriented by the fields of green.

I returned to Ottawa, certain I wouldn't be staying long. Over five years, The Canadian Press had taught me the rigours of journalism more than any degree could, and there I'd found invaluable mentors and lifelong friends. I'd learned extensively about politics, about multitasking and writing quickly, about the art of encapsulating breaking news into one short sentence. Most important, I learned the value of working in a team whose members always pulled in the same direction.

But I wanted to follow the story, and it was shifting to the Middle East. I had not intended to make that part of the world part of my world again. But after September 11, it seemed a foregone conclusion. I quit my job at CP, packed up my apartment, and said my farewells. Armed with vague promises from some newspapers, a freelance contract with the CBC, and approval for an Iraqi visa, I stopped thinking and made my way back.

FIVE

Jordan, Again

ॐ

The cobbler is barefoot,
and the carpenter's door is broken.
—ARAB PROVERB

AMMAN, DECEMBER 2002

I hadn't heard a call to prayer like this in years. When perfected, as this one was, its quarter tones summon the memories of hundreds of years past, an echo of millions of births and deaths and as many misunderstandings. It is a plea—no, a command, a reminder of duty. It is conscience, given a man's voice and amplified by loudspeaker. This call was reproachful and far too close, accompanied by a dissonance of backup callers that, in the dead of night, was nearly deafening.

I knew that somewhere, not far from my hotel, members of my own extended family could hear the same wraith-like chorus beckoning them from slumber. I imagined their movements at the sound of the call: rising out of bed and praising Allah; heading to the wash basin to cleanse; pulling back on hairlines, water dripping from elbows. A well-worn prayer mat is handy, perched on the living room couch, or perhaps near the bed. They pull at it gently, and with a practised flick of a wrist, they unroll and point it in the direction of Mecca. They begin their meditation by raising hands to ears—*Allahu Akbar*—then resign themselves to the Almighty, looking down, hands at rest, minds fully engaged. They prostrate themselves, touching their foreheads to the ground, then sit back up. And again. The prayer ends in a salutation to the angels that sit on each shoulder. To the right: *assalamu alaikum wa rahmatullah.* To the left: *assalamu alaikum wa rahmatullah.* Hands are then cupped on laps in the final act of prayer, asking Allah to protect children, bring success, forgive sins. Make them worthy of heaven.

I was wide awake with jet lag, listening to my imagination, and there was, admittedly, a hint of nostalgia in my imaginings. But I had no love for this place, and this was no happy homecoming. My parents had spurned it, not once but twice. And despite our brief residence here, we would always be, as I was now, only visitors.

I had allowed the prevailing winds to carry me east, in the direction of a coming war, armed with only one conviction: that I might be useful here, at a time like this. Driven by an involuntary compulsion and in a lingering daze, I found myself stepping onto the cold, scuffed floors of the Amman airport, waiting in a queue for official Jordanian sanction of my hare-brained idea. My world had narrowed: everyone—myself included—looked alike, and I suddenly thought I'd made a mistake. Then someone stamped my passport, and I collected my things and headed out in the bitter Amman wind, where I ordered a taxi.

Within a few hundred metres of the airport, the interrogation began.

Where did you fly in from? Why are you alone? Why are you staying at a hotel? Where is this family you're talking about? Are you married?

I'd forgotten that curiosity here went beyond the bounds of what was considered appropriate back home. Frankly, I didn't care to tell my whole story in a country where the habits and traditions generally glowered on a single woman arriving alone in the night, en route to a country on the verge of war. Later, I would change my story depending on the look of the driver, his age, the time of day, and my mood. Sometimes I made a lengthy phone call or pretended that I didn't speak Arabic so I could avoid Taxicab Confession.

"What is wrong with this Bush, anyway?" ventured my current taxi driver.

Arabs talk about politics just as Canadians discuss the weather. It's the region's favourite pastime, an obsession. For a nation of analysts, it's an easy icebreaker, a subject suitable for small talk between strangers at salons, in the bank, at the mosque. *Did you see what happened today at the UN? A shame, isn't it?* And it isn't just the broad strokes. Arabs love the minutiae: a gesture from a politician here, a questionable look there, a stumble, however small—all are worthy of feverish conjecture. Any child old enough to attend school knows the names of the past several U.S. presidents, what the British prime minister last said about the peace process, what might have prompted the latest skirmish. You had to know what was going on, and you had to have a position. If you didn't, then you were clearly a stranger. Or a spy. Or both.

Later, I would learn to avoid discussing politics unless I was working. I was happy to listen to people's thoughts—they were only too happy to share them—but I learned to placate my interrogators with just the right platitudes. I kept any thoughts I had to myself.

This chatty driver, however, wouldn't relent.

"What for do they want to attack Iraq?"

Obviously, Iraq was the subject of the hour. I had my own questions, a journalist's questions. We were being told that there were good reasons for this war-in-waiting, that Saddam had long had this coming. I'd read about how he treated his own people; knew well his adventures into Iran, Kuwait, and Israel; and understood in theory the U.S. desire to depose him. But did Saddam still have weapons of mass destruction? Was he implicated somehow in supporting terrorism, as Washington claimed? Perhaps Iraq needed an earthquake to bring stability to the region, or at least to that country's long-suffering people. But earthquakes also bring disaster and misery. Much as people in this region might have thought otherwise—much as Bush might have thought otherwise—in this, it was already clear there was no black and white.

It was early morning as we approached the city, and the streets were empty and dark. I had dozens of relatives in Amman, but I had told no one that I was coming. I didn't want to explain my career choice and the peripatetic life I would now be leading. So for most of my stay in Amman, I kept mostly to myself. Other foreign-born Arabs of my generation in search of their roots came back and dove right in. I skimmed along the surface, like someone swimming in the Dead Sea. I had not come to find myself. I did not, actually, know precisely what I had come to find.

ℵ

I found a Jordan I hardly recognized. I marvelled at the dizzying signs of modernity: Internet cafes, highways and bridges and endless lines of new cars, thousands of modern new buildings—and a KFC, a Pizza Hut, and a Hard Rock Cafe. There was even a gay-friendly cafe installed in the heart of the old city. It seemed everyone had a mobile phone, when just a generation ago, only the privileged had landlines.

Shrill, bubbly Arabic music blared from storefronts and restaurants, while Western rap music jump-started the souped-up, beat-up Beamers of young men fond of street racing. Taxi drivers I rode with played the Koran, the news, or old favourites like Oum Kolthoum or Fairouz. Though Lebanese, Fairouz was omnipresent throughout the Middle East—as she had been when we were children—her morning music like daytime lullabies for adults. There was a Fairouz song for every occasion. She sang for lovers, for snow, for Lebanon and Amman and Jerusalem, and eventually even for a little house in Canada. And a disproportionate number of her songs were about exile, separation. "They're gone, like a dream, they're gone," she once sang.

On one early morning taxi excursion, I daydreamed to the lilting rhythm of one of her favourites. "Visit me once a year, it's cruel to forget me completely," she sang, seemingly speaking to me. I'd visited Jordan briefly twice since we left in 1983, but I was still astounded by how much Amman had grown. Over several days I took in the changes by car, eventually chancing upon our old neighbourhood of Hay Nazzal. The large fields we crossed on the way to school were now filled with new buildings, restaurants, and drive-through coffee stands. The field at the end of our "high street" was no longer a petrifying stretch of garbage populated by wild camomile and grasshoppers. It was now an entirely new, densely populated neighbourhood, with store upon clothing store and a large souk where women with veiled faces dashed in and out. Downtown Amman looked the same: grimy, congested, and full of aimless young men walking arm in arm in Hashemite Square, near the Roman amphitheatre. After a cursory look, poor, residential East Amman—and Al-Wihdat—also seemed the way I remembered them: beige, rigid, insolent, overpopulated, and dirty. In a petty act of revenge, I rented an overpriced, sterile apartment in affluent West Amman, an antidote to the memories of squalor in the East.

Yet Al-Wihdat *had* changed. Its main thoroughfare was lined with small businesses selling CDs, mobile phones, and stylish clothing. Many homes had shed their zinc roofs, the open sewers had disappeared, and many of the narrow alleys had been paved. Still, nearly two decades after I left Amman, the camps, and their way of life, lived on.

Today's Jordanian kids, though, were obsessed with computers and Britney Spears and the twenty-four-hour TV networks dedicated to children's programming, which even showed the odd episode of the original *Tom and Jerry*. It seemed kids and adults alike had been kidnapped by the expanding world of Arab television. It now included everything from hugely popular Arab reality shows—or foreign ones dubbed in Arabic—to Arab versions of MTV, which played surprisingly suggestive video clips that rivalled even their Western counterparts in gaminess. In our absence, the Middle East had also produced Al Jazeera, a Qatari-owned, pan-Arab network. Its inception in 1996 was hailed by American commentators as the "dawn of Arab freedom." One of the first shows I caught was an hour-long live debate, *The Opposite Direction*, Al Jazeera's flagship current-affairs program. The unabashed criticism of Arab policy, of Arab governments, even of Arab leaders left me in shock—as it did the Arab leaders themselves. An incensed Muammar Qaddafi, Libya's then president, even called in once to join the debate. News shows also interviewed foreigners—including Israeli officials—live, with simultaneous translation, providing Arab audiences directly with information that until then they had only heard second-hand. State television—the brainwashing tool we watched as children— was surely on its way to extinction.

At first glance, to someone who knew a different Jordan, it seemed that the country was making progress in tackling its significant political, economic, and social problems—helped in part by foreign investment and aid, which increased dramatically after Jordan signed a peace treaty with Israel in 1994. The country was booming, and even those in the majority Palestinian population were flourishing. I would later discover that many of my own relatives had left the camps for regular neighbourhoods and now lived in proper homes, some of them in relative prosperity. Not Uncle Hussein, though; he still lived the way he'd always lived, and wanted everyone else in his life to do the same. During the past two decades, time had raced ahead for us in Canada, and for people in many parts of Jordanian society. But like Miss Havisham in *Great Expectations*, Uncle Hussein had, out of what I could only surmise was deep bitterness, stopped all the clocks. It's why I'd vowed never to enter that house again.

Amman was never home to me in the emotional sense of the word. Nor did I feel much warmth there, despite its agreeable climate. It was a tough place, which developed around seven hills, with eight major traffic circles (some of which had been replaced by traffic lights but were still referred to as circles when people gave directions). It was a challenge to drive or walk, and virtually impossible to get ahead without a *wasta* (connection), bribes, or both. There was no official caste system, but there was overt inequity: people of Palestinian origin—the majority—were always a notch or two below the native Jordanians, unless they were wealthy. And sometimes even then.

Though parts of the countryside were breathtaking, Amman itself was generally devoid of beauty. For most of my time in the region as a journalist, it was only a *mahatta*, a station, a place to pass through on the way to someplace else. And so as I rang in 2003 in a hotel room alone, I pledged a kind of celibacy, a departure from my history in Amman, from everyone and everything that had come with it, for the sake of my work. I was visiting the Middle East on my own terms, unencumbered by either habits and traditions or family obligations. This was a job, and I was sure I wouldn't be here for long. A couple of years at most.

Despite the years I had spent here, I couldn't profess to fully comprehend the region and I had come with so many questions. If indeed, as so-called orientalist writers claimed for generations, Arabs had throughout their early history valued liberty and independence above all else, how could they be ruled by autocrats for so long?

How had they endured four centuries of Ottoman rule, and then many more years controlled by European colonial powers? And if Islam were truly the religion of tolerance and brotherhood, why did the largely Muslim Arabs despise one another as much as they did? And how could any Muslim be capable of violence on the magnitude of the September 11 attacks? And if indeed militant Islam was on the rise, how could you explain the simultaneous soaring popularity of figures like the sultry Lebanese singer Haifa Wehbe and her provocative video clips?

I rarely heard such questions answered, let alone asked, in anything I read or watched about the Middle East in the mainstream media. The crises, as always, dominated—and there were plenty of them. Even then, such reports regularly glossed over nuances that mattered—ignoring key historical facts, mistranslating people's words—occasionally significantly altering reality. I thought with my basic knowledge of the region and the language I could perhaps, in the smallest of ways, try to fill that void. It was, by any measure, a grandiose self-assignment, but I intended, after much encouragement from respected colleagues, to give it a try.

ࢶ

It may be one of the world's oldest civilizations, but the Arab world as it exists today is terribly young. Most of its daughter nations only gained their independence well into the twentieth century, having been ruled by the Ottomans and, later, the French or the British. All of them left indelible marks on the region—even the borders were determined by colonial rulers, seemingly blind to the complexities they introduced by drawing them the way they did. Those borders are often blamed as the root cause of the internal strife and regional conflicts those countries would experience later.

In the same post-colonial period, Israel also declared independence on May 14, 1948. Palestinians still mark May 15, 1948, as the Nakba, or the catastrophe in reference to their displacement. Israel's founding was a transformative event that seized the region, with Arabs interpreting the West's steadfast support of the new country as another example of its treachery. That support cemented the widespread modern-day suspicion and distrust among Arabs of Western nations and their intentions. Arab nations sympathetic to Palestinians declared war against the new nation. A year later, armistice agreements between Israel and its neighbours officially ended the fighting, and Israel remained. But the conflict continued to simmer, with occasional flare-ups.

An "awakening" that was sweeping the region in that period in the form of Arab nationalism adopted the recovery of Palestinian land as its cause célèbre. For a time, the nationalist movement's idol was Egypt's president, Gamal Abdel Nasser. Though he was a fiercely controlling autocrat, he was admired as an Arab hero for successfully nationalizing the Suez Canal in 1956 in the face of an Israeli, British, and French onslaught. He was immensely charismatic, well-spoken, and passionate, simultaneously a friend to U.S. president John Kennedy, Libyan president Muammar Qaddafi, and Cuba's Fidel Castro, yet still seemingly connected to the common man. He managed to come across as a playful husband and father who loved music, especially that of Egyptian Oum Kolthoum, whose live concerts he occasionally attended. He took up photography and filmmaking as a hobby. Nasser was repeatedly credited with restoring to the Arab people a sense of dignity, with reclaiming some of their lost glory. And with him at the helm of the nationalist movement, the region's people, especially its youth, felt a surge of hope.

Abdel Nasser's popularity continued to soar—until the 1967 Six-Day War. Nasser and his allies massed troops along Israel's borders, threatening war, when Israel launched a surprise pre-emptive strike, wiping out most of Egypt's air force in a mere three hours. It was the disastrous start of a short war that would end very badly for

Arabs, and with a breathtaking triumph for Israel. In an unusual act of contrition rarely taken by an Arab autocrat before or since, Nasser announced he would step down. Egyptians protested in the streets in response, so he changed his mind and stayed.

Still, it was a stunning defeat, and not just for Egypt. In only six days, Israel had annexed East Jerusalem and the West Bank from Jordan, Gaza and the Sinai Peninsula from Egypt, and the Golan Heights from Syria. A new rush of Palestinian refugees arrived in Jordan, Egypt, and Syria. The events of 1948 may have been described as the Nakba, but this defeat was named the Naksa— the setback—reflecting the deep disappointment that prevailed throughout the Arab world. It is a setback still deeply embedded in its psyche. It signalled the beginning of the end of the nationalist cause—a disappointment ultimately punctuated by Nasser's death from a heart attack in 1970. The modern Arab identity was set, marked by a constant expectation of disappointment, a pessimistic outlook, and a sense of victimization and self-pity.

The enduring disappointment also encouraged the ascendancy of political Islam and the groups that espoused it, who painted it as the only answer to secular nationalism's failures.

⚜

In the years between that war and my return to the Middle East in 2002, a cascade of other events helped entrench and deepen the negativity.

There were regular spikes of violence: the 1970 conflict in Jordan and subsequent eviction of the PLO; the 1973 war between Arab nations and Israel; the fifteen-year Lebanese Civil War, fuelled partly by the PLO's relocation to Lebanon, which in turn invited an Israeli invasion of the country in 1982; the disastrous Iran–Iraq War throughout most of the 1980s; the decisive 1982 Syrian government crackdown against the rebellion in the city of Hama;

the two Palestinian intifadas, or uprisings, against Israeli occupation; the failed Israeli-Palestinian peace talks; the First Gulf War in
1990–91; right up to September 11, 2001.

Oppressive Arab dictators—nationalist strongmen like Iraq's
Saddam Hussein, Syria's Hafez al-Assad, and Libya's Muammar
Qaddafi—and the violence they perpetrated against their own
people ensured any remaining hope was completely snuffed
out. They, along with other autocrats around the Arab world,
ruled through fear, curtailing freedoms and crushing any and all
opponents into submission, often under the pretext of protecting
national security at a time of "war."

In the modern Middle East, Arab presidents were lifers who
preferred their opposition in exile or in prison and groomed their
sons to take their place. Many of the leaders entrenched their
positions by having the West believe that only they could keep a lid
on Islamists and their anti-West sentiments.

Arab leaders rarely agreed on anything, hamstrung as they
were by divided loyalties and the backing from competing powers
that ranged from past colonial masters to new-found international
players with self-serving and often conflicting agendas. And beyond
the long authoritarian tradition, many other hands conspired to
maintain the status quo—the rival influences of various religious
factions, tribal loyalties, the merchant elite, the ongoing conflict
with Israel. There was always something that hampered change
and, by default, favoured the ruling class. So change was elusive.
Nearly impossible.

Yet it was badly needed, because the Middle East in the first
decade of the twenty-first century was in a deep trough, an unmiti-
gated rut—politically, economically, technologically, and socially.

Most countries in the region had loosened up enough to let the
modern world in—computers and the Internet, mobile phones—
though some countries severely limited access. But they were in

decline and lagging behind everyone else in virtually everything that counted: from education to women's participation in the workforce to political freedom. If anyone doubted it, the proof came in a blunt 2002 report prepared by Arab experts for the United Nations Development Programme (UNDP). When it came to political freedom, the Arab world fared abysmally, scoring lowest out of seven regions on the "freedom score" in the late 1990s. On a scale called "voice and accountability," which considered a number of factors, such as civil liberties and independence of the media, the Arab world again came in dead *last*. In both cases, that meant it had scored even lower than countries in Latin America and sub-Saharan Africa.

Arab governments, even U.S. allies among them, became the subject of severe criticism in the wake of the September 11 attacks for failing to democratize, failing to bring economic reform, and failing to improve human rights. In the view of Western experts and many Eastern ones, the widespread disenchantment that resulted from such failures had, over time, bred the fanaticism and extremism that led to September 11.

Arab dictators passionately argued change must be gradual and must come from within. By 2002, many were ostensibly in the process of introducing change. And Jordan was among the first to try to address the criticism blowing in from the West.

"Jordan First!" Everywhere I went in Amman, it was Jordan First: on billboards, lampposts, car windows, front doors. This slick nationalist campaign, the first in Jordan's history, was the Jordanian monarchy's attempt to redefine the relationship between individual and state, to woo Palestinian Jordanians into moving on from their past and putting Jordan first. The government's description of the exercise used unfamiliar words like "democracy," "justice," "equal opportunity," and "enhancing public freedom." It sounded promising, but it was wholly un–Middle Eastern, and therefore suspicious. Skeptics suggested it was simply elaborate chicanery designed to give the *impression* of willingness to change, without actually changing anything. Still, the effort drew cautiously optimistic declarations from within the region and abroad that Jordan—a staunch ally of the U.S. and the West as a whole—was finally engaging in something that resembled a reform process.

Saudi Arabia, meanwhile, revealed a blueprint for what appeared to be one of the most promising pan-Arab reform initiatives in recent years. The so-called Charter for Reform of the Arab Condition not only advocated the creation of an Arab free-trade zone, but also called on all Arab rulers to give more power to their people. It was a bold yet discordant initiative coming from one of the least permissive countries in the world.

"The Arab heads of state decide that internal reform and enhanced political participation in the Arab states are essential steps for the building of Arab capabilities, and for providing the conditions for a comprehensive awakening and development of Arab human resources," said the text, published in the pan-Arab daily *Asharq Alawsat*. Awakening. Internal reform. Political participation. Words that suggested Arab leaders were at least acknowledging the shameful state of affairs festering before their gazes.

But such moves proved hollow, superficial, and very late. Islamist political groups were already well entrenched in countries like Jordan, Syria, and Egypt, and as the only alternative that managed to evolve under the existing regimes—they could crush dissent, but they could not close the mosques—they were growing in popularity. Disenchanted citizens had become more religious, and many young Arabs were far more so than their parents or grandparents. Their votes alone could carry Islamist groups to outright victory were it not for the diligent efforts of those regimes to keep them out of power.

You could see evidence of the resurgence of Islam just by walking the streets. The change in Amman after only a couple of decades was stark: I noticed that many, many more young women wore the hijab, and even the niqab (the face-covering veil) and gloves (both optional in Islam), than before. Many more young men wore beards and attended mosques on a regular basis. But it didn't happen as easily as the experts thought—and not only due to lack of freedom and economic opportunity. Religious zeal was imported by expatriate Arabs who worked in the conservative Arab Gulf region, where religion plays a much bigger role in society and politics. It was also exported feverishly, mostly by Saudi Arabia—in the form of mosques, schools, and money—in an effort to win a cold war against its Shia Muslim rival, Iran.

For some of the young, Islam had also simply become the modern-day communism their parents had embraced as teens, the nationalism of their grandparents. In places like Jordan, it had become cool to be zealous about your faith—even rebellious. If your parents disapproved—which many of them did—then all the better.

For the ordinary masses who'd embraced it, religion had also simply become a cure-all for the poverty, fear, displacement, the dearth of opportunities, and utter lack of say in political matters— a kind of self-administered cognitive behaviour therapy that helped them cope with the unpredictability and anxiety of their surroundings. Religion was the last refuge for the powerless. As a coping strategy, it seemed to some more productive than the endemic fatalism or the widespread drug use.

The political repression, along with the poverty and the maddening stasis, created a populace beaten down by the past and terrified by the future. People were not permitted to move forward, so they were constantly looking back, held hostage to a violent past and present often blamed by their nationalist leaders on "foreign hands." Long dependent on restricted state sources of information, many were given to rumour and vulnerable to conspiracy theories—and still are, even with the Internet and satellite television so widely available.

In the Middle East anxiety is the default emotion, fed by the fear instilled by authoritarian regimes that rule by the application of force. The fear then grows: fear of worsening poverty, fear of instability, fear of chaos, and fear of hope. The future, and any hopes associated with it, can only bring disaster. So it's best not to hope.

And though everyone craves change, they also fear it, too: the growing Western influence and alarming adoption of Western habits, technology, and entertainment, and the fear of the competition between this inevitable "modernity" and traditional values. There's also a fear of persecution, the belief that they, their traditions, and their religion are constantly threatened, even more so since September 11.

During the past several decades, it seemed that every time there was reason for hope—a peace deal, increased political freedom, or even a period of relative stability—a sudden calamity would cause it to evaporate. Religion removes all power from the hands of mere mortals. Everything is decided by god, and justice will be exacted only by him. Those who do not find comfort in him will do anything to escape.

☙

When I arrived in December 2002, the Middle East was experiencing an unprecedented youth bulge, its population the youngest in the region's history. An estimated 30 percent were eighteen or younger, the largest generation of young people the region had ever seen. It was a generation that tried to do everything right. They attained higher education in droves, embraced new technology, were computer savvy, and, thanks to the Internet and satellite networks, were worldly, even if they'd never crossed their country's borders.

Yet in many Arab countries jobs were scarce and poorly paid, and many were forced to work in occupations unrelated to their education, while unhealthy numbers of them were unemployed. Their leaders had done too little too slowly to modernize their economies, to encourage the kind of innovation that creates the opportunities the young people were looking for. So much promise, yet they had inherited their parents' historical discontent.

It didn't help that genuine political freedom and participation remained as elusive as ever—from Jordan to Egypt to Syria. "They just keep us busy with hummus and falafel," Ghassan, a young acquaintance, told me soon after I moved to Amman. He meant that simply getting enough to eat was so challenging, governments had little fear anyone would find the time or energy to protest the impossibility of genuine political participation.

Young people also seemed to suffer from an unmistakable hero deficit—the absence of anyone they could trust to speak on their behalf. The few existing political groups were part of an old order, and one that was more representative of their parents' and grandparents' generations. The true opposition organizations were ineffective because of regime harassment or imprisonment, and if they gained any traction, they were discredited as tools of the West. The only potential heroes left were fighters, the armed "resistance" groups who believed change was only achievable through violence. There were also the Islamist groups, like the Muslim Brotherhood. But even then, many youth had little hope that any political movement or figure could ably represent them, that there was any prospect of bringing about the change they craved.

In survey after survey, young people of the region said one of their foremost aspirations was to leave it, or at least leave their home countries. After so many hopes were dashed, it was the only one that remained.

Gorbah. It's difficult to translate precisely, but it means estrangement, alienation, desolation, exile, even loneliness. It is a word that often appears in poetry or in the many Arabic songs that bemoan separation. As Arabs living in Canada, my family technically lived in *gorbah*, a condition that often elicited sympathy in conversations here, for our being so far away from family, from everything that defines home.

Everywhere I went, the subject of emigration came up. Being a Canadian citizen somehow qualified me to answer all manner of questions. How long does it take to get landed status in Canada? Did I know how to speed it up? Did I know anyone at the embassy who could help? Could I write a letter of recommendation?

It was mostly young men who asked, and they always expressed reservations about living in *gorbah*. Yet they badly wanted to leave. They constantly searched for ways—even as Western countries tightened their immigration policies in the post–September 11 world. Anything—even desolation and loneliness—was better than staying.

ﮒ

And now, with another war looming, anxiety was once again through the roof. Everyone was seized with Iraq, and oil was on everyone's minds: *That's what the war is about—oil, and protecting Israel,* they'd say. Here, many were certain, was yet another example of the treachery of the West. It didn't matter that Saddam was a murderous dictator who'd oppressed his own people. (Many Arabs I met didn't even know that, or if they did, they excused it as necessary to hold together a country as fractious as Iraq.) For many Arabs, this was about a U.S. policy that appeared to be growing more anti-Arab and anti-Muslim by the day—a conviction that deepened with the war in Afghanistan and drove more people to protectively identify with their faith.

The region watched closely as Bush, with the support of British prime minister Tony Blair, prepared for war against Saddam, undeterred by the growing opposition to the plan by critics who argued it was unjustifiable. Bush maintained that Iraq posed a threat because it possessed weapons of mass destruction and refused to give UN weapons inspectors the unfettered access they needed to determine whether this was the case.

Arabs across the Middle East were disturbed by the prospect of another war, and this time around several Arab nations hesitated to get involved. Those that did, like Jordan, joined quietly. The people consulted their talisman, the television, to find answers. Would this war lead to a wider conflict? Could it destroy the economy, disrupt schooling, or destabilize their governments? How many would be displaced? How many more Iraqis would arrive in Jordan, Syria, Lebanon? Who would pay? How much more control would the United States wield over the region once the war dust had settled?

There were, however, Arabs who welcomed the coming war and the American promise to spread democracy in the Middle East, starting in Iraq. So it was difficult to generalize about how Arabs felt. As I began the job of explaining the reaction in the region for the CBC, I bristled every time there was a reference to the "Arab street" and the "Arab view." I struggled to explain that there was no such thing, that if anything defined the so-called Arab street, it was the infinite diversity. The three hundred million people who lived in this region could not be an undifferentiated mass with a single point of view. There was no one type of Muslim—they weren't even all Muslim, a fact that never failed to shock the ignorant—and there was no consensus on any matter that affected the region.

There were many Jordanians and Palestinians who admired Saddam, often for his flowery nationalist rhetoric, or maybe for his Scud attacks against Israel in 1991. Certainly some supported him simply because he was Sunni Muslim, and many of them vehemently opposed the coming war on that basis. Others opposed it simply because it was an attack against an Arab nation, or because it was led by the U.S., or simply because it was war.

But there were Arabs who were eager to see Saddam fall— naturally this included Kuwaitis. There were also religious zealots who relished the fall of a secular dictator and the possible emergence of an Islamic state. There were Shia Muslims in Lebanon and Saudi Arabia who knew of Saddam's treatment of their co-religionists in Iraq and savoured the prospect of revenge. There were many, many pro-reform advocates who saw Saddam's impending fall as the possible start of an Arab awakening, one in which all Arabs might gain some freedom. There were some who were aware of Saddam's atrocities and thought he should be deposed. There were, of course, the hundreds of thousands of Iraqis already living in exile in the Middle East, whose only hope of ever seeing home again was the end of Saddam's reign. And finally, there were also those who couldn't care less—they coped by dropping out, by living apart from the news, soothed by manufactured reality television and racy video clips—though they were surely in the minority.

Ultimately, I could only report that on the eve of war against Iraq, the majority of people in the region were paying attention and were at least suspicious of Bush's intentions. They doubted that he was pursuing Saddam purely to bring democracy to their region. The war could only bode poorly for them, they believed, and many of those I met in Jordan opposed it at least on that basis.

Would they be able to express that view? Some in the Western press predicted "cartwheels of instability" in the Middle East as people rose up to oppose an invasion of Iraq. But I was certain the authoritarian regimes would do everything to ensure that never happened.

The Iraqi visa I had secured back in Ottawa—thanks to acquaintances in the know—was ready for me to pick up in Amman—and unlike the dozens of foreign journalists forced to pay exorbitant fees to extortionist Iraqi and Jordanian fixers, it cost me nothing but an administrative fee—to the chagrin of those fixers.

I got on a plane again, this time to Baghdad, to wait for its latest war.

SIX

Sick

What is written, is written.
There is no escaping it.
—ARAB PROVERB

BAGHDAD, JANUARY 14, 2003

I was appalled upon landing in Iraq by how quickly I was tapped for a bribe.

I'd hoped in vain that being Arab and a woman might exempt me from the treatment to which other foreign colleagues had been subjected at Saddam International Airport. But just a few steps beyond the immigration desk, my satellite phone was whisked away to the customs office, locked, and registered. The "fee" for making sure it eventually got to me at the Information Ministry was promptly requested by the man who occupied the smoky office in the corner.

I rolled my eyes with indignation and protested. "I expected better from my Arab brothers," I said.

He offered platitudes. "*Teddallaleh*," he repeated over and over, which roughly translates to "As you wish." And yet he still put out his hand for payment.

For years, Iraqis had been forced to bribe their way through life. Everyone from clerks at hospitals and university offices to policemen and border guards expected payment. We call it corruption. But in Iraq—and places like Syria and Egypt—under-the-table payments were no longer seen as bribes. They were a part of the paycheque. A lowly government official was lucky to get the equivalent of a dollar or two to grease the creaky wheels of bureaucracy into action. With the lead-up to the war and the mass arrival of hundreds of journalists, officials who had regular contact with them had grown used to crisp $100 bills.

More than ten years into crippling UN sanctions, it was hard to believe that oil-rich Iraq had once been a wealthy country, with one of the highest per capita incomes in the region. It was so rich that the state provided free medical care and education, as well as subsidized electricity and water. But the sanctions (on top of the effects of Saddam's wars) had taken a severe toll. They were punishment for Saddam's intransigence—a litany of infractions starting with the invasion of Kuwait and ending with his refusal to allow UN inspectors to look for weapons of mass destruction. The trade embargo had eviscerated Iraq's economy and made life untenable for its people. But Saddam, his family, and their cronies were immune.

Unemployment stood at more than 50 percent, at times even higher. Poverty and malnutrition were widespread. Inflation hit unprecedented highs, and Iraq's currency crashed, yet the salaries for those who still had jobs—teachers, doctors, soldiers, and bureaucrats employed mostly by the government—had not been adjusted to compensate. So doctors and other professionals were paid the equivalent of five dollars a month; teachers made about three. Many tried to make up the difference by any means available, as they did at the Information Ministry, where officials never tired of informing us of the rules, then asking for money to bend them.

We had to inform them of what stories we planned to cover. They assigned official minders to shadow us, to ensure there were no "misunderstandings." I often got stuck with Abdullah, whose quirky manners and pilled turtleneck made my skin crawl. To give him the slip I often went "shopping," dropping into as many stores as I could without a camera, hoping casual conversation might provide some insight into what Iraqis were truly thinking.

We also had to pay regular visits to more senior officials in order to extend our stay, and they, too, expected to be paid.

"I'd like to renew my visa."

"*Teddallaleh*. But ... where are you from?" the mustachioed man asked me coolly from behind his desk.

"Canada. Canadian television. CBC."

"No. Where are you *really* from?"

Wherever I went in the Middle East, people wanted to know where I was *really* from. Then what religion I was. What sect. Aside from my chat with the pushy customs official, the only other conversation I had at the airport was with our fixer, Ammar, when he asked me those very questions in quick succession within minutes of introducing himself. As an Arab—even a Canadian Arab—I had to be categorized, studied, sussed out. *Is she with us or against us?* I could never simply be Canadian, or a journalist, without an agenda dictated by heritage or nationality. As far as many people were concerned, no such Arabs—and certainly no such journalists—existed. Admittedly, though, even back home that was also often the case.

My satphone finally appeared at the Information Ministry as promised, and I set it up among the jumble of them outside the press office building. As a foreign journalist you couldn't work without one in Iraq. There were effectively no mobile phones and no Internet—a mystery to me, since these were plentiful in Egypt, Jordan, even Syria. Most journalists stayed at the Al-Rashid, an imposing, intelligence-infested hotel reserved for foreigners a few blocks away from the ministry. I moved instead to the Mansour Hotel, a couple of blocks away. Though a handful of intelligence types hung out there, too, the only real annoyance I encountered were the mangy, menacing dogs that hounded us while we walked to the hotel late at night.

Beyond what I'd read, I was still woefully ignorant of Baghdad and its people, the city's rhythms and the country's fabled geography, defined by the ancient embrace of the Tigris and Euphrates rivers. I wished I had known Baghdad before repeated wars claimed its soul, before sanctions depleted its means, and before Saddam's henchmen devoured its spirit. But I could see it only as it was now. Wide boulevards heaving with traffic and bordered by outdated, sprawling buildings. Dozens of scrawny soldiers bracing behind semi-circles of sandbags from a threat that had yet to materialize. Maze-like markets suffocating with vegetables, and women and children cowed by fear of the authorities and yet numbed by repeated conflict.

Everyone knew another war was coming, and they knew this one would be life-altering in a way none of the others had been. And yet little girls with bright white ribbons in their hair still marched to school every morning. The hopeful shoeshiner at the corner briskly cleaned his brushes in between customers. When darkness fell along the river, the *masgouf* (grilled fish) restaurants came to life, full to the brim with people and their chatter, especially on weekends.

Many Iraqis were armed, and they told me they planned to fight with their own hands. You could smell the false bravado. Those staged anti-U.S. and pro-Saddam rallies that the Information Ministry tirelessly put on for our benefit reeked of it. It was clear even to my untrained eye that they were anything but spontaneous—the "protesters" chanted like automatons, and the way they dissipated all at once after an hour or so was almost as if they had been put on a timer. Yet because these protests were repeatedly held outside the door of the ministry, they were difficult to avoid.

So was the poverty. When the UN imposed its sanctions, it came up with a scheme to help mitigate their effect on civilians.

The Oil-for-Food Programme allowed Iraq to export a limited amount of oil, with the stipulation that two-thirds of the proceeds go towards purchasing food and medical supplies for the Iraqi people. Every month, each family was entitled to a free ration of flour, rice, sugar, fat, and tea, in addition to some powdered milk, soap, and beans. The program—like the sanctions themselves—was extremely controversial. Saddam was repeatedly accused of abusing it at the expense of his people. Two of the program's coordinators quit within two years, disturbed at how the sanctions were affecting civilians. The Information Ministry was happy to arrange for journalists to see the suffering for themselves.

The poverty was breathtaking. Nearly two-thirds of the population couldn't live without the rations. An American public health expert on a visit to Baghdad said, "The Iraqi population today is living like people living in a refugee camp." I could see that the first time I visited an Iraqi home, in the upscale neighbourhood of Mansour. Faizah, a mother of four, was well educated and articulate, but her home was worse than some of the worst refugee hovels in Amman. The walls were cracked and peeling, mouldy from the humidity. The curtains and furniture appeared as though they'd been retrieved from the trash. The place was windowless, devoid of air or light, and the kitchen was sooty, primitively furnished with a gas burner, a makeshift counter, and a sink. Even the tap water was dangerous to drink. That was the quality of life Faizah could now afford on her teacher's salary. "Is it possible to live in this kind of poverty in the twenty-first century?" she said to my camera. "It's been thirteen years of continuous torture. As an Iraqi woman, believe me, to live the strife that we live, each day is like a year. I challenge anyone in the world to live one day like we live in Iraq."

With war looming, the government had just started allowing families to double up on their rations. Faizah's war stash was a single bag of flour, perched outside on concrete blocks to keep the bugs away.

With minders in tow, there would be little frank talk of the regime's culpability in the rampant poverty, its oppressive tactics, or how Iraqis felt about the prospect of its demise. I could barely pose such questions, let alone expect people to raise the subject themselves. When it finally did happen, it was in the relative safety of a gleaming yellow taxi. This was new: a driver's confession.

"When Saddam is angry with you, you're taken away, and that's fine. But then your house is also destroyed, your family is harassed and some of them are arrested. And then your neighbour's house is destroyed, then your uncle's and grandfather's houses are destroyed, too. They might also be arrested and tortured."

Ahmad, a seemingly shy young Shia Muslim, was my driver and guide in those early days. Though he was reserved around us, his occasional smile was so wide his cheeks eclipsed the rest of his face, his laughter so hearty it made me laugh in and of itself. Yet he was also a toughie and a maverick: a tall, broad man with a prematurely receding hairline tempered by a bit of a mullet. He was always dressed in a scuffed black leather jacket, boots or runners, and jeans. Ahmad became a close and trusted friend. He also became my first informant, my window on the pain boiling beneath the scripted surface, and my primary source on what people said behind closed doors. That night, Ahmad made the decision—just as we arrived at the hotel driveway—to open up. One grim story begat another. Then the conversation ended with this: "Yes, Nahlah. We want the war to come." Thereafter our forbidden conversations became a nightly ritual.

Not everyone was as brave as Ahmad. Yet once in a while, you could detect a hint of defiance in the words of Iraqis, a dab of derision in a smile while they spoke of Saddam. And yet on the eve of war, as people struggled to put aside money and supplies, Saddam poster sales were inexplicably rising. Authorities had spared no effort at reinforcing the cult of personality: Saddam's image already kept watch at street corners, behind counters, on car windows, and in living rooms, as well as inside textbooks, in newspapers, and always, always, on television. He was shown smiling, shooting, or waving; in military or traditional garb, benevolently staring into the distance. Over cups of tea, the owner of one poster store tried to explain the rise in sales, his darting eyes betraying his insincerity: "I'm not Ba'athi or political, I'm a simple man—but Saddam's the father. If you're a family, whom do the children get attached to if there's an attack? Who is the father in Iraq? So the people are attaching themselves to their father. It's very normal." Ahmad's translation: in the lead-up to the war, the state's paranoia was at an all-time high, which made it more dangerous than ever. People did whatever possible to show their loyalty. And that included proudly displaying pictures of the still-reigning leader.

The government minder then took me to see one of Saddam's most prolific painters: Thaher al-Eboudi, a sixty-year-old artist, responsible for dozens of the leader's most famous portraits. "Saddam is a person who's not easy [to paint]," al-Eboudi reflected. "You must paint him with more glory than necessary, to give him his beauty and his personality." And with a searching look over to the minder, he added, "The leader, god protect him, is always around us, before our gaze. Even when a child sees a picture of him, he becomes happy. He's loved by everyone." What else could he say?

Nighttime cameraless interviews with new Iraqi friends made real for me all that I had read and filled in the cavernous blanks in the official version. They told me how their country was ruled by irrationality and powered by fear. Saddam's Ba'ath Party dictated who succeeded and who didn't. Party members intimidated, bludgeoned, and extorted their way to anything they wanted:

houses, money, women. People simply disappeared, without explanation or process of any kind. Entire families were crushed on
the suspicion that maybe one among them was guilty of treason.
The fear was so intense that a father might inform on an apparently treasonous son, or brothers on each other. The government
successfully played on the people's own fears: of foreign enemies,
of conflict, of poverty, of being left behind in a culture that valued
family and tribes. The regime's henchmen—themselves Iraqis—
killed, maimed, and tortured other Iraqis into submission. They
gassed and bombed them, then buried them in mass graves. And for
more than a decade, the oil-driven plenty of the past was hoarded
by the few. It was a dog-eat-dog world, and if you didn't bare your
teeth, you were devoured for breakfast.

Iraq was also under lockdown, information was as dangerous
as landmines. Unlike even the poorest of their Arab brethren,
Iraqis had no access to satellite television (it was banned) or cellular
phones. They had state television and radio, which peddled the
view of the regime—and apparently resorted to playing Fairouz
songs when war or internal conflict threatened chaos. Internet
access was highly restricted and painfully slow. International travel
was regulated, with the right to it granted sparingly and only after
great effort and more bribes. Leaving the country illegally—as
many attempted to do—could earn you a decade in prison. Iraq
was effectively an island, removed and remote from everyone and
everything else.

The regime imposed the climate of fear to assert its authority,
but it also constantly felt fear. The country had an endless list
of enemies, real and imaginary. It was a paranoid police state,
a panoptical world where one party, the only party, had all the
power. And its leader was most paranoid of all. He was so paranoid
that his reign began in 1979 with a series of executions of fellow
party members accused of plotting against him. And from then on,

the killing never stopped. Saddam was credited with building the modern Iraq, but bringing on wars, it seemed, was what Saddam did best. That, and giving rousing, flowery speeches.

I hadn't been in Iraq for long. I hadn't witnessed any executions or seen the mass graves I knew existed. But it was already clear that Iraq was utterly sick—sicker than I had imagined. The sanctions had done serious damage, no doubt, but so had the regime. The sickness came from within and went right to the core, like an autoimmune disease. And now war threatened to make it even sicker.

𝄐

Ahmad invited me for dinner one day at his home, and I jumped at the chance. He lived in the sardonically named Saddam City, a wretchedly poor, largely Shia Muslim neighbourhood of Baghdad, where people loathed the regime as much as the Information Ministry officials loathed taking us there. Ahmad's crowd of Shia Muslim friends and family who gathered that night were nearly unanimous in the anger and distrust they felt towards their slum's namesake. Their co-religionists formed the majority in Iraq, yet there were aspects of their faith they could not freely practise in public during Saddam's reign. They saw their long-time struggle with the regime as a modern-day extension of the ancient slaughter of Shia Muslims on the plains of Karbala, which they mourned every year, mostly in private.

According to Shia belief, this cataclysmic event happened in the year 680. Imam Hussein, grandson of the prophet Mohammed and venerated by Shia Muslims, was beheaded, and virtually his entire family and all his supporters were slaughtered with him. The incident was rooted in a split among Muslims that dates back to the death of Mohammed. A group of Muslims (the Shia) believed that Mohammed should have been succeeded by a member of his own family—namely, Ali, his cousin and son-in-law. Others (eventually the Sunni) believed that the next leader should be chosen on merit. That prompted a bloody conflict that continued even when Ali was eventually appointed the fourth caliphate and then subsequently killed. His son Hussein, who led the Shia, disputed the successor, the Umayyad tyrant Yazid, and faced off with his army in Karbala, refusing to pledge allegiance. Hussein's murder was considered by Shia to be a desecration of the house of Mohammed and a direct assault on his bloodline. It was a bloodbath that cemented the division between Shia and Sunni Muslims, unleashing centuries of animosity marked by occasional fratricide. When we were regaled at school in Amman with the story of Caliph Harun al-Rashid's friendly gestures to Charlemagne, no one volunteered that the caliph, too, had persecuted the Shia, and was, according to them, responsible for the killing of one of their revered imams, Musa al-Khadim, and for destroying Hussein's mausoleum at Karbala. In fact, no one even bothered to teach us that the Shia existed at all.

Saddam may have led a secular regime, but he was true to his Sunni Muslim origins. He surrounded himself with people of his tribe, and they, like many other Sunni Muslims throughout the region, believed Shia Islam was a blasphemous corruption of the "original." The disenfranchised Shia, historically subjugated by the more powerful Sunni, wore their repeated defeats on their collective sleeve, their religion marked by a seemingly eternal state of mourning. In Saddam's Iraq, new generations of Shia were increasingly turning to their religion as an antidote to the exploits of their leader—often referred to as their own latter-day Yazid.

Ahmad wasn't particularly religious. But his best friend, Waseem, embraced his faith with scholarly zeal. Though only in his early thirties, Waseem was wise beyond his years and appropriately crowned with a head full of salt-and-pepper hair. The two were very different, but they were close and they had at least one thing in common: they'd both refused to get married. I asked Waseem about this in one of our nighttime chats, and he said that he'd actually long been engaged but had put off the commitment until "better days." "I don't want to bring children into this world—not the way it is now," he once told me.

Waseem soon became my resident analyst and friend. By training, he was a teacher, but in practice he was a gifted life guide—to me, to Ahmad, to his parents, and to his students. He himself was an avid student of his people's condition.

"You know in the 1960s, my parents and their generation were not religious at all," he said one afternoon over tea, describing a generation that included my own parents. "My mother wore a miniskirt and didn't cover her hair. It was their children who returned to religion. For us, there was nothing else to hold on to." Waseem explained that the rise in religiosity was a natural reaction to the strict secularism and the oppression they endured from a regime hostile to Shia Muslims.

In recent years, leaders in the region, most of whom were secular, had tried in vain to speak to the new, more devout generation in their language. Saddam had increasingly adopted the language of Islam, and now, on the eve of war, he repeatedly invoked the name of god. "God is the greater, oh brothers and sons," Saddam said in a speech that spring. "Remember the meanings of this great call in accordance with the profundity of your faith." Iraqis privately howled. They also derided his belated claim to be a descendant of the prophet Mohammed, which they believed a self-serving fabrication. Now, they ridiculed his rhetoric about Iraqi unity in the face of impending disaster.

Like the patient teacher he was, Waseem explained to me one night that the coming war and the overthrow of Saddam would unleash a settling of accounts among Iraqis. People would almost certainly exact their revenge for past wrongs, and the country would boil with sectarian vendettas. His analysis would prove to be unnaturally prescient. "It's all waiting for the weakening of the state," he said, pulling in the air at an invisible weakened state with the tips of his fingers bunched together. "When the state is weakened, they will go at each other. They will kill each other," he said. "We will have another war. That will be the most dangerous time. It will be worse than Bush's war."

George W. Bush's war still hadn't started, but it felt close. The rest of the CBC team—all of whom were far more experienced than I—had decided to stay. I resolved to stay, too, partly because of Waseem's advice. But within hours of our decision, that resolve began to unravel. We were warned repeatedly by Iraqi officials not to stay. They said that journalists would be used as human shields, and that women were particularly vulnerable. "Paranoia reigns," I wrote in my occasional diary on March 5. "People getting desperate. Nerves fraying, minds changing every day." We hesitated, then opted to leave in what would be one of the most regrettable decisions of my short career. We tearfully bade our staff goodbye at the Jordanian parking lot where vehicles from the neighbouring country waited for customers to make the desert trek. Ahmad gave me a rosary that used to belong to his grandmother. He and Waseem sobbed like children, everyone cried. We didn't know if we'd ever see them again.

The moment we set foot in Amman, our task was to find a way back to Iraq on our own terms, without the guidance or protection of the Information Ministry.

☆

Watching war return to its doorstep, Amman—indeed the entire region—was restive. Wars or conflicts in the region are lived collectively and owned by everyone—even more so after the advent of pan-Arab networks. People in the entire region, it seemed, were sitting before their televisions, watching and internalizing this latest affront.

As they did around the world, anti-war protests erupted throughout the region. Some of them were tolerated by regimes aware of the need to allow citizens to vent, but there were many crackdowns. And as is typical in times like these, the aggrieved seized the opportunity to rage over other complaints, like their living conditions, their poverty, and their own lack of freedom.

Egypt, for example, saw its biggest protests in decades. One day late in March 2003, a huge gathering of thousands of young people took over a downtown traffic circle by the name of Tahrir (or Liberation) Square, under the watchful eye of riot police. Ostensibly they were protesting the war, but they also shouted for the downfall of President Hosni Mubarak's regime. The next day riot police intervened, chasing protesters away with truncheons, water cannon, and tear gas to prevent them from taking over the square again. Thousands marched in the streets anyway, burning U.S. flags, as well as a poster of Mubarak. As a lesson, hundreds were arrested and tortured in prison.

In Amman, too, there were limits to the kind of anti-war protest authorities would tolerate. Several small protests organized by professional groups like lawyers' unions were allowed to proceed. But larger, more unruly and spontaneous ones were quickly shut down. Naturally, one of the biggest happened in Al-Wihdat, and we went to watch as hundreds of youth gathered to denounce the war, and Jordan's support of it. (Jordan reportedly acted as a secret base for thousands of U.S. and British military and special forces personnel, providing use of at least two military bases and its airspace. Though this was all done in secret, people knew—nothing escapes the Arab street.) Within minutes of arriving, we got caught up in the clouds of tear gas. Needless to say, the young people of the camp were tear-gassed back into their pitiful homes.

We watched the war unfold on television for twenty agonizing days, staying in touch with our Iraqi staff by telephone, before we finally got the go-ahead from Toronto to return. When we drove to the border, the amusing Iraqi information minister, Mohammed Said al-Sahhaf, was still claiming in news conferences that U.S. soldiers were being slaughtered on the outskirts of Baghdad—even as foreign networks reported they were steadily progressing towards the capital. Sahhaf had once served as the obscure head of Iraqi broadcasting. Now he was peddling Saddam's lies live on international television and putting an absurd, comical spin on events—earning himself the nickname Comical Ali.

"We will get them stuck in the mud, and we will certainly defeat them!" he exclaimed. "Iraq will spread them even more and chop them up." The deluded in the Arab world lapped it up, desperate for the kind of victory of which he spoke. The rest of the world watched as British and American journalists arrived in Baghdad along with the American tanks in which they were riding. U.S. troops were fighting at Saddam International Airport. But in Sahhaf's world, "The infidels are committing suicide by the hundreds on the gates of Baghdad. Be assured, Baghdad is safe, protected. Iraqis are heroes."

As the greenest war reporter there by far, I was in good company with the CBC's Don Murray, producer Heather Abbott, and cameraman Sat Nandlall, as well as Mark Mackinnon from *The Globe and Mail* and Tom Kennedy from CTV. Our convoy barrelled into a forebidding orange storm on the horizon before dawn. It was April 8, and at the border checkpoint a likeness of Saddam was still inside the waiting room, watching us from the painted wall. The counters were still manned by Saddam's people, to whom we cheerfully offered our satellite phones to be wired shut, not to be opened except by an Information Ministry official in Baghdad. It was as if nothing had changed in this remote outpost of Iraq's corrupt officialdom.

As we crossed the border in the early afternoon, we knew that we might not make it in time for the 6 p.m. wartime curfew in Baghdad. Conditions were certainly not ideal for a last-ditch attempt to cross six hundred kilometres of desert, and they only got worse.

Once in Iraq, it was all desert but for the paved highway etched in its middle. The desolate road normally offered no aesthetic relief, few diversions besides the occasional rolling hill or a gas station. But on this journey, the monotony was punctuated by the sight of bombed-out cars and buses, and the rare vehicle heading in the opposite direction. We were also surprised to be stopped by what appeared to be foreign special forces soldiers riding in two Humvees—likely New Zealanders, but they wouldn't say. They approached to ask what we were up to. It was a delay we couldn't afford. But our convoy must have seemed as strange to them as theirs was to us—a short ride from the unsuspecting Iraqi border guards and their leader's likeness.

About midway to Baghdad, we were forced to stop again at an Iraqi police station to explain our business. But from there, the trip continued smoothly until we passed Fallujah and were nearly within sight of Baghdad. That's where we came upon the Americans.

The men of the platoon manning a checkpoint on the bridge leading to Abu Ghraib prison were clearly nervous. They trained their guns in our direction, and our convoy ground to a halt a few hundred metres away. The female journalists among us jumped out. I grabbed the makeshift flag—a fat, long metal pipe with a white sheet that said "TV" in wobbly red type—and stuck it into my belt as if we were going on parade. Three of us walked slowly towards the soldiers, who eventually let down their guard as Heather started explaining who we were. Someone had already alerted their captain, and soon we were engaged in discussion about why they wouldn't let us proceed "under any circumstances."

The soldiers eventually allowed our vehicles into their cordon. It wasn't long before Baghdad's wartime curfew came into effect— and our drivers were quietly calculating their next move. I knew what they were thinking. They'd only ever seen these soldiers on television. Now they were right before their eyes, acting as their protectors. It was an excruciatingly uncomfortable position for a band of warrior drivers who thrived on a kind of businessman's neutrality, while almost certainly harbouring—at best—a deep, typical mistrust of Americans.

"We have to turn back. Let's go back to Amman. We have to go back, ya Nahlah, ya Nahlah." It was the Boss, the enormous leader of the drivers, trying to bully me. He spoke no English, so all his complaints were levelled at me. As we argued, the sun was sinking quickly and his men were restless. The Boss threatened to unload our gear and leave us behind.

"*Wallahe*—by God—I am going back. I will not sleep here," he swore. "When the Iraqis on the road see us here with the Americans, they are going to tear us apart. Either we take you to Baghdad, to the Jordanian parking lot, or we leave you here now." The Jordanian parking lot was as far as vehicles from Jordan could get into Baghdad to drop off or pick up customers.

The soldiers helpfully suggested that they might be able to get us an escort into the capital. But eventually darkness fell, and there were still no guides. They told us the ongoing fighting would likely force us to spend the night right where we stood. "There is heavy fighting in Baghdad," I ventured to the Boss, echoing the captain. If he went forward, he risked being blown up by an American bomb, I warned. Go back and the Fallujans might just skin him alive. "It's best to stay here." The Boss wagged his enormous finger. *NO*. It was a tiresome argument, and some time into it I wished he'd just dump our stuff and leave.

The Boss's brother asked to borrow our hand-held satellite phone (the one we'd hidden from the border officials) to call his family. They told him the Arab networks were reporting heavy fighting near the Jordanian parking lot. He repeated this out loud to the rest of the drivers, with an apologetic look towards me. The boss and his men fell in line and broke out their tea and food.

Here were soldiers actually involved in the battle telling us what was happening, and it took an Arab television report—heard third-hand—to persuade these men that the soldiers were right. That moment alone gave me a clear sense of the challenges the Americans faced in "winning hearts and minds," both in Iraq and throughout the region.

We barely slept that night because of the heavy bombardment. A freak thunderstorm and the Boss's snoring added to the strange orgy of noises on that peculiar evening.

On the way into Baghdad the following morning, we were greeted by the remnants of battle. Smoke billowed from charred tanks that littered the road. Bodies, some still smouldering, lay scattered around abandoned Iraqi positions. A fire was still in the process of consuming a tree. The occasional explosion rumbled ahead in the distance.

⚔

Baghdad had gone insane with the chaos that comes with the withdrawal of one power and the arrival of another. Comical Ali had just given his last statement, still maintaining that there were no Americans in the capital, and that the "infidels will be slaughtered." He then disappeared. The bombs were still falling. At the Palestine Hotel, where most journalists had moved to witness the war, the Information Ministry staff was also nowhere to be seen. Our fixer had been waiting there for us, and we went out for a quick tour for Don's evening story. A hysterical man stopped us, desperate for help. Someone—a friend, a brother, a father—was severely injured, lying on the side of the road, splattered with blood. "Give us a ride," the upright man pleaded, "to the hospital." It was already an enormous risk to be out at all. Ammar hesitantly drove on, all of us silently guilty.

We stopped at the Iraqi Olympic Committee building, which was shrouded in flames, while a stone statue of Saddam stood there, arm aloft, his serenely welcoming gesture a surreal contrast to the chaos below. A looter screamed, "This is our oil! This is our oil!" Another levelled a Kalashnikov rifle at a poster of Saddam across the street and, with a maniacal smile, unleashed a barrage for our camera. I acted as Don's translator as we sought to understand what motivated the marauding Iraqis, who were tearing their own city apart as bombs continued to fall from the sky. Occasionally, I would ask our crew to move on when some in the crowds that besieged us began making threats in Arabic. We watched as others dragged away whatever they could find in the various ministries and palaces: televisions, sinks, cupboards, air conditioners, and even doors— whatever they could carry or push or drag behind them. Revenge was sweet, the poor vanquishing the obscenely wealthy, but it was also unsightly and shameful, debased and eminently difficult to behold.

We arrived back at the Palestine Hotel as American tanks were rolling into Ferdous Square towards a recently installed bronze statue of Saddam. Hundreds of people had congregated there, including a lineup of live cameras. I was bursting to report all that I had seen. A growing mob was trying to pull down Saddam's statue with the help of U.S. soldiers, and Don went live on the telephone from the scene of the mob while I went live on camera a few dozen

metres away. With Saddam's statue as the backdrop, I tried to
explain all that I'd seen, but the right words were elusive after two
sleepless nights. I was then struck silent—terrified—when gunfire
erupted about a hundred metres behind me. I stood there mute
until the anchor gruffly prompted me to turn around and describe
what I saw.

I turned around and saw Khaled, a normally chipper veteran
Iraqi journalist, alone at the curb, heaving with sobs. I saw a wisp
of smoke curl up in the distance. I then saw a noose hanging from
the statue's neck, and a raucous melee of people cheering below it.
They were flanked by American tanks that looked out of place. I
saw no gunmen. But I did see clumps of bedraggled little children
looking amused and afraid all at once.

"It must be celebratory fire," I offered lamely. In fact it had
been a firefight—we didn't know with whom. Whatever it was,
it was a footnote given that we had just witnessed the end of an
oppressive regime—and the start of an occupation.

The euphoric cheers, the looting, and the anguish of those
moments mingled with the utter desperation of people who'd lived
most of the war lacking access to electricity, food, and clean water.
Iraqis pained by separation also longed to reach the outside world.
Dozens of them begged us to call their relatives abroad, the ones
who had long ago escaped and avoided this latest dance with death.
They wrote their phone numbers on pieces of paper, the torn insides
of cigarette packs, the sweaty papers inside my flak jacket—even on
my hand—beseeching me to call relatives in Holland, Australia,
the U.K., and the U.S. to let them know they had made it. In every
phone call, I heard immense gratitude in those faraway voices, and
a sad longing for home.

The firefights continued every night, and hungry fires consumed government buildings unabated. People were appalled by
the ongoing looting, and dismayed that no one was stopping it.

It didn't take long for the blame for the pillaging to be shifted from the Iraqis themselves onto the Americans. I heard it happen in a single conversation at a barbershop that had buzzed back to life near the Palestine Hotel. Any hint of celebration had already been swept away with the snippets of hair on the floor. "We have been *destroyed*," the barber said, accenting key words with spurts of water from his spray bottle onto his customer's head. "We want the Americans to restore the electricity, and to bring the situation back to normal. Bring us a good president. What do we want? For them to go *back* to their country. If they stay, the situation will be *dangerous*," he said, with an extra-long spray emphasizing his last word. This was only a few days after the Americans had arrived.

A waiting customer spoke up. "When we went to Kuwait, we didn't steal one screw," he claimed. "We are Muslims—it's forbidden to take something that's not ours."

The customer in the chair piped up from the folds of the black apron draped around him. "Yes. Kuwaitis came with the Americans. The doors to all the ministries were locked. It was the Americans! They broke the locks and let the Kuwaitis steal, then they said the Iraqis did it."

The owner completed the thought. "If America stays, we will wage jihad for God. We will kill them. It's my country—we will defend it. We will not become like the *Palestinians*."

SEVEN

Ghosts

He who is beautiful is beautiful, even when he
wakes up from sleep. He who is ugly is ugly,
even if he washed every day.
—ARAB PROVERB

NEAR HILLAH, IRAQ, MAY 2003

It was only mid-May, but in a barren stretch of desert, the sun was pitiless from above, the sand as hot as coal licking our feet from below. There was not a single sliver of shade, nor any gesture of welcome. But we hadn't expected any in a place whose very existence reeked of callousness.

There were too many people, quiet people moving from plastic bag to plastic bag like shoppers strolling in a market. The earth had spat out maddeningly silent skeletons, coy about their origin. The hopeful fingered the faded ID papers, noted the colour of clothing in search of any clue that a particular heap of bones belonged to one of their relatives. Many walked away with nothing but the unanswered questions they came with.

One woman sat cross-legged on a diminutive hill overlooking Hillah's mass grave, speaking to herself. No one spoke back or answered her pleas, for what she wanted would surely require a miracle. For the duration of our visit that searing afternoon, the black-draped woman remained on her perch, rocking back and forth to the staccato of her monotone banter. She had run out of tears, but there were heaves syncopated with her movements. She looked majestic against the white sky: a kind of mourning queen presiding over a court bursting with the dead and the living dead— an entire village of ghosts swarming at her feet.

It had been only weeks since the larger war ended, but Iraq had begun the war of confronting its past. It would take years: Iraq was teeming with ghosts.

The most pressing concern was finding the missing. There were so many. Their relatives were certain some of them were still alive in Saddam's hidden prisons buried underground, perhaps behind walls at palaces and key ministries, and they flocked to these places, begging the Americans now guarding them to be let inside, to be allowed to dig with their own hands to liberate them. Others knew their brothers, fathers, children were dead and namelessly buried. Still, they wanted to find them.

The Hillah mass grave was one of the first to be "discovered" after the war. Iraqis have always known about these graves, but only now could they see them and be openly outraged. It was proof of the Ba'ath regime's brutality and, they said, the wider world's long-standing indifference to Iraqi suffering, to Iraqi desire for freedom.

The grave at Hillah had been freshly unearthed a day earlier, to get at bodies buried more than a decade ago, witnessed only by a sparse guard of trees. Those who lived near such places knew what the earth held. So great was the fear of Saddam's regime that no one had dared come forward sooner to unearth the missing, to give them a proper burial.

Now, thousands of days later, there was urgency to the task. People had started digging on their own, and dozens of bodies already lay on top of the earth that had suffocated them. Plastic bags kept together the individual skulls, femurs, and spinal columns, as well as bits of tattered clothing, wallets, and yellowed ID cards. Sometimes there were leather belts or lengths of rope, apparently used to bind wrists or ankles. Some of the skulls still wore blindfolds. The bags were left open for people to sift through and decipher, like jigsaw puzzles. Among the throngs of people searching, there were children. I wondered what went on in their heads now.

Foreign-aid workers had counselled against the disorderly exhumation, but nothing and no one could stop this. Someone even thought to bring a tractor. It roughly scooped out mounds of earth to turn up yet more bodies: dry, unknowable bones that might still contain a marrow of truth and yield closure. Try all you want, it was hard not to breathe in the sand and dust kicked up by the digging. So you stopped trying, inhaling deep on the dust of the dead, allowing it to settle inside your lungs and, for the first time in years, be warmed by a beating heart.

Prior to the war, you could read extensively about Iraq's mass graves, but until you saw one, they were just words on paper. Contemplating a mass grave—and everything it took to create one—is disturbing enough, but watch it excavated and you wish you would be struck blind on the spot. Still, we tiptoed into the field and hunched over the remains of the dead to elicit interviews from the living.

Much as I wanted to, I couldn't bring myself to approach the woman on the hill. How do you do that? No journalism class teaches you that. We walked instead towards a middle-aged, sweaty man in a white *dishdasha* crouched over some of the plastic bags, surrounded by a coterie of family and the curious. I cast a shadow over him, and in the meekest of voices I asked for an interview.

First, he wanted to determine the extent of my guilt. "Canadian," I answered, truthfully. A citizen of that vast world that averted its eyes as Iraqis were being slaughtered wholesale. I, too, could have some culpability in this man's morbid odyssey among the plastic body bags of Hillah.

But where are you really from?

At my answer, he expressed dismay. Saddam was a champion of the cause of (mostly Sunni Muslim) Palestinians, and that made them detestable to many of Iraq's disenfranchised Shia. It didn't matter that this hadn't the slightest influence on my life, or the life of any of my family—in the Mideast you are the sum total of the blood that runs in your veins. The man's reaction stirred the group that had gathered around us, and their curious expressions gave way to looks of disapproval. I shifted out of nervousness. We might have just offered ourselves as convenient targets for the rage percolating under the surface at this highly sensitive moment.

So I pushed back. "I lived most of my life in Canada. I know what he did, and it was wrong. Do you want to do this interview and tell the world what's happened to your family, or not?"

The man squinted in the sunlight and looked at me hard. I stared right back. He looked down, thinking, then his face softened and he started telling his story. Jim Hoffman, our cameraman, who had a gift for reading silence as well as body language, started rolling unprompted. The tension in the crowd eased, and the focus shifted from me to the man unfurling old wounds.

"Two of my brothers went missing in the 1991 uprising," he started. "They were civilians, living with their children." His brothers had gone out to find food for their families. They sped away into streets strewn with bodies and never came back. The man said that when he went to look for them in the capital's prisons, he was arrested himself and tortured, then warned never to ask about 1991 again.

"Let the world see," he remarked over and over. Reaching deep into one plastic bag, he delicately retrieved a skull he thought might belong to his brother and set it on the ground. "Look at this. Don't Iraqis have human rights? Saddam used to torture us. He put us in prison. He took our salaries. He hurt us, hurt the Iraqi people. Let the world see. The United States of America, Britain, and all the countries in the world. Let them see and judge whether we suffered."

Soon he was crying, still talking but no longer to us. He then quietly slipped away to continue his search. The mourning queen was still talking to herself.

ℒ

The 1991 uprising in Iraq, just after the end of the First Gulf War, and the merciless crackdown that followed were on a scale rarely before seen in the Middle East. The closest, perhaps—though much smaller—was the post-uprising crackdown in Hama, Syria, in 1982. Sunni Muslim residents of that often restive city had revolted against strongman Hafez al-Assad, and he sent in a massive military force to raze the city, killing thousands.

Both were rebellions of discontent, demonstrations of the people's desperation and dissatisfaction with the authoritarian regimes that ruled them. In both cases, most of the rebellious belonged to religious majorities that were politically disenfranchised by the tyranny of a minority. As they happened, both uprisings were out of the reach of most foreign reporters, who had trouble getting into those repressive countries even in peacetime. But the message was in the subsequent crackdowns, and it was abundantly clear to anyone else with revolutionary thoughts: speak up and you will suffer unspeakable consequences.

The Iraqi uprising and Saddam's ferocious effort to snuff it out, however, dwarfed all others that came before and most that came after.

With the war over in 1991 and Iraqi forces unceremoniously turfed out of Kuwait, masses of Iraqis rose up to try to topple

Saddam in his moment of weakness. They were, it seemed, partly encouraged by the U.S. president's statement that urged them to depose Saddam. The revolt began in the Shia-dominated south, where retreating soldiers spontaneously took aim at state institutions. They were joined by civilians, many of them young city-dwellers, who attacked Ba'ath party offices and officials, confronting Saddam's impressively thick layers of security forces and liberating significant portions of the country. In the north, it was the long-suffering Kurds who revolted, sending Saddam loyalists fleeing. But Baghdad, the capital, remained out of reach without outside help—and the U.S. subsequently refused to get involved in what Washington labelled an internal Iraqi affair. Saddam's Baghdad loyalists retaliated, swiftly recovering lost territory, indiscriminately flattening homes, hospitals, and many religious sites, and hunting people down—rebels or civilians, it didn't seem to matter—with machine guns, tanks, and helicopter gunships. Tens of thousands were rounded up and executed, then buried in mass graves like the one in Hillah, one of the cities where the uprising had been fiercest. Hundreds of thousands of Iraqis left their country to escape Saddam's wrath.

I once met a survivor of that clampdown in Paris. Sadeq had the large doe eyes Iraqis are famous for, scruffy salt-and-pepper hair, broad shoulders, and a warm, fatherly smile. He was a Sayyed, a descendant of the prophet Mohammed's family, but one who still enjoyed the odd glass of wine and made a living selling wholesale clothing. He wasn't religious, but he was proud of his heritage. He said that the Sayyeds were among the first Iraqi communists, and that his grandfather was the first in town to educate his children. His father's generation spawned judges, professors, and artists, making them natural targets for Saddam Hussein's paranoid regime.

"Intellectuals scared Saddam. Every aware person became a threat," Sadeq told me. This was especially the case at times of unrest, when such intellectuals threatened to channel and encourage the people's rage, just as he once did.

Over the several meetings necessary to tell me his entire story, Sadeq explained that in 1991, Shia Muslims were motivated by a desire to avenge all those who had died in Saddam's brutal wars, his brutal prisons, his brutal witch-hunts of their religious leaders. When it happened, Sadeq worked behind the scenes, helping form a plan to control his Southern Iraqi city when the regime fell. He then encouraged his people to revolt. "I yelled in the streets, 'Fight this regime that destroyed you ... Don't be afraid.'" They rose up, and for a fleeting few days, their success was breathtaking. But then Saddam's men arrived to unleash a bloodbath.

Sadeq was among those who escaped. He said he shelled out stacks of cash for a passport and left the very day he got it, taking a taxi north to Baghdad, then another on to Amman and finally to Beirut, where he settled for some time, completely cut off from his family. Feeling threatened even in Lebanon, however, he eventually schemed to leave for Europe. He told me that he and another survivor, Ali, along with two others, snuck into Beirut's port and sealed themselves inside an empty shipping container. They had bread, water, candles, a lighter—and a whiff of hope. As the ship sailed, they struggled with seasickness and the small panic attacks they suffered from the lack of space. Soon, Sadeq started having disturbing heart palpitations. They were running out of air.

They'd noticed plastic plugs in the metal wall of the container and managed to poke a few out to avoid suffocation. When the ship finally stopped, they knocked on the container's walls to draw attention after nearly a week of silence. The ship's captain brought them on deck and they continued to Marseille, where they were accepted as refugees.

Sadeq thrived in France. He kept insane hours at work, and that helped keep the pain of separation at bay—returning to Iraq was out of the question. Ali, meanwhile, never quite fit in. Within minutes of meeting him, I could see he was troubled. "They thought that I was involved in the Concorde crash and the Toulouse bomb," he told me, referring, apparently, to the French authorities. "They interrogated me. They are in cahoots with Saddam's men. They are all *mukhabarat*. They have tapped my phones, and they watch me. They tried to kill me, you know."

Adel, another Iraqi exile, looked sadly at his friend. "Saddam is no longer," he said. "He's gone. No one is coming after you."

Ali just wouldn't believe it. He was so paranoid, his friends later told me he believed even I was a spy.

In extreme cases, post-traumatic stress disorder manifests itself as severe paranoia, a constant, irrational fear of impending disaster. Ali was a classic case. He could not keep a job due to his condition. He may have survived Saddam's worst atrocities, but their memories would remain with him forever. He was certain that one day, "they" would eventually get him.

𐤉

Iraq's nightmares came in many forms, the legacy of a state that excelled at terrorizing its own people. It was in the ease with which you could end up in a prison, the speed with which you'd be tortured before you could even dream of a judge hearing your case. One man I met in 2003 who'd had his ear cut off for deserting the army told me he would go through it all over again—even losing half of his ear again—if only he could erase the memories of sleeping one night in one of Saddam's cells.

Abu Ghraib, an imposing building on the edge of the capital, was perhaps one of the most notorious of Iraq's prisons. If you were arrested, you prayed never to land there because there was every chance you'd never leave—and even if you did, the experience would haunt you forever. But Saddam's prisons and torture chambers dotted the country, and they came in many incarnations—even in the midst of a posh neighbourhood like Mansour, in a benign-looking house with a neat garden and a rare green lawn.

The house once belonged to a middle-class Shia family, who had it custom-built like an American bungalow back in the 1970s. Authorities seized it after some members of the family were branded traitors and sent either to jail or into exile. It was then transformed into the neighbourhood interrogation centre. Neighbours heard screaming and muffled cries at all hours, the homey facade belying the ghastly crimes committed inside.

We'd heard about the house and went to see it. Dia'a al-Hariri, the owner who'd come back to reclaim it after Saddam's fall, had thrown the doors open for anyone who cared to delve into the dark corners of their darkest days. The rooms were crudely equipped to administer punishment: hooks fastened to the ceilings from which to hang prisoners; pegs in the ground to which they were shackled for weeks at a time; car batteries provided the electricity to shock the reluctant into confessing. The walls were etched with the slogans, sketches, and signatures of the hopelessly incarcerated.

Amazingly, former prisoners did visit. Ali Raad, a sprightly, tough-looking man, wandered aimlessly through the house, a cigarette leaving his mouth only when he spat out a few words. He had been held in solitary confinement there for an entire month, forced to lie down under the stairs, shackled and handcuffed. He slipped himself under the stairwell for us, re-enacting his confinement as beads of sweat formed on his brow. "The cheapest thing here was human life," he said. "We weren't human—we were like insects."

We also met Hyder Mohammed, who said he was nineteen when he was brought there on suspicion of belonging to a religious opposition group. Like a real estate agent, he took us from one room to another, explaining in broken English how each one was used.

Here, twelve of them were made to sleep together "like sardines," he explained. Over there, he remembered a woman being tortured in a room with a door that had a small window, through which her husband was forced to watch. Now forty, Mohammed still has nightmares about hanging from the ceiling with his arms behind his back, being beaten with iron pipes and cables.

Al-Hariri, the bespectacled, greying Iraqi Brit who was the owner now, estimated that thousands had been interrogated in his childhood home. Hundreds of them are believed to have died or gone missing at the hands of the bungalow torturers, among them al-Hariri's own brother, cousin, and uncle, whose fates are still unknown.

"I feel every person who went through this house," said al-Hariri. "I came here because I wanted to say [that] we have won. Saddam is gone, and people shouldn't be afraid of these thugs anymore."

Yet this could never again be a home—it seemed to me it would remain haunted forever.

Torture was endemic in prisons throughout the Middle East, but in places like Syria and Libya it was routine and inhuman and sometimes fatal. Even in Amman I'd heard stories as a child of friends or distant cousins who disappeared and endured torture for months, always the subject of whispered conversations but never, ever of newspaper headlines or a court case. Yet it was only now, standing there inside that house of horrors with Ali and Hyder, that I saw direct evidence of that reality. I was daunted thinking about the kind of trauma the survivors must have endured, the anger they must harbour for the rest of their lives.

Salim, an Iraqi man I met in Lebanon, had plenty of it. He was an army deserter under Saddam, and he lived through months of agonizing torture and humiliation after he was captured. He told me he was often beaten at the height of the day's heat, which is legendary in Iraq's sweltering summers. He said he was forced to crawl into a hole full of mud, gasping for breath, while his torturers laughed, smoked cigarettes, drank tea. He said he was made to carry a heavy bucket filled with sand around his neck and spin around until he dropped. And again. He said he was also electrocuted repeatedly with cables, which eventually put him in a coma that lasted months.

He said he then woke up a different, volatile person, regularly erupting into fits of rage, viciously beating his wife and children. I had never heard an Arab man admit to beating his wife, even though domestic abuse is widespread. But Salim did, breaking down in tears as he described the violence he dispensed at home. Out of continuing fear of the authorities, he took his family and snuck into Lebanon, where he had yet to heal.

"There are things inside me that I can never forget."

ﺀ

Saddam and his henchmen routinely appropriated Iraqi homes at will. Decades ago, my friend Reem and her family were suddenly forced to vacate their home without explanation. Reem was a university-trained English–Arabic translator and a mother of two. After Saddam's fall, she worked with journalists as a translator and fixer, and after I met her through a colleague, we became fast friends. By reputation, though, Reem was a prolific poet well known for her lyrical compositions about love. One day in late 2003, she told me the story of the house, which used to sit near Saddam's presidential compound. If it still existed, it now lay within the Green Zone, home to U.S. troops and civilians and the seat of the fledgling Iraqi government.

One quiet weekend we set out to see if we could find it, armed with old documents proving ownership and a satellite image from her father that showed its exact location. It was supposed to be right at the southern edge of the Green Zone, with a magnificent view of the Tigris. As we approached a bend in the road flanked by the mighty concrete blocks that now enclosed the zone for security, Reem spotted her house and recognized it instantly: a bungalow perched on a slope and, just as in the satellite picture, nestled in a tree grove separated from the rest of the homes nearby. Reem had not seen that house in nearly twenty years. We got out to take a look. There were construction workers all over it.

"What are you doing?" Reem screamed at the men. I hadn't anticipated her emotional reaction. "This is my house! Oh God, what's happening to my house?"

The men ignored us, mixing concrete outside and polishing the floors inside.

Reem had brought her photo album and frantically pointed to the real-life versions of things shown in the photographs. There were the built-in bookshelves her father had installed himself. Over there were the generous sliding windows. She broke into tears, yelling in English: "Tell them to stop! What are they doing?"

One of the men told us they were fixing it up for the use of an American contracting company. Reem vowed to make a legal claim, then fell silent on the way home.

The subject of Reem's stolen home first came up shortly after I had inadvertently become her tenant. The hotel I was staying at had received a threat one night, forcing dozens of us journalists to seek immediate alternative shelter. I was alone and had nowhere to turn, and so at first I ended up at Ammar's house on the outskirts of Saddam City (now renamed Sadr City). Reem found this out through Waseem, and offered to put me up in a tiny, empty apartment next to her own and closer to the centre of town, and I readily agreed. There I found companionship, comfort, and the beginnings of a long and intense friendship, my first with an Arab woman since I left Amman twenty years earlier.

It was Ramadan at the time and Reem and I spent many late nights talking and laughing, our closeness heightened through our shared anxiety over the dangers that lurked outside our common home, the nervousness we felt at the sounds of the ongoing battles between American troops and insurgents in the Dawra neighbourhood nearby.

Reem and I were also bound by space, the wonderful meals she cooked, and the curses we both unleashed when the power cut out (always at the most inconvenient moment). Electricity was essential for my work, my computer, and my satellite phone. For Iraqis, it was above all about safety—they simply needed to see what lay around the next corner. The availability of power seemed to determine their mood. Once, just after the war ended, a bunch of us journalists were invited to the home of our fixer, Ammar, for lunch. The power was out. Before his wife had served a single dish, intense shooting broke out right outside the windows. *I knew it*, I said to myself. *This was a bad idea.* As the shooting got worse we cowered uncomfortably in our seats. *Who was fighting? How would we get home?* But it turned out that the power had just returned for the first time since the war. *That* was celebratory fire. I made a mental note for next time. It was the happiest I'd seen Iraqis since I arrived.

But the power continued to be erratic, and on those dark nights, Reem would remain anxious until Sadeq, her husband, came home, each errand a life risked. Yet despite the dangers, many evenings Reem's living room came alive with visitors: writers, thinkers, journalists, artists, and self-described philosophers. Her sister was an accomplished painter whose depictions of women's bodies were among the best I had ever seen. In Reem and Sadeq's living room, surrounded by their vast library, music, and friends, I discovered a side of my native culture I hadn't fully explored before.

Reem's intellect and profound love of country touched me at the very core. Her poetry—and spontaneous delivery of a suitable line or two at appropriate moments—reminded me of the pivotal role poetry played in our own upbringing, as avid readers. Unlike the turgid lines recited by children at school, Arab poetry was owned by all the people, memorized, and delivered with pride, and it was all the more appreciated when the words implied dissent and thinly disguised defiance—it didn't matter to whom: foreign colonizers, overlords, or Arab dictators. As children, we had memorized stacks of verse and competed in games designed to test our poetic knowledge. Music could be serious only if it was inlaid with the profound words of Arab poetry. Oum Kolthoum, the revered Egyptian singer, immortalized some of the Arab world's most beloved poetry with her explosive voice. In a region where leaders of virtually all colours spouted lies, poetry continued to thrive as some of the truest words spoken in Arabic. The classical singers who put those words to music became among the few who could truly speak for the people.

Reem's poetry spoke to and for Iraqis, and all about them: their isolation, their fatigue after a lifetime of wars. "We grew up on wars. I opened my eyes to war," she once told me. Even as the sectarian clashes intensified, she was certain that the unrest would be temporary, that Iraqis would swiftly move on. "Iraqis learn quickly," she observed. "They never make the same mistake twice." And when things began to seriously unravel, she insisted that Iraq was not beyond redemption, and that she would stay to see it come back to life. "This is my home. I did not leave before, and I will not leave it now."

Though they feared otherwise, Iraqis wanted to believe the worst was now behind them. And more than ever Iraq now needed what remained of its intelligentsia to stay and rebuild. In the course of gathering stories for the CBC, I met lawyers, businessmen, doctors, and intellectuals who swore nothing would budge them. Jim Hoffman and I met and filmed a group of surgeons who selflessly offered free cosmetic surgery to those disfigured by Saddam's torture, doing their part to help Iraqis heal. While gathering a story on schools, we met teachers who vowed to brave the increasingly dangerous streets to ensure that Iraq's children were educated and a man with a Kalashnikov who stood alone outside to keep troublemakers out. I met policemen who were certain that with a bit of effort, traffic could be organized again and crime could be beaten. Policemen like Amin and Nidal, whom I'd met on an earlier trip with Don Murray at a U.S. police retraining course, and with whom I stayed in touch. Such people came from all over Iraq, and from every one of its sects. The key, many of them said, was to purge Iraq of its demons. And to find Saddam, who'd gone into hiding since his regime fell.

They were still afraid of him—even when the Americans finally found him in December 2003, dishevelled and disoriented, in a hole leading to a hiding place near his hometown of Tikrit.

It was one thing to witness Saddam's mighty, seemingly unshakeable regime fall like a house of cards. But to see a once-powerful and mercurial man passively having his teeth checked by an American soldier on television was deeply shocking to many in the Arab world. Some Iraqis and many other Arabs were incredulous—insisting to me that the man shown on television had to be a fraud. *It can't be him! The Americans are lying!*

Of course some still viewed it as the West vanquishing an Arab, yet again. Yet his capture marked the first time the modern Middle East had seen one of its strongmen humiliated, weakened, and undone. It was a profound lesson, a precedent. An idea had been planted.

☙

When Saddam was caught, I was in Jordan, at Petra, the spectacular ruins of an ancient Nabataean city south of the capital, which we'd never visited when we lived in Amman as children. I was forced to return to Amman immediately, to file and to make plans to head to Iraq the next morning.

Though I had already taken the highway to and from Baghdad several times, I always dreaded the long, dangerous road trips. The journey often began from my Amman apartment, which coincidentally lay in the midst of a mini Iraq, a new upscale West Amman neighbourhood whose streets were all named for Iraqi (and, unsurprisingly, mostly Sunni Muslim) cities—a kind of Jordanian ode to its generous neighbour and once its source of virtually free oil. I walked Ramadi Street on the way to the corner store, crossed Fallujah when I wanted to grab a taxi, and lived on Al-Habbaniyah Street, named after a Sunni enclave in the heart of Al-Anbar Province.

As my virtual Iraq receded behind me, I had time to slowly ease into the real one, the long journey helping smooth the transition from safe and staid Amman to otherworldly Baghdad. A convoy of GMC utility vehicles hired by a number of journalists would gather before dawn to try to get to the border by daybreak, travelling together for safety. The Jordanian crossing first made way for Rutbah, a tiny village near the Iraqi border, and after that, it was nothing for miles and miles. Eventually, the edges of Ramadi appeared, and you knew you were close. Restive Fallujah flashed by, and you were thankful for that, and then finally an inhospitable Abu Ghraib gruffly welcomed you at the threshold to Baghdad. By then, seven or eight hours would have passed and I'd be ready to see it.

Working in a country I was still getting to know, and in a medium I was still learning, had its challenges, not least with the mounting dangers. At first I found marrying images to words difficult—each was an art on its own that I felt sullied the other. More experienced journalists said that it would take time, that the art was in saying as little as possible and allowing the pictures to speak.

It seemed illogical to me: if pictures were truly worth a thousand words, then for God's sake, let the pictures speak and leave me be to write it all longhand and fill in the edges, the parts beyond the frame. I also constantly wrestled with the decades of historical facts crammed in my head, forever frustrated as I tried to jam in whatever would fit into two minutes and thirty seconds. It made for awkward television, mediocre at best.

"Your last story was better," one of our senior broadcasters told me over the phone as I stared into the brick wall across from my window at a Baghdad hotel in late 2003. "Just try to relax when you read. And by the way, next time, don't talk about Sunni and Shia Muslims—that's too complicated. Try to simplify."

I was gobsmacked and I protested, explaining that the distinction went to the heart of the Iraqi story. He insisted that I avoid it as much as possible. I was furious, but it was early going. Eventually there would be no debate over making such distinctions.

Television was also a tribal medium, each bit of it best created through the cooperation of several individuals. Early on, before Jim joined me, I made television alone—save for the help of a fixer and the occasional sympathetic vetter on the desk in Toronto—awkwardly interviewing while filming, listening while trying to remain in focus. I'd had only a few days of training on a small camera, and a handful of grave lessons from a master on the art of writing for television, before heading to Baghdad. But I hadn't been prepared for all that on top of doing my own translation and editing (for TV and radio), even my own standups. Needless to say, while I researched endlessly and sought out the best stories I could, the execution left them wanting. I lacked confidence and my voice intoned inexperience. I felt that my journalism was being sacrificed to the logistics of making television, and of working in a troubled place. Logistics—like where to live—were everything; the journalism, in fact, seemed always to come last.

Over time, I lived in several places in Iraq, with Reem's house just one in a kind of musical hotels tour of Baghdad. There was the Hamra Hotel, which I left behind to stay at Reem's, and which was eventually attacked by a car bomb. There was the Rimal Hotel, the Palestine, and another smaller hotel in the Karrada district, all of which were eventually attacked in one way or another. Nothing was immune, and with every journey came the inevitable game of hotel roulette, a game you didn't want to lose.

After the fall of Saddam, car bombs, mortars, RPGs, and firefights became a regular part of life in Baghdad and beyond. Much of my work centred around visiting the aftermath of such acts: the charred, broken remains of the Red Cross headquarters; the UN building that had toppled over after a powerful explosion; the remains of car bombs that unleashed chaos and death in the streets. The central morgue became a regular stop for me and for the Iraqi families who went to claim the bodies of civilian victims of the casual killing sprees of terrorists.

Funerals were even worse. Back home in Canada, I could easily stop mourning women from beating their heads and chests into awakening my own early memories of mourning—I simply changed the channel. But as a CBC employee, I was now paid to chronicle such events and bring them to television screens across Canada: the daily harvest of young men and children in the streets of Baghdad, of people who had taken the ordinary risk of going to the market; the families at the morgue, rigging an orange-and-white taxi for an extra passenger to ride in a box up top. We witnessed countless funerals that followed the annihilation of worshippers by unholy bombs blowing up in holy places; we talked to the distraught relatives of those killed by a bomb lying in wait not for them, but for some marked politician. In person, those images became real people, their screams piercing and their sunken eyes challenging my own. They were as inconsolable as those of us watching were helpless. Months and even years later, their faces were unforgettable.

To escape the chaos and death, an increasing number of Iraqis were making journeys across that desert. In their quest for some measure of peace, they tried to leave even for just a little while by travelling for the sake of it, the first time for many of them.

In the fall of 2003, the Coalition Provisional Authority (Iraq's transitional, American-run administration) approved temporary free travel documents for all Iraqis without passports, which was likely the vast majority because under the previous regime, passports and permission to leave the country were not easy to obtain. The four wickets at the Directorate of Citizenship Office in the Karrada neighbourhood were immediately besieged with people: women in flowing abayas; mustachioed businessmen in suits; farmers and shopkeepers in *dishdashas*; a young man in a knock-off Armani baseball cap. Overwhelmed by the din, the staff members inside occasionally yelled in vain for order. "Please go back! Please move back!" But no one moved.

The back offices were crammed with mounds of paper in bundles as large as encyclopedias, stuffed into folders that in turn were held together with twine. Iraq's bureaucracy had not yet discovered computers, so the staff did everything manually. The Interim Travel Document was simply a sheet of white paper, lined up top with the red and green of the flag, and good for only one trip. The men and lone woman in the back stuck pictures in a square on the left side of the page using stick glue. The picture was then stamped, covered with plastic, and imprinted with a seal. Still, they had managed to issue more than twenty-five thousand documents in just a few weeks, and in the process, they'd helped eliminate what had until then been a thriving trade in passport forgeries.

"For more than twenty-three years we were forbidden from travelling," Jamil Mubarek, manager of the passport section, told my camera. "Now even women can travel alone without an escort. This is democracy!" He said this with a smirk, seemingly unconvinced that this kind of freedom was necessarily a good thing.

Outside, enterprising freelance application writers helped customers ensure their papers were in order before they joined the chaotic queue. A silver-haired man wearing a blue shirt methodically stapled pictures to applications and placed them neatly in a folder for his customers to take to the window. Next to him I met Bashir Khaled Shabib, who was leaving the next day on a religious pilgrimage to Iran. "It's the first time in my life," he said. "I have never travelled to any country."

Such a simple desire—to see some other place, to visit relatives they hadn't seen in decades. Or perhaps to catch their breath, to sleep soundly and securely, to enjoy twenty-four-hour electricity. When Reem once came to Jordan and dropped by to visit me, she insisted on keeping all the lights on—all the time—just because she could. The borders were now heaving with Iraqis, not exactly refugees—for many of them planned to return—but undoubtedly haunted people seeking refuge.

�

As the chaos intensified, many other Iraqis sought refuge in religion.

The first time I saw Shia Muslims in a public display of ritual mourning was in Baghdad shortly after Saddam's fall, in the very spot in Ferdous Square where his statue had been toppled. Young men dressed in black marched in a haunting procession, slowly swinging thick chains onto their backs in an act of self-flagellation. It was days before Ashura, the tenth day of the Muslim new year and one of the most important dates in the Shia calendar that commemorates the murder of Hussein, the prophet's grandson, in Karbala. Such public displays had been forbidden in Saddam's day. But here they were, sombrely walking to the hypnotic beat of a mournful chant. It was a powerful display of the Shia revival following Saddam's defeat.

A year after the regime's fall, elaborate plans were made for a large public marking of Ashura. We stayed in Baghdad to watch the proceedings at the Khathem shrine, where it's believed that two Shia imams, both killed by Sunni Abbasid caliphs, were buried centuries ago. The night before, a rare quiet descended on Baghdad and the neighbourhood of Karrada, where I was staying. I listened to the chants waft through the windows and caught the aroma of pots of stew being stirred on the sidewalks outside, where whole families would spend the night. The entry in my diary that evening was hopeful. And even though it was the eve of a sombre occasion, the mood on the streets was one of contentment.

Early the next morning, Jim and I and four Iraqi colleagues joined tens of thousands of people in the old alleys of Kathimiya, intending to visit the golden-domed shrine that gave the neighbourhood its name. I'd been to the area only one other time, three months earlier, to meet with a kindly Shia cleric to talk about Saddam's capture. Waseem and I had found Sayyed Ali al-Waeth sitting on the lush, deep red Persian carpet that dominated his office, legs crossed before a tiny, intricately carved wooden desk on the floor. He wore dark robes and a black turban—another descendant of the prophet. His face was very fair and partially covered by a grey beard. He was advising a woman who appeared to have come to discuss a marital dispute. He gestured for us to sit on the floor against the wall until he finished.

"So you're the journalist," he began with a welcoming smile. "You knew you were coming to see a Muslim, didn't you? You're not dressed properly for our meeting."

Though I abhorred the idea of having to wear the hijab, I had always made a point of observing religious and cultural standards while working in the Middle East—as I would anywhere else I worked, out of respect for the people who followed them. Yet the large black scarf and the long sweater I wore that day were apparently not enough, and I had offended this pious man in his own office.

"Let's get you ready for our interview. Don't worry. The girls inside will take care of you." He made a quick phone call, and out of nowhere a man appeared with a used version of the requisite outfit and handed it to Waseem to hand to me. Al-Waeth gestured to a second door. "Go there. I will be waiting here when you're done."

I pulled at the handle, eager to get out of view and into the room. I slammed the door and turned around quickly—and found myself face to face with about thirty young women in what appeared to be a religious class.

"The imam told me to come in here so I could get dressed properly for our interview," I stammered. "I'm a journalist," I added.

A few girls giggled. The instructor broke into a smile and immediately welcomed me. One of the students helped me drape the navy *jilbab*—a kind of coat—over my shoulders, pulling it over all the other layers. Then they placed the headpiece on my face and pulled back the edges of the garment along with my hair. My face finally emerged, taut, like a fingertip poking out of a torn glove.

When I came out, al-Waeth approved. At the end of our interview, he wouldn't hear of taking the outfit back.

So that was what I wore that day as we walked into Kathimiya. Dozens of gunmen stood as security on the outskirts of the neighbourhood. Their presence was a comfort given the likelihood of violence, even though many of them belonged to the rebellious Mahdi Army—whose maverick leader, Muqtada al-Sadr, I had interviewed in Najaf only a few days earlier. (Once again, my being female threatened to derail an interview. When we arrived, al-Sadr's handlers begged Ammar, our fixer, for a different interviewer. Wasn't there a male who could ask the questions? But we persisted.

Al-Sadr eventually emerged, walking in his flowing abaya with not a hint of a smile. He refused to look at me, and throughout most of the interview, he stared at his feet.)

Outside Kathimiya the security men checked vehicles closely, but subjected people on foot to little more than a cursory pat-down—and then only the men. We, however, were delayed repeatedly as they checked our equipment and vehicles. But we finally got through: two cars and six people, four of them Iraqis—including Waseem, and Ammar's brother and nephew—who came along as our security.

Once we'd made it through, we walked along the ancient alleys until the beautiful golden dome of the Khathem shrine finally appeared, gleaming in the distance. For centuries, Shia Muslims had come here to be blessed, to pray, to ask for forgiveness, for help, and for healing. Jim set up his tripod to take a long shot.

As I looked ahead, I saw a plume of what seemed like dust burst out of the windows just below the glittering dome. Seconds later, a big fireball erupted from it. The shrine was under attack. I was concerned there might be other bombs, so my immediate instinct was to hang back, and I asked everyone on our team to do the same. Jim and the guys said they would move forward just a few metres to film the chaos that had erupted. I told them I would get out of the way of the fast-moving, retreating crowd to get on the phone to the CBC. By the end of the phone call, Jim and the others had vanished from view.

Wailing people ran past me, pleading for god's mercy. Then I saw them: two young men looking at me suspiciously and talking to each other. I was on the two-way radio, trying to reach the crew, and, sensing danger—and vulnerability—I deliberately spoke louder in Arabic. Then a third young man, in fatigues and armed with an AK-47, walked purposefully in my direction. He silently grabbed my left arm at the wrist and started dragging me up the main road towards the shrine.

I asked him what he wanted. He told me not to be afraid, said that he just needed to check the radio, which he'd yanked out of my hand. "No problem," I said, "but please slow down. I don't want people to think I'm being arrested." It was apparently what was happening, though, because he wouldn't let go and wouldn't slow down.

Where were we going? "To the al-Sadr office," he said finally. Good, I thought, he's from the Mahdi Army. I told him I'd just interviewed al-Sadr. He smirked in disbelief and continued to drag me with him. He became rougher as we approached the shrine and stumbled into the carnage that had just been unleashed. It was still only minutes after the explosion. People on the ground were soaked in blood, some writhing in pain, others completely still. Angry men hauled bloody ones on blankets down the street. Body parts. Screaming. Hysteria. I was nearing that state myself. He yanked harder. People noticed.

A balding man with white hair approached us first. He said something out loud. That got more people's attention. I pleaded with my captor to keep things calm. As we rounded the corner, several people were already following us. And then the beating started. First it was a shove from behind. Then several blows to my head, and someone pulled my hair. Someone else kicked me, and something struck me on the back and head. The sequence repeated itself, and suddenly I was being pulled in a thousand directions. I heard myself yelling, "I'm a journalist! I'm a journalist! I didn't do anything!"

Earlier I had offered to show the young gunman my papers, proving my identity. I told him that I was with a cameraman, and that we had permission to be there but had gotten separated. He didn't believe me. He wasn't interested—it seemed he, and those now beating me, believed I was somehow involved in unleashing the unholy violence in their holiest of places, but I couldn't know for certain. How was I going to convince an entire mob that I was telling the truth when we were surrounded by carnage?

The punching became fiercer and the situation seemed to be spiralling out of control. I caught sight of my free hand and, seeing red, realized my nose was dripping blood. My head throbbed and I ached all over.

Just then, a man in a white *dishdasha* soaked in blood appeared at my right side and pulled at me. I thought he was about to deliver another blow. "Come with me," he yelled. But the gunman still had my other aching wrist. He in turn warned that if the man took me away, he would shoot both of us. He released my wrist and cocked his gun. Everyone moved back. Closing my eyes, I waited for the shot. I wondered how my mother would cope when she heard.

But there was no shot. In that split second, the man in the bloody *dishdasha* yanked me and we ran for a few metres and ducked into a hotel. He bolted the main door and dragged me into one of the rooms and started with a rough barrage of questions. *Who are you? What are you doing here? Why did you come?*

I was hysterical now. He demanded identification. I gave him my backpack and told him to look—there was nothing suspicious. "I am a journalist and have done nothing wrong," I said. He fingered my passport and put it in his breast pocket along with my press pass. He looked through my wallet and handed me all the cash and said to put it in my pocket. I could see the man was unsure what to think. He told me not to worry, but I *was* worried. I stared at the blood on his *dishdasha*. He disappeared for a while and then came back saying that the young gunman had come to the door and threatened his life. I could hear a howling woman in the lobby demanding that I be thrown back out. I could hear shooting outside.

My telephone rang, instantly sobering me, and I saw that it was Ammar, our main fixer. I told the hotel man to answer, to explain to him where I was, and to have Ammar confirm my story. I could see the hotel man now believed me. Ammar arrived some time later with his brother, having also lost Jim and Waseem. He went off to al-Sadr's office to show them the document that gave us permission to be there, and to persuade the armed youth, who was still lurking outside with his mob, to relent. Ammar sorted it out and came back. The young man was called off.

I finally learned my saviour's name: Hajj Salam. He said that I should leave immediately. He put my backpack into a plastic shopping bag, and we ventured out of the hotel, walking single file, quickly, with Hajj Salam either beside me or behind me to protect me from curious eyes and the mayhem that continued to engulf the area. He walked with us until we got to the car, where we offered our profuse thanks and left. Ammar's brother drove me back to the hotel, while Ammar stayed behind to look for Jim.

Once out of the perimeter, I dialled Toronto again. With the help of the desk at the CBC, I made calls to everyone who mattered—the U.S. forces, the Iraqi forces, the Mahdi Army office, and other television networks—to be on the lookout for Jim and Waseem. Several nerve-racking hours passed before Waseem finally called to say they were on their way back.

Jim and Waseem were much more badly hurt than I was. Moments after we were separated, they had been overpowered by a crowd of angry worshippers who didn't like either Jim or his camera. Both he and Waseem were bitten and badly scratched and bruised. A passing cleric stopped and saved their lives. Waseem said it was just in time, because someone had pulled out a knife and was going to stab Jim in the back. The cleric personally brought Jim all the way back to our hotel in Karrada. I couldn't find the words to thank him. He smiled and said he was just doing his duty.

Jim needed stitches on his head. Yet despite all that had happened, we filed a story—though, despite tremendous pressure from Toronto, I refused to talk on air about what had happened to us that night. Nearly a hundred people died in Kathimiya that day, in what turned out to be at least three separate explosions, and many more died in simultaneous bombings in Karbala. It was the bloody start of an intensely violent period in Iraq, and in my view what happened to us was tangential. The next day, I photographed Jim's injuries for him to keep on file, including the teeth marks on his back, then watched him get ready to go on air to talk about it all on the CBC's morning show, parting his boyish hair to the side and putting on a nice shirt. He did a wonderful job. We agreed to stay in Iraq for the rest of our scheduled time. Despite our tearful protestations, Ammar sacrificed a goat to give thanks for our survival, right outside the hotel. Our only consolation was that he distributed the meat to the poor in Kathimiya.

Before we left Baghdad, Jim returned to the neighbourhood to see the cleric who'd saved his life and thank him. Ammar asked if I wanted to see Hajj Salam, but I couldn't bring myself to do it. Many times in later years, I regretted that decision. I concluded that Jim's approach had been much wiser.

We left later that March. It was 2004, and it would be well over a year before I returned to Baghdad. I remained haunted by the memories of that day, and left certain that Iraq's ghosts wouldn't leave its people in peace either.

EIGHT

On the Run

꽃꽃꽃

Contentment with what you have
is a treasure that never runs out.
—ARAB PROVERB

BAGHDAD, DECEMBER 2005

I hadn't seen Iraq from the air since early 2003, long before bombs
rained down on Baghdad, before the concrete barriers ruined its
boulevards, and before kidnapping became a way to make a living.
You wouldn't know any of that went on, peering now from a
window seat high above—you could be anywhere. From up here,
Lake Habbaniyah glimmers invitingly, the villages make-believe
friendly. The palm groves look more like secluded resorts than
hiding places for vengeful men with rocket-propelled grenades.

The plane was just about to begin its corkscrew descent, an
approach intended to throw off such assailants—and redefine
vertigo in my vocabulary—when my mind conjured up Latif
al-Ani. He was the very first Iraqi to photograph Baghdad from a
plane. I'd tracked him down once after seeing one of his black-and-
white photographs in a cheap calendar, and went to his home to
interview him. We chatted about his long career as a photographer
and the merits of sitting at a window seat. His first official photo,
he said, was of Iraq's King Faisal back in 1954, a picture that started

a career that spanned a good portion of Saddam's reign, and during which he photographed notables ranging from Charles de Gaulle to Gamal Abdel Nasser to the Shah of Iran. If there was beauty in Baghdad, the city he adored, it too was captured by al-Ani's lens.

In the 1960s he produced harmonious images of Iraqi musicians—a man hunching over an ornate qanun, and a young woman embracing an accordion player. He captured a poetic portrait of a Baghdad fountain lit against a dark sky, and the iconic image of a worker galvanizing steel inside a pipe under construction. He even saw beauty in a window display of dozens of ladies' shoes hanging on to a rack in disarray.

But his Baghdad had fallen on seriously hard times and was now grossly disfigured. A team of four of us had come to cover the election of the first full-term government since Saddam was ousted, and there was a modicum of hope hanging in the air despite the growing insurgency. Still, the concrete barriers had multiplied like weeds, snarling traffic, surrounding hotels, keeping neighbours from each other. The streets were jam-packed with cars—a sign of progress, to be sure, but since the fall of the previous regime, they flooded the country unchecked, further polluting air already choked with dust and sand. The machinery of the U.S. forces was still everywhere, creating knotty bottlenecks of traffic and damaging Baghdad's sidewalks, roads, and what little greenery there was. Satellite dishes—illegal until the fall of the regime, unless you painted one green and hid it in the bosom of overgrown bushes, as one family I knew did—now competed with palm trees as the dominant feature on Baghdad's horizon. Burned and bombed-out buildings completed the sad picture, and with the addition of garish new advertising billboards, Baghdad was as unsightly as I—and al-Ani—had ever seen it.

The insurgency played a central role in this degradation, by stepping up its attacks against Iraqi civilians and foreign soldiers alike. Insurgents had discovered improvised explosive devices (IEDs), and rigged them up wherever they could for another blow. Mortar and rocket attacks were a daily ritual, and they inflicted untold damage. Then there were the occasional—but sadly commonplace—huge bombs that signalled the involvement of al-Qaeda and badly bruised Baghdad and its people. The city's overworked hospitals and Baghdad's morgue would bear witness time and again to the carnage they together inflicted.

Every time we returned and reconnected with our Iraqi colleagues and friends, someone we knew had in some way been touched by the violence. Every time we visited, someone was always in mourning. Amin, the policeman, survived an assassination attempt, getting away with just a shot in the leg. Then they killed his brother instead. Jumana, one of our translators, told us her brother was kidnapped and held for ransom, beaten, and then left for dead. He left Baghdad and moved to Fallujah, which weeks later erupted in exceptional violence. Jamal, Ammar's young nephew, who had been one of our security guards on that awful day in Kathimiya, was killed in a car bombing. When we saw him, the young man's father, Mohsen, looked like he'd aged ten years. The light had been stolen from his eyes. The light was eventually gone from al-Ani's eyes too. His thirty-seven-year-old son was also killed by a bomb planted in his car. No one could understand why. Meanwhile, Reem's father was kidnapped and held for ransom. The moment they got him back, he left the country.

And Waseem, my resident analyst, who still worked with our team as a driver, lost both his brother and his best friend in one cruel afternoon.

Waseem, his brother Khalil, and Ahmad, my driver and infor-mant before the war, had together bought a large utility vehicle that they drove on that wretched desert highway between Baghdad, Jordan, or Syria, on roads that were no longer safe for us—for anyone—to travel. But at a loss for any other way to make a decent living in the new Iraq, Khalil and Ahmad did, often together— for the company and for safety's sake. Sometimes, when their customers brought them to Amman, we would gather at a cafe to share dessert and tea.

One morning, Khalil and Ahmad set off towards the Syrian border and disappeared. Their customer managed to get away, and he told this story: A gang of armed men standing in the middle of the road intercepted the vehicle near the Syrian border. They seized Ahmad and Khalil, while allowing the passenger, a Sunni Muslim, to escape.

Surely they were all right. Surely they'd be back any minute. Waseem and I, over the phone, had tried to keep calm.

A number of us at the CBC got involved, and we tried everything to find out what had happened to them. I repeatedly contacted the Americans—perhaps they had mistakenly ended up among their prisoners? Nothing. Waseem inquired among the tribes in the area where they had disappeared. Nothing. He checked local hospitals, even morgues. Nothing again. Waseem's mother cried ceaselessly and went on an impromptu hunger strike. And still, maddeningly, absolutely nothing. Weeks turned into months and we all lost hope. Khalil, a father of two, was gone.

Gone too was Ahmad, my smiling, irreverent friend, who'd sworn off marriage but had recently relented and become engaged, to Waseem's sister. He was now just a memory, an entry in my mobile phone's address book. Once in a while, I try to call. The line is still shut.

⚔

So much had changed. With hotel bombings and kidnappings on the rise, staying at unprotected establishments like Reem's was no longer an option—and working as I used to, mostly alone or with Jim, was also impossible now. We were back at the insufferable, but relatively well protected Palestine Hotel: Sat Nandlall, then one of the CBC's finest cameramen; Edith Champagne, a seasoned producer; and Margaret Evans, one of the network's most prolific foreign correspondents, in addition to two armed men whose sole purpose was protecting our lives. We moved in armoured cars, dressed in bulletproof jackets. There were interviews in some neighbourhoods we simply couldn't do—it was too dangerous—so our religiously mixed staff did them for us, or else they brought the subjects right to our hotel. It was a frustrating way to work after two years of exploring all parts of Baghdad and beyond.

The extreme security precautions that U.S. and Iraqi authorities took to protect voters during the election provided some relief. They banned cars, for one, and Baghdad's streets suddenly fell silent. On voting day, we could walk to polling stations, as Iraqis did. We lingered to watch them come out with wide smiles, flashing fingers made purple by indelible ink, welcoming what they described as the birth of a new Iraq.

Though the Americans were still present, the election was a process that was largely administered by Iraqi authorities, and for the first time since Saddam's ouster, Iraqis had an opportunity to choose their own permanent government. It would be hailed as the first free election in Iraq—indeed in the whole Arab world—the long-awaited "dawn of freedom."

At the end of that hopeful day, we walked back to our hotel, waving at the children playing football in the streets, watched over by mothers sitting at doorsteps. It was pleasantly quiet—too quiet for Baghdad, even when there was no violence. But the quiet was temporary.

On the morning of February 22, 2006, any pretence that one election could solve Iraq's problems swiftly evaporated with one powerful explosion.

The target was an important shrine in the city of Samarra, where Shia Muslims believe the last of their twelve imams, Muhammad al-Mahdi, disappeared. The golden dome of the Al-Askari mosque, rebuilt a century earlier, collapsed from the force of the blast. I'd seen first-hand how passionate Iraqis can be about such shrines, and memories of those explosions we witnessed in Kathimiya came rushing back. "This," I told our foreign editor, Brien Christie, over the phone, "is going to be huge."

Thousands of Shia Muslim men and women were on the streets within hours, and though many beat their chests in the traditional show of mourning, it was anger they came to vent. Many others— mostly the armed and barely controllable gangs of self-proclaimed vigilantes on both sides of the Muslim divide—lashed out with the blindness of vengeance. By the end of that day, dozens of Sunni mosques had been damaged, burned, or blown up. A wave of counterattacks blew over Shia areas and mosques. Dozens of people were killed on both sides.

We returned very shortly thereafter to an Iraq well into civil war. Hate had overrun the streets. Bodies, mutilated bodies, were discovered daily: shot in the head, limbs cut off, dumped in the river, dumped by the side of the road, dumped on their families' doorsteps. Waseem had warned this would happen, three years ago, when the sectarian powder was still dry. The hate was now out in the open, unsightly and corrosive. "They [Shia Muslims] are like animals. They are not really human. This is no life—we can't live with them," a Sunni Muslim journalist told me one day at the Palestine Hotel.

In another room, in another hallway, a few days later, a Shia colleague confided in me his opinion of Sunnis: "They're not true believers in god. They have no religion. They have no soul. They are the devil." Until then, it seemed they all believed the U.S. occupiers had been "the devil," a common enemy. But in the wake of Samarra, Iraqis had turned their attention to exorcizing one another.

To be sure, that campaign had begun some time ago—despite extensive and long-standing marital and family ties between Iraqis of the two sects. Shia Muslims blamed every attack on their neigh-bourhoods, mosques, and shrines on disgruntled Sunnis and their co-religionists among al-Qaeda. Sunni Muslims made the same allegations about the Shia, and accused them of marginalizing them out of their rightful place in Iraqi society.

Many Sunnis and their political leaders had chosen to boycott the elections in 2005. They refused to join the army or the police. But they said a large part of their exclusion could be blamed on the now Shia-dominated authorities. A Sunni family we interviewed said they were even afraid to take their son, who'd lost a leg in a bombing, to certain hospitals because they were Shia-controlled and they'd heard Sunnis were refused treatment. Others insisted they couldn't rely on the assistance of police and government officials because they were largely Shia.

Many Sunni Muslims complained that they were being painted with the same brush as al-Qaeda, simply because they belonged to the same religious sect. "All eyes are on you," said Abu Ahmad, a father of four who was threatened into leaving his hometown, only to settle in a Shia area of Baghdad just a few weeks before the Samarra bombing. No one needed to tell Abu Ahmad that he was unwanted—that as a Sunni, he, too, was guilty.

"Who is committing the violence in Iraq? They're going to assume it's the Sunni, the Sunni, the Sunni. Of course [as a Sunni], you're going to be afraid." So, in the hateful wake of Samarra, he packed up his family and moved to Jordan. Abu Ahmad said he used to feel Iraqi. Now his identity had been stripped down to one, small facet of it: he was only a Sunni Muslim, responsible for the ruin of Iraq. He reached into his pocket and pulled out a laminated card. It was a UN-issue ID card, certifying that he'd also become a bona fide refugee. Going back, he said, was not an option.

"How can I be optimistic?" he asked.

Sunnis also charged that they were overrepresented in Iraq's jails. One former prisoner I spoke to alleged that he had been arrested purely because he was a regular at a Sunni mosque that had been pegged by the Americans as a centre for insurgent activity. Omar maintained his innocence, but he was apprehended and then handed over to the Interior Ministry—once a terrifying institution under Saddam—where he says he was tortured because of his religion. He showed me scars that were caused, he said, by cigarette butts his captors had pressed into his flesh. Omar said they ridiculed him while he prayed. He said he'd never before thought of joining the insurgency, but his experience in custody could very well change his mind.

There was no question, though, that Shia Iraqis bore the brunt of the violence. The police, who were mostly Shia, suffered terrible losses from the start. Seen as collaborators, partly because many of them had been retrained by the U.S. military, they became a favourite target—especially for al-Qaeda loyalists who had entered the fray and targeted Shia Muslims just as they did foreigners. Dozens of Shia were killed in bombings at recruitment centres, police stations, and checkpoints—and even in their own homes. Nidal, one of the two policemen with whom I'd stayed in touch, was as adamant now about leaving as he was about staying when I first met him in the fall of 2003. Amin, the one who'd been shot in the leg in an assassination attempt, had switched jobs to get off street patrol and out of view of his would-be assassins. Their threats had forced him to relocate to Najaf for two years without his family.

He, too, was desperate for a way out. He asked me for help in
getting a visa to Canada.

Ordinary Shia neighbourhoods were targeted, as were Shia
families living in mixed neighbourhoods. Threats had become
a daily occurrence. Sometimes they came in the form of text
messages or scraps of paper left on car windshields or doorsteps.
Sometimes they were the briefest of heart-stopping phone calls.
The calls and notes would demand that the recipients relocate
to areas populated by their own sects. Many Iraqis did it anyway
without any prompting.

Baghdad was coming apart. At the height of the carnage, the
violence had sifted its people according to religion and sect, pulling
them swiftly apart the way DNA separates in a dividing cell. Mixed
neighbourhoods were targeted to extinction in a violent ethnic and
sectarian cleansing worse than anyone imagined possible. Some of
those driven out of their neighbourhoods ended up as refugees on
the other side of town. Agencies sprang up to arrange house swaps
between families who, depending on their sect, were suddenly
living on the "wrong" side of town. Baghdad was becoming a
collection of ghettos. The lines had been drawn, and god help you
if you crossed the wrong one. Thousands abandoned the capital
altogether and headed for the provinces, back to areas where they
knew they indisputably belonged.

Hundreds of thousands of Iraqis left their country for good.

☆

You couldn't really appreciate the scale of the Iraqi exodus after
Samarra until you stood at the border and watched people stream
out. Brien, our foreign editor, sensing a dramatic story unfolding
all the way from Toronto, encouraged me to do just that. I travelled
to Syria with Zouheir Bizri, our French-Lebanese cameraman, and
from there we made our way to the Al-Tanaf border crossing at

the edge of the Syrian/Iraqi desert, six hundred kilometres west of Baghdad.

The lineup of cars stretched far into the horizon, a caravan of citizens who had given up on their country. They were loaded with belongings of every description: blankets, baby carriages, and swollen suitcases. One sported a modernized decal of the Iraqi flag. "God is *greater*," it reads—"*Allahu Akbar*"—a phrase that the normally secular Saddam ordered imprinted on the Iraqi flag in 1991, and that is often uttered as a rallying cry in times of calamity. In those contexts, it meant God is *greater* than violence, *greater* than evil, *greater* than the evildoers, but also greater than any of man's greatest creations. It's also a phrase uttered when one beholds beauty, hears riveting poetry, or admires great achievement. That's the essence of the phrase, one of the most inaccurately translated by the world's media.

Allahu Akbar, they muttered when they got out of their cars and saw the endless lineup at the immigration wickets. They came from all over Iraq: Sunni, Shia, and Christian; teachers, drivers, labourers, even a bacteriologist. Most told me their move was temporary. I could see in their eyes they didn't believe their own words.

There was something amiss in the way the people carried themselves that day, something beyond the obvious regret they brought with them across a border that marked their departure from home. Some of the men sat out on the curb, smoking, silent unless they were briefing relatives over the telephone as they waited. Others hid in the small slivers of shade made by big cars and the tiny kiosk that housed the customs office. A bare-headed woman in modern attire sat quietly in the shade of a car's backseat, resting her chin on the flat of her palm. Another, covered completely in a black scarf and abaya, grimaced at the sun as she shepherded her children into the building. I realized that, strangely for a crowd of Arabs, they all kept to themselves, the usual small talk between strangers so ordinary in the Middle East completely absent.

Even at the Syrian border, the distrust hung in the air.

"It's a tragic situation," Kareem Khalil, a displaced man from Ramadi, said succinctly. With a look around him, he added, "You don't know your enemy from your friend."

Several of them described themselves as *musharradeen*—displaced. Implicit in the word is an invisible hand that commits the act, and in Arab parlance that hand is often assumed to be foreign—evidence of many Arabs' enduring and illogical refusal to believe that fellow Arabs could slaughter one another without foreign encouragement or involvement.

We spent an entire day speaking with the *musharradeen*. By listening to those refugees at the Syrian border, I was actually getting a clearer picture of what was happening in Iraq than if I'd been there in the flesh. That day I also learned that the Baghdad I knew no longer existed.

꙳

Here at last was Baghdad. With its tea stalls, fresh fish peddlers, the aroma of *sammoun* bread, the flowing black abayas, and the Iraqna mobile phone stores. And that accent. Iraqi colloquial Arabic is unique, more guttural and harsher than, say, Lebanese or Palestinian Arabic. But it has a distinctive lilt that makes it almost playful. When addressed by an Iraqi, you feel as if you are receiving a kind of spoken nudge. You could hear it everywhere here, sung in a cacophony of nudges all over the street.

Only this wasn't Baghdad. It was Syria, just a short drive from the heart of ancient Damascus and the tomb of Salah al-Din (Saladin) al-Ayoubi. This new Baghdad was far safer than the original, and though just as divided in reality, here its residents were all simply Iraqis, desperately nostalgic for home.

A short distance away, I found Syria's Kathimiya: crude concrete hovels crouching in tiny alleys busy with bicycles, and small shops selling cheap goods to the poor—all of it built around a mosque, a temple to the revered. For a moment my heart jolted at the sight of the golden-domed shrine, this one dedicated to Sayyeda Zeinab, the daughter of Ali, the first imam of Shia—it conjured up memories I'd rather have forgotten. Yet I felt oddly nostalgic for the original, even though I'd never been inside it.

In the relative safety of Damascus, I decided to go in. I put on an abaya and entered the shrine alone, simply to satisfy my curiosity. The inner chamber shimmered with intricate silver work and mirrors, yawning well above the heads of the worshippers and giving way to an ethereal din. There are few places in the Middle East safer than the woman's section of a mosque, and though I'd seen only a handful in my lifetime, I always felt secure, untouchable in a way that's almost impossible to feel anywhere else. I was indistinguishable from the crowd of mostly Iraqi women, but also Iranian and Lebanese Shia, who were mainly on pilgrimage that day. The tomb, the focus of attention, was encased in delicate lattice wall that kept the worshippers at a respectful distance. Some of the women threaded their fingers through the latticework; others kissed it, muttering prayers. One woman tied a green ribbon through it, while another leaned against it reading the Koran. Inside their cocoon of devotion, they seemed at peace, temporarily unburdened of the anxiety and mundane chores of their everyday lives.

As soon as I sat down on the mosque's carpeted floor, an older Iraqi woman struck up a conversation. She had been in Damascus for ten days. I asked how things were in Iraq, and she said she was dreading the return trip. "God protect us," she said ominously. "We have been shaken."

Despite myself, I closed my eyes and yet again imagined Kathimiya and the hysteria unleashed by the explosions.

Outside in the courtyard, I tried to focus on the blue and green mosaics and sublime arches. Nearby, a man sang a *latmiya*, a Shia mourning chant. A small group of worshippers sitting on the cool stone floor swayed and gently beat their chests. A few of them had tears in their eyes. I wondered what scenes were playing in their minds.

In the surrounding neighbourhood, alleys wet with wash water were littered with garbage. A small store displayed live chickens tucked into stacked cages. Store names were slashed in paint right onto the buildings that housed them, along with meaningless graffiti. Girls dressed in hijab dodged the passing cars. Two boys struggled to strap a large canister of cooking gas to the back of a rickety bicycle. A few blocks away, a stroller meant for two held a lone little girl dressed in red. There was no guardian nearby. The baby amused herself watching the traffic splash through a nearby puddle of mud. A rusted sign barely hanging from a lamppost declared: "*Al awn billah.*" Assistance comes from god.

The neighbourhood of Sayyeda Zeinab was home mostly to the poor. And full of Iraqi refugees. It all looked so familiar, like Al-Wihdat and Kathimiya rolled into one.

Deep in one of those alleys was the home of Mona, her husband, Thafer, and his elderly mother. Everyone stood up when Zouheir, my cameraman, and I walked in, except for the mother leaning against the wall, a thin white veil barely covering her grey. A part of her body was no longer functioning. She wore only half a smile and her left hand rested limply in her lap. She sat cross-legged on a worn mattress on the floor, underneath a small window that offered an unobstructed view of the shoes of passersby. Across from her sat a couch the colour of mould. A fan in the corner wheezed next to a giant, ancient refrigerator that whirred like a truck. It felt like I'd been here before.

In typical Middle Eastern fashion, the couple deferentially used words to make up for their poverty.

"We're sorry you have to endure this. Please forgive us for not living up to our obligations." (We're too poor to entertain visitors.)

"Please sit on the couch." (It's the best thing we have.)

"Please do not take off your shoes." (The place isn't worthy of your clean socks.)

We did not take off our shoes, but as a compromise, I took a seat on a stool. Mona left to make coffee. Thafer, her husband, sat on the couch a proper distance away. His elderly mother eyed us from her looking-place. Zouheir started rolling.

Thafer started at the beginning, patiently explaining his religion. They belonged to a tiny minority, he said, numbering only a few thousand in Iraq. He had lived and owned a thriving store in a majority Muslim neighbourhood, and he had always gotten along with his neighbours—until the regime fell and his fortunes changed. He asked me to reveal neither his religion nor too many personal details. None of his new Syrian neighbours knew his religion. His family kept to itself.

Just weeks after Saddam's fall, Thafer's store in Iraq was ransacked and destroyed, his safe and inventory taken away. He suspected he was targeted because of his religion. His fears were confirmed when his daughter was subsequently kidnapped. Masked men put a gun to her head in the middle of a congested street. Her friends called out for help, but no one dared intervene. They disappeared in an instant. When she heard the news, the girl's grandmother passed out from shock and woke up to partial paralysis. She now mostly sits in the sorry living room, quietly weeping. Mona is back with the coffee. She too cries.

"They called and said, 'If you want to see your daughter, then prepare the ransom,'" he told me, his eyes too welling up at the memory. A few days later, the price was even higher: Thafer had to convert to Islam before he ever saw his daughter again. "They said, 'Do you want your daughter? Then you should come to Friday prayers and see her. If not, we will give her away to one of the fighters to marry and publicly announce her conversion to Islam.'"

Thafer said he had been raised to be protective of his dying religion. To be absorbed into the Muslim mass, even as a pretence, was too high a price. "I *have* a religion," he said.

The family decided to flee Iraq, hoping that their daughter might be spared a fate worse than marrying against her will. I was astounded that he would give up his only daughter for his faith. But then I knew nothing about the demands of protecting a minority religion and the kind of pressure that comes with that. People also regularly killed in the name of religion, and that too was a state of mind I could never comprehend.

A few months later, other family members found the daughter's body at a Baghdad morgue. She had been beaten to death. Thafer refused to return, and left it to his family to bury her.

Her grandmother could no longer remain silent. "She was so beautiful," she said, interrupting her son's story. "They are monsters, monsters. Not human. Would you want to live with them?"

So home now was a one-bedroom apartment barely big enough for the couple and their grown children—who hadn't been in school since they left Iraq. The family applied for asylum to a Western country where they have relatives. They were rejected. So they registered with the United Nations and became official refugees. And waited. They were not allowed to work legally. So Thafer and his son did odd jobs under the table. Mona shopped at the end of the day, when the leftover produce was likely to be cheaper. Even so, she deliberately picked out fruit that had started to rot, to lower the price. She opened the whirring fridge to show me: half yellowing apples with the rot cut off.

They did not live in a tent in a refugee camp. But they endured the worst form of refugeehood: their suffering was invisible.

ఋ

At its height, the crisis forced some forty thousand Iraqis to cross into Syria each month, the large majority of them from Baghdad. This was in addition to the two million who had been displaced internally in just over a year. It had become one of the largest ongoing displacements of people, and at the time it created one of the world's largest urban refugee populations, at 4.5 million. Certainly it was one of the largest the Middle East had seen, despite its long history of conflict and displacement.

Around the region, I had seen the modern history of Iraq told through wave after wave of immigrants and the displaced. Iraq had erupted in violence with metronomic frequency, each time scattering another wave of immigrants, refugees, and the politically persecuted around the globe. They were everywhere in the Mideast: working construction in Beirut's Shia-dominated neighbourhoods; strolling with family in Cairo's leafy suburbs; watching a cellphone video of a wedding on the Qasyoun Mountain overlooking Damascus; selling cheap packs of cigarettes lined up on towels on an Amman sidewalk. I saw them at every border and airport. And my encounters with them changed the way I saw the Middle East and its future. But it was only after I visited that Syrian–Iraqi border that I started to see it all as one heartbreaking narrative.

The U.S. Committee for Refugees and Immigrants estimated that prior to 2003, there were already as many as two million displaced Iraqis who had a "well-founded fear of persecution if they returned." That's only a fraction of the overall number of Iraqis who no longer lived in Iraq. Further, according to the UNHCR, there were more Iraqis seeking asylum in 2002 than any other nationality in the world. More than fifty-one thousand had applied to some thirty-seven industrialized countries—*before* the latest war even started.

After the war, CBC correspondent Don Murray and I first met some of the internally displaced in the bombed-out headquarters of Saddam's air force club in central Baghdad, back in the fall of 2003. I remember the deferential man who appointed himself our guide to the small village that had formed there in the aftermath of the war, smiling and gesturing to the new living quarters as though he were showing us a newly acquired grand home. The squatters, who'd come from the south, made full use of whatever they could find, forging a shantytown out of the remnants of an institution in which Saddam took particular pride. They had no running water, little food, and were desperate for blankets. No aid organization had yet discovered them.

Most of those displaced after Samarra were welcome in Jordan and Syria, and they elicited superficial empathy from their fellow Arabs, who now added Iraqis to the list of those hard done by, aggrieved. Yet they would not be allowed to become naturalized citizens, only temporary "guests" with no rights to legal work or permanent stay. They could be deported in a heartbeat, and many have been, in flagrant disregard of international laws prohibiting the deportation of refugees back to countries where their lives were at risk. And as their wait to go home grew longer, their hosts became openly hostile. Wherever they landed in the Arab world, Iraqis were blamed for all society's ills, from skyrocketing housing prices to increasing levels of prostitution. Syria, which never requires a visa from any Arab citizen, began demanding one of Iraqis a year after bearing the brunt of the Samarra tidal wave.

Still, the vast majority of them remain in the Middle East, where they have formed little Baghdads far from the original, because they have no other choice.

Close to Damascus I found a replica of Karradah, that busy

Baghdad neighbourhood that was my home for many a night. Here in Syria, it was Jaramana, a largely Christian area with a significant population of the previously displaced, including Palestinian and Syrian Druze.

The Ibrahim Khalil church looked like any you might come upon in the Middle East, even in Baghdad. It was an unremarkable modern building adorned with stained-glass windows, with a large stone depiction of Mary cradling her dying son out front. The grounds were spotless, a stark contrast to the muddy, littered street outside. Each Sunday, the parish made room for Iraqis to pray. And virtually every Sunday, an Iraqi priest made room in his service for the names of the dead back home. The day I visited, his voice was tinged with melancholy as he read them out loud, one by one. The worshippers, mostly elderly women, crossed themselves with the gravity of the bereaved. They could do nothing but mourn, and listen as the priest's voice soared along with the incense smoke.

The priest, named Arkan, leads the Iraqi Assyrian community in Damascus, now numbering more than two thousand families. The population of Christians in Iraq had dwindled from around 1.5 million before the U.S. invasion to a few hundred thousand and was still falling. Sitting in one of the pews after the service, the priest told me he found it hard to accept that so many Christians were leaving. But he could do nothing to stop it. And at the rate things were going, Christians in Iraq would soon exist only as a memory.

One of those I met in Damascus was twenty-seven-year-old Bassam, who had left Iraq three months earlier. The guilt and embarrassment he felt at abandoning home was still fresh. "I had said that I wouldn't leave Iraq. There's work, and plenty from god," he said in his brother's living room in Jaramana. "But I will not go back. After what I saw, there is no point."

He said this as if he had committed treason by leaving. And his attitude wasn't unusual among displaced Iraqis. Even those who had suffered the worst, like Bassam, felt the need to apologize for leaving home behind. This was especially true of Christians, whose way of life was already endangered in a country dominated by Muslims. But the campaign against them started early: bombs at their churches, in their neighbourhoods, at their homes. Then the threats came.

Leave the country.

Get out of Iraq.

You will be killed.

Bassam and his elder brother, Fouad, received them by text, which was now one of Iraq's favourite modes of communication, even for the criminally minded. The young clothing merchants decided to ignore them at first. But then four men dressed in police uniforms walked into one of the family's stores one day, brandishing guns. Bassam escaped and ran full throttle down the street. The assailants, joined by five others who were waiting outside, followed him. One shot him in the back, just below the shoulder blade, the bullet exiting from his chest. Out of sheer terror, he picked himself up and continued running until he made it to the second store, where he fell into his brother's arms. For some reason, the men gave up the chase. Bassam spent seventeen days in hospital, where a miraculous operation saved his life. On the seventeenth day, his family brought him home for just a few minutes to gather some things. Then they drove to the airport and put him on a flight out. His brother and his young family followed shortly after.

Their crime, as far as Bassam could tell, was being Christian. But all Iraqis, his brother maintains, were fair game. "If you don't hurt anyone, the problem comes to you. If you have money, you have a problem. If you have a good place, you have a problem." And if you dared to hope in the new Iraq, you had the biggest problem of all.

The brothers had dared. They'd carried on with their business, even aspired to expand. Yet now they had no homes and no work. That, for the brothers, was most humiliating of all. "We're used to working, not used to sitting," Bassam said. "Here, we sit. I am filling my time talking to you."

To fill up more time, they also constantly watched television, as so many displaced do. The brothers seemed to do it partly out of a need for affirmation, in a search for more proof that they'd made the right decision. But like so many of the displaced, they also watched for news about their neighbourhoods, the friends and families left behind. It was strangely cathartic to know there were others who were suffering as they did. There was comfort, too, in simply knowing that their story was being told.

"I'm sure you're listening to the news," Fouad says. "All Iraqis cry when they see the news.

"A fish, when you take it out of the water, she dies. Ask the children," he said, "where they want to live. Disneyland? They will tell you Baghdad. They want Baghdad."

In the end, though, home became the U.S.

⚸

Many Iraqis who had exhausted all other means of survival in Syria lined up at the UNHCR office, hoping they would be among the lucky ones to be spirited to a faraway place and a new chance at living a decent life. Wrapped up against the cold of the early Damascene morning, they were dressed in their finest, proud people, mostly educated middle class. Some covered their faces whenever a camera came along to record their most shameful moment. I asked them where they wanted to go. *Sweden. Canada. Anywhere that will take us. Even the U.S.* But the UN was able to resettle very few. No country was willing to take more than a token number, and then only the worst cases.

Many of the displaced fell prey to unscrupulous people who

promised them a safe berth elsewhere. In Damascus, producer
Stephanie Jenzer and I, along with Zouheir, met one of them:
Mustapha, a young Iraqi who had been kidnapped, tortured, and
left for dead on a Baghdad street. Immediately afterwards, he
moved to Syria and started working to save to get back to university. What he wanted more than anything, though, was to leave
the Middle East and its troubles behind. Some of his friends had
made it to Europe, and a man he was introduced to said he could
help Mustapha follow—for a $15,000 fee. Mustapha made a down
payment of several thousand dollars, savings he'd painstakingly
accumulated over two years of working odd jobs. The man took it
and disappeared.

These schemes claimed more and more victims, partly because
some of them actually worked. One man I met told me he'd
walked—*walked*—all the way from Baghdad to a major city in
Western Europe, initially with the help of guides to whom he paid
a large sum of money. He was a friendly waiter at a cafe, uncomfortable in a red vest and baggy trousers better suited to the bustling
kahwas of the Middle East. For his protection, I will refrain from
naming the city where he now lives.

"From Iraq? You walked here from Iraq?"

"Yes. I am not the only one. It happens."

I had heard rumours of Iraqis fleeing their country on foot. It
certainly happened under Saddam's rule, and during the country's
other conflicts. But I had never met an Iraqi who'd actually done it.
How do you walk from Baghdad to Europe? I explained that I was
a journalist and wanted to hear his story. He took this as his cue to
walk away, refusing to meet me again.

"There's no reason to come back," he said brusquely. But then
he returned to give me a brief explanation. When the war started
in 2003, he said, "I walked. In the bush. We slept out in the cold.
I left Iraq with a compass and the clothes on my back. That's it."

An army defector? A Saddam loyalist? I pressed him with questions. Clearly irritated, he asked me what else I needed to know. "That we saw dead bodies on the way? [Those] others who tried and didn't make it? That we saw death with our very eyes? That there are people who will promise you the world, take your money, and then leave you for dead? That's the whole story. I now live in a subway stop. I am illegal. I don't need trouble," he said, emphatically wiping the adjacent table. A spring drizzle had just ended, and so had our conversation. I returned once a few days later to see him, and he turned me away before I said more than hello. I have no idea what became of him.

But his chances were still markedly better than the chances of those stuck in the limbo of the Middle East. As they waited to return home, many of them fell on hard times. One Damascus-based UN psychologist told me that on the occasional days when the UN offered counselling services, they could get up to five hundred people waiting in line. Some who showed up included the completely paranoid, women whose husbands had been killed, and whole traumatized families who'd watched a loved one die. Among them were also downtrodden men who had lost everything in their exodus and yet still received threats. Others confined themselves to their apartments, economically powerless, while their women and children, who found it easier to get illegal work, earned a paltry living.

I could see their disquiet even in the fleeting interviews I'd have with them all over the region. The tearful man who followed me for an hour in Damascus, begging me to help him get out of the country, or at least find a job. The family I met in a Damascus suburb who'd lost one son to the violence in Iraq, then another one, later, to suicide. His anguish at losing his brother was so deep that he could no longer bear living.

Suicide attempts had grown in number. Divorce and separation were on the rise, along with alcoholism, drug use, pill-popping—and domestic abuse. Families found it harder to protect and contain their youth, as they in turn became more hopeless and easier prey not only for drug pushers but also for extremists and radicals. And most important, added the psychologist, they were troubled by the opacity of their future and the fresh pain of the past.

Several international organizations have warned of the consequences. This was a terribly distressed population with rates of depression and anxiety much higher than those encountered among other displaced people. The International Crisis Group warned that these refugees were becoming desperate and destitute. The Washington-based Brookings Institution called it a looming crisis, one that required urgent attention not only out of compassion, but also because it was a fundamental security issue: security for Iraq, for the region, and for the Western world as a whole.

⚷

The region is no stranger to this type of crisis. There have been significant waves of displacement: the Palestinians in 1948 and 1967; the Lebanese between 1975 and 1990; the Iraqis in 1991, and again in 2003 and 2006. And in between, Arabs from various countries have consistently been seeking refuge from political or religious persecution, or simply seeking opportunity. According to that report prepared by regional experts for the UNDP in 2009, the Arab world is home to the highest number of refugees and internally displaced people in the world—some *seventeen million* people—not to mention the untold millions of other Arabs who have relocated abroad. And in the wake of the horrific events of September 11 and the wars that followed, more Arabs are out of place, around the world, than ever before.

Iraqis were now ominously being called the new Palestinians.

Palestinians were once considered to be among the most educated in the Arab world. These days, more than six decades after the first Palestinians became refugees in Lebanon (where they still have few rights, no citizenship, and are excluded from society), they are among the least educated, least employed, and most heavily armed. Extremism has at times easily festered in their midst. In Palestinian towns and villages, in the refugee camps of the West Bank and Gaza, and even in Israel proper, youth suffer from post-traumatic stress disorder, rampant unemployment, rising drug and alcohol use, and growing fundamentalism. Will that be the fate of displaced Iraqi youth another sixty years down the road?

This region was and is still defined by war. It was shaped, and continues to be shaped, by the resulting displacement. Dispossession has been the dominant theme and challenge for generations—both physical and political. It seemed to me that unless some solution was found for the displaced Iraqis, the prevailing hopelessness would only be magnified. And from hopelessness, there can only come desperation.

But I had also come to realize the sad tradition in the Middle East was that war and its consequences, no matter how far back in the past, never stop giving. It's the way it's always been.

꙼

I had one more chance to see the real Baghdad, in September 2007. We arrived to discover an unnatural peace, brought on partly by the departure of so many.

By then, many journalists had given up the so-called Red Zone in favour of the Green one. But our team stayed at a rented house right by the river—walking distance from the Palestine Hotel and surrounded by high concrete walls. We managed a few outings, including a rare U.S. helicopter journey to Jurf Al Sakhar, south of Baghdad. Flying in a twosome over fields of duelling palm trees and satellite dishes, we left behind a trail of flares to throw off potential strikes. For years I'd watched the duos of U.S. helicopters fly above us in Baghdad's skies in a kind of synchronized dance, yet this was the first time I could see that dance from their vantage point. Admittedly I was nervous the entire way, but then I had hardly been myself since that awful day I was beaten in Kathimiya.

We landed not far from Hillah, where that mass grave had been unearthed four years earlier, and we could now hear the familiar sounds of war over the horizon. U.S. soldiers had started paying and arming Sunni residents in Jurf Al Sakhar to turn against al-Qaeda in what Washington would call the "Sunni Awakening." The U.S. credited the awakening, and the deliberate surge in the number of U.S. soldiers, for the relative quiet that now prevailed.

Early on, we also took the short drive to the Green Zone, where I interviewed Prime Minister Nouri al-Maliki. He insisted that the worst of the violence was over, and that the country was now somehow suddenly unified. His upbeat prognosis was at odds with Baghdad's Red Zone reality.

By then, Baghdad's ghettoization was complete: Shia and Sunni were as separated as they could be (by an actual concrete wall in one neighbourhood). Even so, there were enough bombs and IEDs to keep the morgues busy. Four years after Saddam had been deposed, people also still struggled with erratic electricity and unsafe water—and the insecurity of living in what was still a very dangerous place.

Saddam was now dead, hanged at the gallows on December 30, 2006, a year earlier. It was another first for the region—or at least for those who actually believed the gruesome mobile phone video showing him being led to the gallows. It was satisfying revenge for all those who had suffered under his rule, especially those forced to leave the country they loved because of him. But that too failed to quell an insurgency and a civil war that had taken on a life of their own.

Over the years, we had met many Iraqis who made valiant efforts to move their country forward even as they were being forcibly pulled backwards. They created new institutions, new television networks, and newspapers of every stripe, while many others gave themselves over to the arduous task of building the new, democratic political order. None of their efforts can be discounted. But these days, many Iraqis were voting with their feet.

Even those who had refused to leave during the worst of Saddam's reign were now gone. Two of those were Reem and her husband—they moved their family to the safety of another Arab country, preferring the uncertainty of refugeehood to the unpredictability of war. She penned a poignant new poem that encapsulated the despondence of so many who had left.

Waseem and I read it together at the CBC house one night. He too had repeatedly tried to leave, running by me a few outlandish and expensive schemes that I counselled him not to pursue. In the end he accepted his fate and remained, largely because after Khalil's disappearance, he was the only son his mother had left, and she couldn't bear losing him, too. By then, he had married his fiancée of five years. (Waseem later told me that when they were finally alone on their wedding night, she had apparently broken her silence with this: "So where have you been for the past five years?") With his wife, Waseem finally brought children into the world—two of them—even though he still believed it wasn't a world worthy of welcoming new life. I only met his young family over the telephone; much as we would have liked otherwise, even Waseem counselled that a visit to his house these days was out of the question. Maybe later when things improved.

But it would be my final visit to Iraq. Lake Habbaniyah, reflecting the sun, winked at me one last time as we made our way out of the country on that small plane. The highway that I had travelled so many times hurtled away at an unnatural speed below. Even as we were still gaining altitude, Baghdad was already a memory—a powerful one, to be sure, and one I could reconstruct in my mind any way I liked. Some days it was just a dot on a map, a place I'd once been. At other times, it was the fabled capital of modern Arab and Muslim knowledge that we learned about at school, the centre of Arab poetry and music, a city replete with splendid libraries and ornate mosques, in a time long before it was sacked by the Mongols, when they sacrificed its libraries and the Tigris ran black with the ink of the city's precious books. Other days it was the way I first knew it: the rivers I'd boated across, the alleys I'd wandered, the smoke-filled cafes, and the thousands of books for sale on ancient Mutanabbi Street, displayed out in the open just as they had been for centuries. Baghdad was where I'd really grown up, where my heart and friendships had flourished, where I had, for the first time, known what it was like to lose your nerve. It was where for the first time I'd lost a friend to violence and had seen death up close. After nearly five years of frequenting its homes and hotels, I found leaving Baghdad exceptionally difficult. I couldn't bear to imagine how its born-and-bred sons and daughters felt leaving it—and the rest of the land of the Tigris and Euphrates—behind.

NINE

A Protest to End All Protests

$\approx\approx\approx$

God spare us the evil of this laughter.
—ARAB PROVERB

BEIRUT, LEBANON, OCTOBER 2004

Nearly two years after I arrived in the Mideast, I moved to Beirut in search of a semblance of peace and purpose in between trips to Baghdad. By then I'd become accustomed to the sounds of war, but as I was lying half awake in my hotel room one morning days after I'd arrived, I thought I had misheard what sounded like an explosion.

Minutes later the phone rang. It was Hussein, the driver who'd picked me up from the airport and had been helping me find a home since.

"There's been a bomb …"

By the time we pulled up at the beautiful seaside Corniche Beirut promenade to watch, the dead and injured had been evacuated, the road up the slope where it happened blocked by a police cordon. It had been a roadside bomb, timed to explode as a two-car convoy passed by. The apparent target, former cabinet minister Marwan Hamadeh, survived, but his driver didn't. This was the stuff of Baghdad, yet here I was, standing before the familiar charred remains of a moving car arrested by the detonation of explosives, with the Mediterranean, instead of the Tigris, as the backdrop.

Kasem, a much wiser journalist/producer and veteran of all of Lebanon's recent troubles, ambled over to chat. "This is just the start," he said ominously. "You just wait and see."

I liked Kasem. He was earnest, kind, and hard-working, with large, shy blue eyes and a lean face lined with experience. He was also generous with his war memories, and Lebanon's war stories intrigued me. He'd worked with Clark Todd, a CTV journalist, when the latter was injured in the Chouf Mountains during a particularly vicious fight between Christians and Druze Muslims in 1983. His crew had been forced to leave him behind—it was impossible to get him down a steep escarpment under fire—and Todd died before help could get to him. Kasem repeatedly described how it went down, openly sharing the guilt that's racked him for more than two decades.

Kasem had an uncanny knack for reading Lebanon's tea leaves, but he had elevated the Lebanese habit of forecasting doom by using cogent arguments to back up his dire predictions. Still, I didn't believe him that day. This bomb was just a one-off. It happens, in this stunning city of intrigue and never-ending feuds.

⚔

Unless you counted Fairouz and her melancholy morning music, I knew no one in Lebanon, had no history there, save for that brief stopover at the airport on the way back to Canada in 1983. The civil war had ended in 1990, more than a decade earlier, yet I arrived to find ample evidence of that complex, drawn-out battle that the Lebanese had endured for fifteen years, and that defies simple explanation.

I took it all in on house-hunting journeys, riding around the fishbowl that was Beirut in Hussein's champagne-coloured Mercedes. Hussein was a quietly shrewd, war-tested fixer and driver who would become an essential part of the CBC team and a steadfast friend. Every nook in Beirut had a name and a civil war story, and like many Lebanese, Hussein loved to tell them. Over there, in the neighbourhood of Raml al-Zarif, René Mouawad, Lebanon's president for only seventeen days, was assassinated by a car bomb. In Ain Mreisseh, someone kidnapped Terry Anderson, the chief Mideast correspondent for the Associated Press at the time. Over here in Sanayeh, PLO leader Yasser Arafat narrowly escaped a bomb. On the Avenue des Francais along the coast, the American embassy was blown to smithereens. Within striking distance, the old Holiday Inn still stands, entirely pockmarked, as a reminder of the "hotel" phase of the civil war. Farther down on the Corniche, near Al Manara, is where a Syrian tank, nicknamed Abu Abdo— apparently after the man who operated it—was stationed during the civil war. The gunner would start lobbing shells at Christian East Beirut in the afternoons, and at his most destructive, Hussein said, he fired every thirty seconds. And on and on. I often asked Hussein how he could see downtown now without imagining the Green Line, how he could still drive on the bridge where dozens of Lebanese were killed on the spot for carrying the wrong ID. He just shrugged his shoulders and moved on to the next story. In my first few weeks of discovering Beirut, I'd formed a mental map of the city's bloodied past long before I had nailed its major intersections.

"*Tinzakar, w ma tin'ad.*" At any mention of the war, Lebanese would often say, "To be remembered, but not repeated." And yet in telling their harrowing stories, they invariably looked wistfully at each other and admitted there were, despite the unspeakable carnage, some good memories from war.

During the conflict, Hussein was a linchpin of the Commodore Hotel, the Hamra-area establishment where dozens of journalists stayed at the height of the civil war in the late 1970s and early 1980s. His job was to keep the hotel working and especially to keep the power on even as it was cut repeatedly in the neighbourhood.

He later branched out and got into the lucrative generator business, providing entire streets with power when the state supply shut down. He had a thousand stories about how he and his family managed to survive such lasting hostilities. Once, in the panic of trying to escape as shelling started anew, he and his wife ran downstairs to the basement, only to discover they had left their newborn behind. He loved describing the occasion when he and some friends gathered in a closed basement Hamra bar for an evening of music to ward away the sounds of conflict, and he told of many risky adventures crossing into East Beirut and points beyond simply to go out for dinner. Hussein was street smart, a keen observer who was attuned to subtleties most others would miss. He was a survivor, a chain-smoking, hard-working father of five, and an encyclopedia of everything Lebanon.

It wasn't hard to get people to talk about the war. It became a habit every time I went to Habib's, a dimly lit, wood-panelled pub/restaurant on a side street in West Beirut. The place smelled slightly of mould—until it filled with customers, and the odour of smoke, food, and alcohol overwhelmed all else. Old empty wine and champagne bottles were stacked up on shelves, testimony to the revelry of nights gone by. High up in another corner hung a small television, and for most of the evenings I spent there, it was muted, silently tuned to Fashion TV—unless there was a major crisis, and then it was tuned to the news.

A Lebanese friend once took me to Habib's, and thereafter I became an occasional customer, drawn as much by Habib's war stories as I was by his *sahras* (soirees) of live Arabic music. I'd never been much of a fan of such music, but the resident oud players changed that. A couple of times a week, Khodor or Abbas took the tiny stage and regaled appreciative listeners with memories of the past—playing everything from the traditional Egyptian music of Muhammad Abd Al Muttalib to songs by Ziad Rahbani, son of Fairouz and father of modern Lebanese music. On the good nights, when the singer's voice soared and the customers were at the height of their inebriation, Habib would tug at the old-fashioned bell hanging from the bar to acknowledge a moment.

Habib's was a favourite among local residents with a penchant for late *sahras* and ordering hard liquor by the bottle. Predictably it also appealed to loners, as well as the eccentrics and refugees that Beirut tended to attract. On busy nights, Abu Mohammed, an Iraqi who had an uncanny resemblance to a young Saddam, would invariably be there in a crisp suit along with his well-coiffed Lebanese girlfriend. At the other end of the bar, the Poets would quietly slip into their seats late, after midnight, shy and reserved until they downed a few straight Black Labels. Then she-Poet would venture to the dance floor while her Poet partner tried to focus with one eye to watch. From some corner, you would eventually hear "Pavarotti" about halfway through the night, when the mood suddenly struck him to start singing along in a laughably dramatic tenor, while his companion tried awkwardly to belly dance, clearing out the floor with her flailing arms and terrible timing. Late, late, the regular we called the Gulf Princess might show up with her "chaperone," who would be forced to sit alone with a bottle of local beer while she chatted up Khodor and stuffed dollars in his breast pocket so he would sing what she wanted. She never, ever came in sober.

Habib had the impressive distinction of being one of the only Hamra barmen who stayed open throughout the civil war. He loved telling stories of shilling whiskey and champagne to journalists, fighters, soldiers, police, and ordinary folk alike, while the shells screamed outside. You were always more than welcome at Habib's, no matter your origin, religion, sect, or nationality. He was Christian, his employees were largely Shia Muslim, and these days most of his customers were Sunni Muslim, a small cross-section of one of the smallest yet most sectarian countries on earth.

The Lebanese will tell you that one of the best things about Lebanon is that rich sectarian mix, its tolerance and ability to embrace so many different people, vexingly, those same qualities that drove them to kill one another. It is a country whose citizens still carry some ID cards that identify their religion and their sect—a government-imposed life sentence that defines you and holds you responsible for your forebears' deeds, no matter what you eventually turn out to be. Yet many Muslims told me they wouldn't accept living in Lebanon without its Christians, and some Christian friends acknowledged that Lebanon wouldn't be Lebanon without minarets among its churches, and chadors among the miniskirts. It's that modicum of tolerance—just a shade removed from the bigotry—that also made Lebanon a long-time refuge: Persecuted Arab intellectuals, artists, and political dissidents found freedom here they could not imagine in their home countries. Somehow little Lebanon also made room for hundreds of thousands of displaced Kurds, Palestinians, and Armenians who'd managed to escape the Turkish slaughter. Egyptian labourers, six hundred thousand Syrian workers, even war-weary Iraqis found space in tiny Lebanon's warm embrace.

Yet it was a painfully subdivided nation, and as civil wars went, Lebanon's was among the most uncivilized. There were endless militias—Lebanese, Palestinian, Sunni and Shia Muslim, Christian, secular, nationalist, communist—and at different phases of the war, most of them had fought against every other. Several countries were also involved as backers of one side or another, or as ostensible peacekeepers. Syria was both a peacekeeper and at times a party to the conflict, its troops initially pouring into the neighbouring territory at the request of the Lebanese president in 1976. Iraq, Egypt, France, the U.S., Russia, Italy, and, of course, the Palestinians and Israel all had a hand in Lebanon's ruination. In such a tiny country virtually every citizen was directly affected.

Between 1975 and 1990, between 150,000 and 230,000 people died, and perhaps as many as a million were injured. Thousands of people went missing, either dead and unaccounted for, or imprisoned in Lebanon, Israel, or Syria. And at least one million Lebanese were uprooted.

You could see remaining traces of them on virtually every block. Brittle buildings and once-elegant estates waited for them, some of their gates still dutifully locked, gardens overgrown, balconies still decorated with potted plants, long ago desiccated and dead. Such buildings, still wearing the war's graffiti, were now home to bold bats and monstrous mosquitoes. Others still sported the old television antennas, the flimsy T-shaped masts that picked up the last war news their owners heard before they locked their doors and left their homes prey to squatters. Oversized 1970s cars remained parked out back, windows long ago busted, letting in years' worth of dust and rain.

Some of the owners—from all sects—had relocated within Lebanon, hoping it would be temporary. For others, the journey away from home had an abrupt finality: they left the country altogether, giving up the draining battle to out-will the war. Many who chose exile left through the only functioning land border, to Syria, traversing dangerous mountains and valleys to get there and move on to faraway places. When the Beirut airport was open, many managed to get on planes, but often only after passing through a gauntlet of checkpoints manned mostly by armed and dangerous children. There was only one other way out of Lebanon, and that was by sea, perhaps the most treacherous route of all. Yet thousands made their escape on chartered ships to Cyprus, the gateway to the rest of the world, far enough away and over the horizon that the black smoke that rarely left Beirut's skyline was no longer visible.

Within days of my arrival, I was assigned to cover the twenty-second anniversary of the Sabra and Shatila massacre that had interrupted our television viewing as children. It was odd finally seeing the camps in their modern-day incarnation: a stark, lively contrast to the lifeless black-and-white television images still stuck in my head. They were a stone's throw from some of Beirut's most expensive and coveted real estate, yet the moment you passed the entrance, you left behind any appearance of opulence; it was as if you'd even left the current century.

Inside, teetering apartment blocks were stacked so high they blocked the sun, forced so close together the only view possible was of someone else's wall, or if you were exceptionally lucky, someone else's window. Jumbles of electrical wires hung low over the alleys, vineyards of cables that haphazardly brought power to homes but occasionally jolted unsuspecting residents, even killing an unfortunate few. Open sewers ran like little rivers through the alleys. Children played everywhere, even atop a mound of garbage at the edge of the camp, swatting flies in between swatting each other. It was disturbingly similar to the Al-Wihdat I remembered. Only that was three decades ago.

Youth armed with AK-47s stood guard at the various party headquarters, a testament to both the political division among them and the general lawlessness that prevailed unchecked. Occasionally the various parties clashed here as they did in some of the bigger camps down south, and occasionally those clashes claimed lives. Invariably, residents also had to contend with the growing influence of extremists, who naturally thrived amid the disenchantment and disorder. Sometimes their battles spilled out of the camps, and on at least one occasion, they invited the Lebanese army's attention and artillery. A camp in the north was badly damaged in one such episode in 2007, the conflict claiming the lives of Lebanese soldiers as well as Palestinian civilians.

Palestinians in Lebanon's camps lived like unwanted visitors left to languish at the edges of civility, with no rights to citizenship, forbidden from owning land or property, and barred from dozens of professions, all in the name of keeping alive their hopes—protecting the possibility—of return. They waited still, generation upon generation doomed to an appalling existence that, nearly six decades later, many still insisted on calling temporary.

Like Al-Wihdat, the camps here were all about remembrance: of the losses, of the various conflicts their people endured. A mass grave sat right at the entrance of the Shatila camp: a small, starkly well-maintained memorial enclosed within a grassy compound of crudely laid bricks and adorned with placards carrying photographs of slain and discarded bodies. On this day, the field was dominated by a small stage and a sparse crowd of the living: a mix of Palestinians, a few supportive Lebanese, some foreign pro-Palestinian advocates, and war tourists in shorts and sunglasses, some of them wearing the Palestinian kaffiyeh in a show of sympathy. I was jarred by all this. In my head this was still Sabraandshatila.

I knew more about the massacre now—that it was carried out by Christian Lebanese militiamen with the knowledge of the Israeli army, which had invaded Beirut to destroy the PLO. I had learned, too, that it was an apparent response to the assassination two days earlier of Phalangist chief Bashir Gemayel, who was about to become the Lebanese president, and to avenge massacres perpetrated by Palestinian fighters and Lebanese Muslims, which had in turn been committed to avenge other massacres, and so on.

Every side was in the right in Lebanon, *their* losses most grievous and only *their* acts of retaliation just. Back then, as now, the Lebanese could never agree on how the war unfolded, who was right and who wasn't, what had happened and why. And so to this day, they do not teach their schoolchildren about the war: there is no one narrative on which they can concur, no textbook they could ever adopt as the truth. So kids are taught about Lebanon's history until independence from the French in 1943, and that's where the history lessons stop. The rest they learn from their parents, whose version of the truth varies according to their birthplace, their last name, their sect and political affiliation.

The war might have been over, but the divisions, the terrible memories of a painful history, lingered.

♐

And yet Lebanon is a sublimely beautiful place, blessed with fertile valleys, soaring, snow-capped mountains, and a sinuous coastline hugged by the sea. It is a ski resort, beach hideaway, shopping mall, dance club, and casino rolled into a place about one-tenth the size of Newfoundland. Its people—men and women—are worldly, multi-lingual, and cosmopolitan, the women beautiful and exceedingly attentive to their looks. When it comes to entertainment, it is a place that caters to every taste and budget. If you want women or drugs, it is easy. And if you want to laugh, there is no shortage of laughter in Lebanon—someone, somewhere is making people laugh at the expense of politicians, especially, but everyone was fair game. It's a place at once capable of producing Hassan Nasrallah, the militant chief of the armed Hezbollah, and Haifa Wehbe, that sultry chant-euse whose singing skills are blatantly secondary to her plunging necklines and smoky eyes. It's new and old, east and west, quiet and yet insufferably noisy, a tinny blend of car horns mixed with English, French, and Arabic assaulting your ears around the clock.

It's such an infinitesimal place, a small world made even smaller by geography. In Beirut you could easily bump into the famous, at restaurants, cafes, even the Sporting Club on the Corniche, where some of them liked to play cards. You were almost certain to run into Ziad Rahbani if you dropped into one Italian restau-rant tucked in behind a modern high rise in the neighbourhood of Clemenceau. Yet while you could run into the same person two or even three times in the course of a day of errands, you could also hide from view for weeks if you knew your way around the city's hidden stairs and meandering alleys. And yet small and labyrinthine as Beirut was, its people still had a serious penchant for big cars that hogged the roads and challenged the dozens of buzzing mopeds and the aging *serveece* taxis that snarled traffic every time they stopped for a customer.

I had arrived in Beirut many years after the war nearly killed it, but it was clear that Lebanon was well on its way to returning to its place among the living. Large swaths of Beirut had already been restored or rebuilt, and restaurants and bars were packed again with tourists, expatriates and foreigners alike, thanks mostly to the country's long-time postwar prime minister, Rafic Hariri. Yet despite the gushing magazine articles about Lebanon's return, live here for a while and it soon becomes clear that all is not well.

Lebanon's problems are as diverse and breathtaking as its variegated landscape. It was, in reality, a failed state, home to a collection of individuals who might on paper share a heritage but were forced to fend for themselves. I learned early on that the majority of people refused to drink the water that came out of the taps because they didn't trust it to be clean enough. The Internet and phone systems were unreliable yet expensive, and they faltered with the smallest hint of a rain shower. You couldn't really function unless you had a generator to light your building when the state's source cut out—which could happen twice daily, sometimes three times, since the civil war had wrecked an already outdated system and no one had bothered to fix it. Many, if not most, Lebanese sent their children to private schools and chose to be treated at private hospitals, such was the state of public education and health care. Drug use was beyond rampant, and so was the use of anti-depressants. Unemployment was high, particularly among the young (as it was in the rest of the region), and even those who had jobs were poorly paid—unless of course they were well connected, or rich enough not to worry about finding jobs. The economy was not growing the way it should, and much of it was propped up by remittances from citizens abroad. As a result, though proud of their country, many Lebanese seemed to feel no civic responsibility; they were loyal to the nation and fellow citizens in spirit, but not in practice. They had become accustomed to breaking rules, to finding shortcuts to get things done. You could see the evidence of this in everything from flagrant violations of the traffic rules to using connections to get out of prison, get ahead in line or obtain exemptions from taxes or fines. This was a country where car owners could rent a headlight or a bumper for just long enough for their cars to pass the annual safety test. If you had money and connections in Lebanon, you could just about get away with murder, and over the years, many apparently did.

The country is also saddled with an arcane constitution that virtually ensures the government will always be ineffective. It provides each of Lebanon's main religious sects with what was once a proportional say in the upper echelons of the government, meaning that every decision has to be made by consensus, which is nearly impossible to achieve with such disparate loyalties and interests. So governments accomplish very little. The constitution is also based on a census that was held in 1932—the last count the Lebanese have ever had, out of fear of upsetting the consti-tution's delicate sectarian balancing act. And for all the boasting about Lebanon's long-time democracy, elections were traditionally a series of mini-coronations, just as they were in most of the rest of the Middle East. The leaders were invariably small-time chieftains from clans that have ruled for generations—Gemayel, Jumblatt, Chamoun, and others—many of them in positions inherited from fathers. They represented various sides of each sect, expected blind, unwavering support from their co-religionists, and ran the country with little regard for their people. Virtually all played their part in the civil war, some of them dividing the place into cartels:

The airport, road construction, the port—each had an "owner," Mafia-style.

Lebanon was also prone to an alternating pattern of prosperity and ruin. Big earthquakes smashed its mostly coastal cities at regular intervals at least as far back as the sixth century, sending the country into episodes of famine and economic stagnation. Then came the various occupiers and their battles: everyone from the Romans to the Ottomans to the French. In the First World War, Lebanon's waters were blockaded by the Turks, and tens of thousands of its residents died of starvation and the plague. As a microcosm of the region and its various religious and political rivalries, forever-divided Lebanon was also often the scene of proxy wars, where outside tensions had unpleasant and often violent consequences. But little could parallel the sudden and intense devastation the Lebanese brought on simply by fighting one another.

So while things were relatively calm when I arrived in Lebanon, the people nonetheless constantly fretted about the next political impasse and dreaded the next war. Many put more trust in religion (as some liked to say, "*Allah ma biyansah hada*"—God never forgets anyone) or the New Year's Eve predictions of a famous clairvoyant than they did the proclamations of their own leaders. I once met and interviewed the psychic Michel Hayek, and he claimed that he saw a bright future for Lebanon, but not before the country passed through a dark tunnel first. The Lebanese took his pronouncements seriously and worried about what it all meant.

Collectively, Lebanon's problems seemed insurmountable, and occasionally people protested in the streets, often about political matters. With nearly a third of the population living below the poverty line, though, they also protested economic woes, like the rising cost of fuel and bread. But their most common form of protest was the most emphatic kind: leaving Lebanon behind.

They'd been doing it for centuries. The Phoenicians, the

original Lebanese, fashioned intricate boats and rode the waves in search of trade and adventure. Their descendants took steamships to Africa, Brazil, the U.S., and Canada to find their fortunes. They were labourers, teachers, and even poets like Gibran Khalil Gibran, whose world-renowned verses and art emanated from Boston and New York, not the Lebanese mountainside town of Bsharri from which he hailed. In more recent times, a failed economy and lack of opportunity drove many Lebanese to Gulf States like Saudi Arabia and the UAE. They were hardy seeds, thriving wherever fate took them, adapting swiftly to snow, monsoons, or hurricanes and delving into business, commerce, and even politics. Today, there are at least four times as many Lebanese living abroad as there are in modern Lebanon itself. They were so good at leaving their own country that a monument of a Lebanese dressed in traditional garb to commemorate expatriates was erected near Beirut's port, from which so many had left, never to return. An inscription reads: "From Lebanon, to the world."

I found myself a home office not far from that port, in the hotel district, on a desolate street that was still in the process of postwar renewal. For a view I had mostly abandoned buildings with only bats for residents, and the broken sign of an old bar across the street that had once been fashionable. But I liked the space, especially the sun that flooded through its wide panes from every angle. There were only a handful of tenants in the building; on the main floor a young couple had just opened a new salon and we quickly became friends, keeping each other company in the loneliness of Yassin Building. Down where the road met the Corniche, a quaint hotel that had been occupied by civil war squatters had recently reopened, the loud, thumping music drifting from its rooftop terrace on weekends a reassuring sign of life.

I managed to set up a bed and a desk before having to leave the country on assignment. More than two months later, I was transiting through Amman, on the way back to my new sunny home, when I heard that another explosion had torn through central Beirut, right in the heart of the hotel district.

⚹

This was no ordinary roadside bomb. Eighteen hundred kilograms of TNT exploded at the juncture of the hotel district and the Corniche that day, powerful enough to radiate destruction for kilometres, shattering picture windows and tugging hard at still-raw nerves. I landed a few hours later and went to survey the scene: Yellow police ribbons criss-crossed the district, where the Phoenicia and the Munroe hotels had been relieved of their glass and opulence, and abandoned by the swanky cars that normally parked in front. The vacant St. George Hotel and the neglected but lovely Victorian building at the corner were grossly disfigured, even beyond their civil war injuries. It was Valentine's Day, and Beirut was as confounded as it was frightened. A cloud of black smoke and melancholy lingered over its skyline. Kasem's prediction, it turned out, was bang on. All those anxious Lebanese who were certain "something" was coming were also vindicated.

My apartment, fifty metres from the explosion, was caught up in the destruction and police wouldn't allow me in. This had been my worst nightmare, what I had feared most since I started covering foreign conflicts. In Baghdad I had learned the difference between the distant thud of artillery, the nearby crash of RPGs, and the thud-crash of mortars. More than once, I had been jolted by the thunder of a nearby car bomb, choked by the acrid smell of burning tires and flesh. I had witnessed the fireball—and carnage—that a suicide bomber unleashed when he detonated his belt, and I had felt its boom in my very temples. What I feared most was the *kaboom*—is that how it would sound?—of a bomb at my doorstep, under my balcony, near my car as I drove by; the wind-sucking rush of explosives at close range; the fireball, the cloud of smoke, and the sinister shrapnel they would send my way.

But I hadn't been there to hear it. If I had arrived, as scheduled, a day earlier, the terrifying noise would have been the least of my concerns. I realized that when I finally saw the inside of my place.

There were shards of glass the size and shape of daggers in piles all over my apartment. Smaller, more insidious shavings nestled into my bed, my duvet, the towels in the bathroom, and the dry kitchen sink. Gravel-sized cubes of glass—heaved straight across my bedroom along with the blinds, which were now twisted and torn—sat in heaps against the walls like mounds of ice that wouldn't melt. When I turned the lights on, the entire place shimmered. A healthy chunk of a door and its handle had also been blasted clear across the office towards the desk, where I would have surely been sitting. I had locked the balcony doors and windows before I left, and many Lebanese told me that if I'd left just one open that would have relieved the pressure and lessened the damage. That's when I acquired the habit of sleeping with one window open at all times.

It was Monday, but Beirut was Sunday quiet that night. The entire population had rushed indoors, huddled in darkened rooms lit only by television blue. Across the various channels, there was only one story: Rafic Hariri, former prime minister, was dead.

The last glimpse Lebanese would get of their long-time leader would be the charred remains of his distinctive ample shape lying on a blackened bend in the coastal road in West Beirut, the plaid blanket that covered him lifted just long enough to make the AP photo, which was displayed on the front page of the *Al-Nahar* newspaper the following morning. Twenty-two other people also died that day: Hariri's security guards, companions, and drivers, as well as ordinary passersby. It was the second bloody mark on my personal map of Beirut in modern times. I saved the front pages.

༄

I was shaken by the turn of events, and I was once again homeless. So I moved into an apartment hotel as I tried to keep up with a fast-moving story. I worked out of the offices of MTN, a small production house ably run by veteran journalist Weeda Hamza, a diminutive, kind, and sharp woman who taught me valuable lessons about Lebanese history and hospitality. With the turn of events, Toronto decided to send out a producer, Corinne Seminoff, to join Zouheir and me. The three of us, along with Hussein, were inseparable for the next month. Despite the upheaval, for the first time since I started working in television, I began to feel perhaps it was doable now that I had able assistance.

Lebanese were old hands at dealing with sudden death at regular intervals, and yet Hariri's funeral was extraordinary, the kind of dramatic, emotional farewell you'd expect for a man who was larger than life and in death had become a *shaheed*, a martyr. As it made its way through the crowd, the coffin was showered with rice and serenaded by doleful prayers from the mosques and the toll of nearby church bells. Occasionally it was shaken by those carrying it in a traditional show of grief, a sight that gave me the shivers. For weeks afterwards, thousands lined up to enter the gravesite, right beside the ornate blue mosque that Hariri was still in the process of building at the edge of Sahat al-Shuhada, or Martyrs' Square. Tearful mourners shuffled by the huge bed of flowers under which Hariri had been laid to rest, alternately crossing themselves and lighting candles or, with palms upturned, reading the Fatiha, a sura that begins the Koran and with which Muslims always mark the start of a marriage and the end of a life.

But once the initial shock wore off, the sombre candlelit vigils gave way to indignant protests that grew steadily with a velocity unknown in the Middle East. Martyrs' Square, the large stretch of land in the middle of downtown Beirut where Hariri was buried, became the protesters' favourite gathering place. It seemed fitting: the square was home to a bullet-ridden monument to Christians and Muslims who were hanged there following an uprising against the ruling Ottomans nearly a century earlier. The statue's location, near the old Green Line, had once been the subject of a bitter postwar dispute between Hariri and Émile Lahoud, the country's president. In the end Hariri prevailed, and the monument to martyrs was moved into the heart of the square, where so many now gathered to protest his death.

Long before I ever set eyes on it, downtown Beirut was home to a bustling old Levantine souk, the likes of which now existed only in Syria and Jerusalem. During the civil war, it became the frontier that divided East and West Beirut, and every conceivable form of man-made destruction was inflicted upon its ornate build-ings and well-worn roads. Hariri presided over the restoration of the ravaged buildings back to their original opulence, but he then installed in them high-priced cafes and restaurants and high-end shops whose monthly rents were greater than the average Lebanese worker's annual income. Gone forever, too, were the big palm trees that used to shade Martyrs' Square, as were the merchants who peddled spices, material, livestock, and perfume from nearby stalls.

After Hariri's assassination, going down to the square became a daily duty for me, Zouheir, and Hussein, as it was for many Lebanese youth, who set up camp near the monument. The protesters wanted the Truth, *al-haqiqa*, the uncovering of the identity of Hariri's assassins—though most had already concluded that Syria was behind the killing. Soon, their chief demand was an end to what could only be described as Syria's occupation of their country.

Unlike other countries in the region, Lebanon was not officially ruled by a homegrown despot. But it was effectively controlled by a dictator all the way from Damascus, just under one hundred kilometres away. Syria's Bashar al-Assad viewed his tiny neighbour as a lowly province. Some fifteen thousand of his troops and intelligence agents made themselves at home in Lebanon, headed by the Ba'athist government's agent, who ran Lebanon on Damascus's behalf and effectively made all its political decisions. Syrian troops entered the country in 1976, a year into the civil war, and they and their arms stayed on, seemingly to keep the peace, even after the conflict ended in 1990. In exchange for this lopsided arrangement, Syrian authorities helped themselves to all that Lebanon had to offer, including cash, kickbacks, secret banking, and international connections. Lebanon may have already been rotten at the core, but Syria's omnivorous presence ate away at whatever was left.

Lebanese citizens were routinely harassed and abused by Syrian troops and intelligence agents. Some were taken away, never to be seen again—either dead or, if unlucky, perhaps rotting in one of Syria's notoriously hair-raising prisons. In recent years, opponents had mounted brave yet small protests against Syria's presence, but they were harshly shut down while the world turned a blind eye. The prevailing view in the West was that Syrians were there legitimately, because the Lebanese president had invited them. No amount of lobbying in Washington *by* Lebanese, it seemed, would change that view.

So the influence of the Assads—first Hafez, then his son Bashar—lingered in Lebanon. Bashar was featured in a large poster prominently displayed in the Corniche al-Mazraa neighbourhood, confirming Lebanon's allegiance to its sisterly neighbour. In those days, there was still the odd Syrian checkpoint, but most of the troops were stationed in the Bekaa Valley. Intelligence offices were nestled inside neighbourhoods like Jnah and Hamra, where civilian clothes failed to disguise the marquee moustaches and black leather jackets of those in the service of the Assads.

In the fall of 2004, Damascus had apparently decided that the term of the current Lebanese president, Émile Lahoud, should be extended, in direct contravention of Lebanon's constitution. A small group of Lebanese lawmakers openly opposed the idea, and they eventually voted against it. Among them was Marwan Hamadeh—the ostensible target of that first bomb I heard—who resigned when the resolution was passed. Hariri, too, had opposed Syria's intervention, and he had quit his position days after Hamadeh was nearly killed.

Rafic Hariri was one of the most successful members of Lebanon's diaspora, the eldest son of an ordinary Sidon family who had made a name for himself—and a sizeable fortune—by leaving for Saudi Arabia. He came back a self-made billionaire and a behind-the-scenes power broker whose money, philanthropy, and negotiating skills earned him wide attention and, later, the premiership of his native land.

Hariri—whose last name aptly meant "silky"—was no traditional Lebanese chieftain. Yet by 2000, a decade after the war ended (with his help), he had become one of Lebanon's most influential prime ministers, using money and shady deals to lift the country off its bloodied knees. A smooth operator, he was comfortable in any circle, and had allies in Lebanon and abroad. "Mr. Lebanon" had the ear of, and lent an ear to, all of Lebanon's factions, earning perhaps not their respect, but at least grudging acceptance of his leadership. He was variously reviled and loved, but he knew how to keep his countrymen at a reasonable distance from each other. His death raised the spectre of renewed sectarian division. Instead, at first, it seemed to do the opposite.

Several of Lebanon's establishment parties, Muslim and Christian, joined forces in protest after his death, among them some of the very same chieftains who'd fought bitterly during the civil war. They united in blaming Damascus for Hariri's murder, calling for its troops and agents to leave Lebanon, and for the sitting pro-Syrian government to resign. Their voices were bolstered by much of the international community; the pressure on Syria was greatest from France and the U.S., the joint authors of an earlier UN resolution making the same demand.

But it was the youth of Lebanon who were now driving the movement, entranced by their sudden ability to loudly channel frustrations shared by so many. They came from the alleys of Hamra and some of the poshest homes in Ashrafieh; all the way from Tripoli, that restive northern city dominated by Sunni Muslims and hardline Hariri supporters; and from the mountain, where they backed the Druze Progressive Socialist Party. Together they formed a generation that mostly did not know the war but had always lived in its shadow. They knew and lived the inerasable divisions among their people, and suffered their violent legacy. Yet they now emerged to tell the world that they refused to belong to one sect, that they were casting aside years of inculcated mistrust of the Other. Even as they waved the flags of the same old establishment parties, they claimed that the old divided Lebanon was no longer, that perhaps in unity they could finally tackle the country's myriad woes.

Beirut was electrified, possessed by the young men and women who prowled its streets, joyriding, honking, and waving flags, just as they would when their favourite soccer team won. They in turn were high on hopeful speeches and pronouncements from their leaders, like those of Gebran Tueni, a Christian newspaper publisher and columnist who led them in an oath to remain forever united, Christian and Muslim. They spoke of revolution, of a political sea change, mulling it over even in the late-night cafes and nightclubs they packed to dance the revolution away. Some of the more dedicated among them put jobs on hold while they haunted Martyrs' Square night after night, listening to revolutionary, nationalist music that echoed from the Ring road at one end of the square all the way down to the coast. One of the most often repeated was a song based on a famous poem that was once an anthem for Arabs fighting for independence from colonialism. The defiant words were written by Tunisian poet Abu al-Qasem al-Shabi. He had died at age twenty-five in 1934, but his memory survived for generations in the powerful words of this one poem: "If one day a people desired life / Then fate must respond / Inevitably night will be dispelled / Inevitably the shackles will be broken."

On one of the busiest nights in the square, we met Tariq Germanos, a twenty-year-old who'd been camping out for a week. Like all the young people we met there, he exhibited an astute understanding of the political situation, and yet tinged by a misplaced optimism that the ouster of the Syrians would be the end of Lebanon's problems. He believed their sit-in could determine the country's fate. "It's my future. I'm building my future," he insisted. "Here you only see Lebanese flags. You don't see the division we had in war."

His friend Sharif Masoud said that for the first time in their lives, they felt they had some purpose. "We all have a cause now," he said. "We want all the Syrian troops to leave us. They are the ones who are choosing our ministers and president."

For its part, Syria vehemently denied it had anything to do with Hariri's killing. In a widely anticipated televised speech, President Bashar al-Assad declared that his goal was always eventual withdrawal, but slowly, so that Lebanon's stability wasn't compromised. He announced that his troops would pull back first to the Bekaa, and then slowly to the border. No one was convinced by the speech, or impressed much by his sluggish plan. It was clear that the Syrian regime simply abhorred the idea of capitulating under popular or international pressure. It was a regime that thrived on instilling fear, and it didn't relish an act that would diminish its power, influence and reach—especially with Israel as a neighbour.

The protests grew even larger. I had never seen anything like it—no one had—in the Middle East's modern history.

Tens of thousands of people—mothers; doctors; labourers; energetic young university students; gorgeous women, some in hijab, others in tank tops; priests and imams, arms linked; even prim old ladies accompanied by their maids—all flocked to Martyrs' Square to peacefully demand change. "Freedom, sovereignty, independence!" became their uniting cry. At their largest, the protests overtook downtown, a sea of red, green, and white as far as the eye could see. In addition to the outrage they felt at Hariri's brazen murder, demonstrators were also protesting the series of unsolved assassinations that came before. It seemed an all-out people's revolution.

I occasionally dropped in to see Habib during this time, and he was often in a foul mood, unimpressed by any revolution that adversely affected his business. He waxed on about how these developments were edging the country back towards conflict. Despite the show of unity, Lebanese still feared that Hariri's murder would mark the beginning of the country's descent back into troubled days. The civil war was on Habib's mind—and everyone else's. Even if I didn't ask, in interviews people inevitably brought it up.

Ranya Choueiri, a young mother who came back from Canada to open a jewellery shop in Beirut's Ashrafieh neighbourhood, wanted affirmation that her return wasn't a naive and costly mistake. She was only fifteen when her family left Lebanon at the height of the civil war, and she'd never contemplated a coming back until she married a Lebanese man and together they decided to try. "It's my country!" she said, slapping her hand against her chest. "I feel threatened here. I do not want my kid to live what I lived, and I do not want to live what my parents lived as parents."

She closed her shop and joined the crowds. The apparent unity was as heartening to her as it was surprising; it flew in the face of everything she had been taught growing up. "We never had this in Lebanon. Never! And that's why I hope—and I keep hoping—we'll really reach somewhere."

The anti-Syrian coalition called for a huge protest to be held on February 28, 2005, to mark the second week after Hariri's murder. The night before, in a weak attempt to wrest back control, the government issued a decree banning all protests and warned against any further gatherings. That night I took a tour of the city, and it was clear the warning would go unheeded. Buses were already lined up downtown, filled with people who had come in from outside the city for the demonstration.

Our car was one of the few on the road the next morning, because the entire city was shut down by a general strike. Once downtown, we watched from the bridge as throngs of people arrived—some carrying huge posters of Hariri, others draping long banners that demanded Syria leave. Over the course of the morning, the protest swelled to hundreds of thousands, a peaceful uprising of the people, shouting in Arabic, English, and French. *Syria out! Syria out!* On that day, there was a thicker deployment of the army, even some riot police, but they would stay out of it. There was a thrilling feel to the gathering, born of a certainty that no one and nothing could stop them.

Inside Parliament, opposition members added to the pressure. One after another they stood up, calling on the pro-Syrian government of Prime Minister Omar Karameh to resign. Under siege in Parliament and on the streets, the government had no choice that day but to resign, marking the first time in the Arab world's modern history that popular protest successfully brought down a government. The entirety of the Middle East took note.

🧍

Bringing down a government was a dream of many Arabs in countries where a demonstration was an achievement.

A few months earlier, I had taken a trip to Saudi Arabia with Samer, our Ramallah cameraman. It was one of those increasingly rare assignments when we were free from the demands of news and could focus simply on telling good, informative stories about a place and its people. At that time, Saudi was definitely of interest. Of all the places I had worked in thus far—and all the places I would work later—Saudi had to be one of the most restrictive. Most of the time we were accompanied by government minders, and while we were able to work around them to interview reformists, we were rarely allowed to film on the streets. The only place we were permitted to get people shots was in one of Riyadh's sprawling malls.

A few days into our trip, we heard that dissidents were planning an anti-monarchy protest for December 16, 2004, to call for the establishment of a democratic government. If the chatter was accurate, thousands would be attending. We were eager to cover such a rare event—but since we were barely allowed to film on the streets on ordinary days, we couldn't imagine we could cover *this*. Samer was more accustomed to the chaos of the Palestinian intifada, and after all the ridiculously brave things he'd done to get the CBC some of the best pictures of those events, little dissuaded him and he insisted we had to try. He spent the next hour on the telephone, trying to secure permission for us to go out. He finally came running to my room to say they were allowing us to go. I was stunned and excited.

At the appointed hour, we rushed out to get our story. But in the very square where thousands of protesters were supposed to gather, we found hundreds of armed riot police and soldiers instead. Thanks to the vast network of checkpoints that Saudi's authorities had set up, there wasn't a single demonstrator. A few dozen people had managed to show up in the city of Jeddah, and they were pursued in the streets with gunfire. Several were arrested and that was that. No wonder we got permission.

Later that week, I had a short interview with Saudi's de facto ruler, Crown Prince Abdullah, who had allowed limited reforms under the pressures of the post–September 11 world. At the time he was also feeling the effects of Osama bin Laden's violent campaign to topple his regime, which a week earlier had manifested itself in an armed attack against the U.S. consulate in Jeddah. The crown prince told me that Saudis wanted change, but that it had to be slow and in line with the country's "internal situation and circumstances." Protests, the regime believed, were not in their society's interests. In fact, they were illegal.

The un-protest was a disappointment from a journalism point of view, but it was my first practical lesson in the lengths some Arab countries will go to prevent public displays of dissent. Lebanon still stood at the other end of the spectrum from Saudi where protests were concerned, and certainly after the pro-Syrian government fell, nothing could stop the growing outcry—now labelled by Washington (not the Lebancse) as the Cedar Revolution. Bush's administration insisted that Lebanon had become the first beneficiary—after Iraq—of the president's vision of a liberated and democratized Middle East.

For some in the Arab world—and certainly in Lebanon—this was confirmation that the revolution had been made in America. You couldn't demand change to the order of things in the Middle East without being accused of sowing seditious seeds or having mutinous intentions. In some segments of Lebanese society, you couldn't espouse freedom or democracy without being labelled pro-American, just as you couldn't propose the resettlement of the wretched Palestinian refugees without being labelled pro-Israel. When you asked certain people why Syria wouldn't give up Lebanon, they explained that the two countries were once one, and that the borders were artificially drawn by colonial powers to serve their own interests. If you offered that this was ancient history, the Arab-Israeli conflict invariably came up. If you thought the

Israeli-Palestinian conflict was a vexing subject of discussion, try having a conversation with certain Arabs about their own state of affairs without going around in futile circles.

Still, some commentators were furiously speculating that the dramatic change in Lebanon might be the start of a cascade of events that could alter the political map of the region, maybe even for the better. Perhaps change was possible in the Middle East after all. Perhaps a tragedy like Hariri's killing could alter at least some of the rules that normally prevented it.

But nothing here was ever quite that simple.

As the anti-Syrian protests were gathering momentum, Hezbollah and its supporters stirred. The group, which had long been backed by Damascus, called for demonstrations to compete with the anti-Syrians as the "true" voice of Lebanon. The group and other pro-Syrian elements believed that the anti-Syrian protests were the work of "foreign hands," and that the ultimate aim in calling for Syria's withdrawal was the implementation of that U.S./French UN resolution, which would pave the way for Hezbollah's disarmament—to Israel's benefit. "Behind all this talk of withdrawal is the attempt to get at Hezbollah's weapons and the resistance," Hussein Al Hajj Hassan, an outspoken Hezbollah MP, told me in an interview. "It will not be easy without giving Lebanese assurances about the danger Israel poses."

Hezbollah—also known in Lebanon as Al-Muqawama, the Resistance—thrived on the existence of an Israeli threat. During the civil war, Hezbollah was thought to have been behind the 1983 bombing of the U.S. embassy and an attack on a Beirut barracks that killed 241 American servicemen. Unlike most of Lebanon's militias, Hezbollah retained its impressive arsenal after the war, reserving the right to protect Lebanon as it saw fit. After repeated attacks against Israeli installations in the south, its fighters took credit for bringing about Israel's withdrawal in 2000, following an eighteen-year occupation. It had many supporters among Lebanese, but also many detractors, who resented the "culture of the Resistance" and saw in its weapons and secrecy a dangerous state within a state that threatened to hamper the country's progress and independence.

Hezbollah often organized its own rallies and protests, but they were almost always held in Dahieh, the southern suburbs of the capital, or in south Lebanon, both strongholds for the group. Now they were planning one in the heart of downtown Beirut. It would be a dual message of thanks to the Syrians, for sending their troops into Lebanon during trying times, and a show of force by Shia Muslims, who had often been cast aside in Lebanon's endless power struggles.

On March 8, 2005, the pro-Syrian gathering drew hundreds of thousands of people, and in a Middle East tradition obsessed with dates, the March 8 movement was born—allied to Syria, linked to Iran, and vehemently opposed to U.S. influence, and, of course, to Israel.

Hezbollah chief Hassan Nasrallah—one of Israel's top nemeses—made no secret of who he believed the real enemy was. "We have defeated the U.S. in the past, and if they come again, we will defeat them again," he thundered.

More Hezbollah protests followed. Corinne and I drove down with Hussein and Zouheir to attend one of them in Nabatiyah, the capital of southern Lebanon. When heading south, you felt as though you were travelling through the country's history. It was home to silent ruins and ancient stories, at times host to the Romans, the Palestinians, even Jesus, and many others in between. As a foreigner, you had to secure the army's permission to visit: a bureaucratic acknowledgment that you knew the risks and, despite your own embassy's advice to avoid travel south of the Litani River, you were going anyway.

In Nabatiyah the people welcomed us, though we were chased by children who kept trying what sounded like Hebrew words on us, to see if they could blow someone's cover. In these parts, foreigners and journalists in particular are often suspected of being spies—partly due to prior experience, partly due to the Middle East's predilection for conspiracy theories. In the south and in many parts of Lebanon, that predilection was as entrenched as the hospitality.

Among the thousands who attended the rally that day we met Osama, a handsome and well-spoken owner of a mobile phone shop on the main drag. At thirty-four, he was the father of two and had lived through much of the Israeli occupation. He said he owed Hezbollah for his ability to walk down the street safely now. So when Hezbollah called for a rally to bolster Syria's position, he felt it was his duty to attend. "All these people, they went down first, for Sayyed Nasrallah, to support the decisions of the Resistance, and to refuse the UN resolution. We should be honourable and loyal to Syria," he said.

Like his counterparts at the rival protests, Osama said there could be no going back to war. "It's forbidden to destroy Lebanon. Forbidden to tear it down. Forbidden that the civil war returns." At least the two sides agreed on something.

But on March 14, one month after Hariri's death, the anti-Syrians mounted their largest protest yet—if you believed the estimates, a quarter of Lebanon's population had gathered and the March 14 movement was born. It was an astounding sight. Looking across a downtown filled with people, you could no longer see individuals—it was a sea of flags and people consistently on one message: a demand for "freedom, sovereignty, independence." Put that simply, it didn't seem a lot to ask.

Assad capitulated. He was forced to speed up his soldiers' withdrawal. It was a feat of people power hitherto unknown in the modern Middle East.

Just under a month later, I attended the elaborate draw-down ceremony at the Riyak military base near the Bekaa Valley. Syrian troops gave their final salute, and then they were gone. Assad's poster at Corniche al-Mazraa had disappeared. Syrian intelligence headquarters in Jnah and the office down the street from my hotel were both vacated. It was over. Or at least it seemed that way.

Hariri's son Saad and his supporters—the March 14 bloc—won the election that summer, and one of the elder Hariri's closest confidants, Fouad Siniora, became prime minister. They vowed that Hariri's assassination would be investigated and the perpetrators taken to court by an international tribunal. March 14 had prevailed, for now.

But a new line had been drawn between the Lebanese, not in Beirut but in Damascus. Lebanon was intractably split again, more or less down the middle. And naturally, more violence intervened to deepen that split.

By the end of 2005, fourteen bombs had exploded in various parts of Lebanon, four of them targeting vocal anti-Syrian figures and blamed on the Syrians or their agents, despite Syria's repeated denials. Predictably, they included those who were or had been writers or journalists. One of them was Samir Kassir, an outspoken critic of Syria's presence in Lebanon who had written extensively about the sorry Arab condition and the rot that had festered under the repression. Ironically, Kassir, a Christian Lebanese citizen, was half Syrian, and his father was Palestinian. A bronze likeness of him was installed in the shade of a tree, in the shadow of the *Al Nahar* newspaper's building in downtown Beirut.

Next was a television personality, blown up in her Range Rover, just one suburb away. I'd watched May Chidiac, a well-coiffed middle-aged journalist, level mordant questions to guests about Syria's possible involvement in Hariri's killing. She'd done so once more on her show that day. She appeared again on television the night of the explosion, but lying on a stretcher, hair dishevelled, oxygen mask eclipsing her face. She lost a leg and an arm, but survived.

On December 12, it was Gebran Tueni, the Christian publisher
of *Al Nahar*, a leading independent Lebanese daily long known
for, among other things, publishing oratories of dissent by Syrians
opposed to their own regime. I had met Tueni once, during the
2005 election, when he ran as an MP under Saad Hariri's ticket,
sticking by that oath he led in Martyrs' Square after Hariri's death.
He was an attractive, charming man with an electric smile and an
easy manner. He was also among the most outspoken early critics
of Syria's dominion over Lebanon. His voice, too, was silenced.
A gigantic poster of his likeness was draped over the newspaper's
building downtown, the latest addition to a growing menagerie of
martyrs that now dotted the streets of Beirut.

As time went on, there would be many more spots on that map
in my head, several more posters and statues and monuments to
the new martyrs, to remember the fallen in Lebanon's latest war.
And with every bomb, every brazen murder—and there were more
in the coming years—Lebanon's divide grew deeper.

᠅

Once the authorities had allowed residents to return to their homes
in the hotel district, Toronto gave me the option of moving house.
I thought about it and decided to stay—with one modification:
Because there was so much glass in the place, friends advised
covering it with anti-blast film. I was now convinced that as Kasem
had predicted a few months earlier, more violence was almost
certainly coming, so I had blast film installed.

The old rivalries *had* begun to surface after all, along with the
army checkpoints, which were intended to reassure people and yet
served only to heighten their anxiety. Lebanese on both sides were
certain their country was slowly heading for another internecine
conflict, and they were at a loss for what to do about it. For the
Lebanese who had been through the worst of the civil war, even this

long afterwards it was especially worrisome, and they instinctively recoiled at the kind of sectarian and political tension that was now on the rise.

Richard was one of those people whom you immediately pegged as a talker, the kind who would address you long before you thought of an opening line for him. And that's exactly what happened when we arrived in the southern Christian village of Damour.

"*Ahlan wa sahlan*," he said with a gregarious smile, opening his arms to show his round body and wearing a genuine smile. "*Ahlan bi al-Damour.*" Welcome to Damour.

It was just after Sunday mass, and the town didn't look anything like the dead village I had been told it was. Perched halfway up a small hill with a magnificent view of the sea, it was full of new stone houses, some fully built with gardens and ample garages, others half-finished, waiting for renewed attention from their owners. The church in the middle of town was almost completely renovated. A couple of open stores and a thriving banana grove down at sea level provided abundant signs of life. But it was Sunday, and Damour's lost children visited only on Sundays. The rest of the time, they lived elsewhere in Lebanon, or far beyond.

This was delicate territory. It isn't easy for Damourians to talk about what happened, even this long after the event. But Richard agreed to speak to us.

Damour had often been caught up in Lebanon's violent episodes, as far back as the nineteenth century. It was an isolated Maronite Christian outpost at the bottom of a mountain populated by Druze Muslims, their historic foes. Early in the civil war, in 1976, Damour was overrun by Palestinian gunmen and some Lebanese allies bent on avenging an earlier massacre perpetrated by Christian militiamen against a Muslim enclave populated mostly by Palestinians. Hundreds of innocent civilians were killed in both massacres. In

Damour, the cemetery and most of the homes were ransacked. The church was destroyed. Damour became a ghost town.

Richard was only thirteen at the time, and he survived along with his family only by running to the coast under cover of darkness and taking boats to safety—a voyage, he said, that he could never forget. As he told the story, his younger sister, who was just visiting for the day, wept. Richard asked me if any pictures of that escape might exist in our archives, and later I did find some. Grainy shots—who would have taken them?—showed children and women, some of them crying, piling into a small boat, then riding off away from the beautiful coastline. You wouldn't want to see yourself in such pictures. For some reason, Richard did.

The surviving Damourians ended up in East Beirut and points farther north and east, where they were cared for by their co-religionists but never truly felt at home. Many of them ended up abroad. The vast majority will only visit, and refuse to stay. "I'm a stranger in my own village—it's sad," said Richard's sister, speaking through her tears. "Wherever you go you feel lost. You don't know where your roots are. They've been erased."

Yet just before Lebanon's latest political crisis, Richard, nearing middle age and now a father, had decided to take the unusual step of moving back. "I was born and raised here, and played here. Is there anywhere more beautiful? All the trees, the nice climate, the nice people. What more could you want?"

Richard's family, like others in Damour, had been comfortably wealthy, owning acres of land and a grand old house. But the family was forced over time to sell it, bit by bit, to stay afloat while they lived away. Richard now rents in the town where he was born. "We need to sacrifice. Who do we leave Damour to? Let us at least die here instead of Beirut," he said.

But now, with the country in upheaval and openly divided, Richard questions his decision and is racked by doubt. Was it premature? Would he be displaced again? Would his children go through what he went through?

"I was born Christian. What should I do? Should I take a beating every day?" he says in one breath. Then he wavers again. "In the end, I prefer my children leave, so they don't live what I lived. This is Damour. It's empty and no one is coming back."

He concluded by saying that he would stay in Damour alone if he had to. But once I had put my notebook away, he asked whether I thought Canada might accept him as an immigrant.

It was a thought that was running through the minds of many Lebanese now. Once again, getting out was the best option. A protest to end all protests.

TEN

Escape Route

He who drank the sea
won't choke on the stream.
—ARAB PROVERB

BEIRUT, JULY 2006

"You must come back. Now."

On the phone was Samer, the CBC's cameraman and fixer in Ramallah. It was 5:30 a.m., and there was only a hint of light outside. I was on vacation in Toronto, sleeping on my sister's couch.

Samer made it clear that there was no room to prevaricate, and he had never before steered me wrong.

"Hezbollah has abducted two Israeli soldiers. Don't even think about it. Just come back."

I knew that what was coming was significant, and as the CBC's Beirut correspondent, I could not sit this out. I called the man in charge of news that day.

"Paul, it's going to be a bloodbath. I have to go back."

He didn't commit right away. "Let's wait," he said. "Watch it and see what happens."

The death toll mounted. I called again, but still no decision. I gathered my things and made flight arrangements, then sat there staring at my sister staring at me. The call finally came.

"You'd better have a story when you get there."

When I landed at Heathrow, all the televisions in the terminal carried the red breaking-news tag. Israeli fighter jets had already bombed the Beirut airport. I would have to get back to Lebanon by road.

I boarded a flight to Amsterdam and from there to Amman, where I would take a car to Lebanon through Syria. In Amman I filed a voice track and a stand-up from a satellite feed point and then sat for two hours in the same hotel that had been my shelter when I first arrived in the Middle East, watching the war unfold on Al Jazeera. The driver was late. We got on the road only as the first rays of sunlight emerged.

This time, there would be no crew, no colleagues, no convoy, and no flak jackets—just an unwieldy backpack of holiday clothes and an unknown driver whose name escaped my memory the moment he said it.

It was hard to get through to Lebanon, to the two people whose advice I needed: Hussein and Weeda. There had been airstrikes on the usual route from Syria to Beirut, a major bridge had been destroyed, and I didn't know which way to take in.

Once I got through they both advised me to avoid the highway and take Tarik Tarshish, a winding mountain road that had been a lifeline for Lebanon's Christians during the civil war. It went through several Christian villages, and was therefore unlikely to be bombed by the Israelis in this current conflict. From Zahlé, the so-called Bride of the Bekaa, you drove over Jabal el Kneisse (Mountain of the Church) to Tarshish, the highest point on the road at more than fourteen hundred metres. You then started the slow descent through Aintoura, Choueir, Bikfaya, Beit Shebab, Rabieh, Antelias, and down to sea level and the main seaside avenue that took you into Beirut. The Lebanese had pulled their old maps out of the vault of war memories. Their forgotten but trusted escape routes were being pressed into use once again.

I trusted both Hussein and Weeda implicitly. But I did not know this driver, and I didn't like his rusting, un-air-conditioned Chevy. I liked him less when he admitted he wasn't entirely familiar with Tarik Tarshish. But as soon as we crossed the border, it was easy to find.

Thousands of civilian cars were inching their way, single file, in a line that would guide us through the tiny villages all the way home to Beirut. We stopped briefly to phone in a report and watch the mournful parade before continuing on our way. The occupants all looked defeated and resigned, staring straight ahead toward their final exit.

It was a long trip—much longer than the highway. In the yawning valleys, the red terracotta roofs bade the fleeing passersby farewell, while welcoming us, the lone car travelling in the other direction. Occasionally, abandoned old mountain houses grimaced in the distance, baring their old war wounds like an animal might bare its teeth. The mountain's green vistas waved us through, followed by Bikfaya's low-rises. Finally, I could see the road leading to the upscale Beirut neighbourhood of Rabieh, and the sea winked at us from below. Antelias was a blur, and soon we were along Beirut's abandoned coast.

☆

Beirut was in a black mood, wearing an unfamiliar sullen expression. The wide Corniche promenade was vacant but for a couple of old fishermen who must have lived through so many days like this they no longer felt fear. The public beach was deserted, the only movement that of the lapping waves and the faded Lebanese flags fluttering in the hot wind. The patios were empty, umbrellas folded as if it were winter. Chairs were stacked on top of tables, shop doors firmly shuttered.

It was too quiet for a Friday, a day when children normally kicked around a soccer ball in the parking lot behind my apartment. All I could hear now was the familiar chirping in the tree in front of my building and the rising voice of my nameless driver, who was arguing about why he had suddenly quadrupled the price on which we'd agreed. Exasperated, I handed over the cash. I hadn't slept in more than two days, so when Zouheir and I finally finished filing, I gave in to a deep peacetime sleep, then woke up just before dawn to the familiar sounds of war.

War is noisy, but it begets silence, and on the famed Hamra Street, silence normally has no place. The honking cars, shoppers, beggars, and shoeshine boys had all abandoned their posts; gone, too, were their dancing shadows on the cobblestone street in the late afternoon sun. The newspaper kiosks were closed, and gone too were the lotto men—the old guys who'd have you believe you could be Lebanon's next millionaire, if only you'd stop and buy a ticket. We found just one store open among Hamra's shuttered shops— Lou and Lou. I couldn't resist the old, balding man sitting alone in a plastic lawn chair out front, legs crossed, wearing a pressed pink shirt and a dour expression.

Ahmad al Saba'a lived around the corner, and three days into the war, he'd grown bored. So he'd opened shop as usual—and hadn't received a single customer. Not a surprise, given that Lou and Lou was an old-fashioned perfumery, but you never knew what people might crave in times of conflict, especially in temperamental Beirut. Al Saba'a said this was the worst war he'd witnessed in his seventy years of living through them.

"It's too much like this, too much," he said. "We've had nearly twenty years without war. Now, war has returned to us. We need a while to readjust."

"And the solution?" I asked.

"The solution is with God," he said, finger pointing upwards.

"Because our Arab brothers, they are sitting quiet. I imagined this operation five or six months ago," he added, predictably.

I asked if he was afraid.

"Of course there's fear," he said, his face softening. "Same on the other side. They, the Israelis, are suffering, too, like us." Then he furrowed his brow. "But what does the airport have to do with it?"

Israeli jets had bombed the airport within the first few hours of the conflict, ostensibly to prevent Hezbollah from spiriting the two soldiers it abducted out of the country—and in the process making my return unnecessarily dangerous and complicated. Virtually every bridge from the border in the south all the way to Beirut was also bombed, and many major highways in the south were, too. But few things about war enraged the Lebanese more than the airport's closure—except, perhaps, for food shortages and civilian casualties, and those, too, would eventually come. Under such circumstances, the airport was one of only two practical ways out of the country. Disabling it made escape harder and more perilous, and the Lebanese did not like being penned in. Now, with Israeli warships also imposing a sea blockade, there was effectively just one way out—by land, through Syria, the way I came in—and that could also be closed at a moment's notice.

Beirut's airport sat just fifteen minutes from downtown, in the largely Muslim southwest of the city, right on the coast. On final approach, planes elegantly skirt the coastline, in plain view of both chic seaside lounges and unsightly tenements. After Hariri's death, its name was changed to the Rafic Hariri International Airport—one of the most coveted stretches of Lebanese real estate.

During the civil war, controlling routes in and out of Lebanon was every militia's dream. Controlling access to the airport could be used to exert control, to extort, to bring in supplies, and to make money. Even in modern times, blocking the road to the airport was one of the most popular forms of protest in Lebanon. And for these highly mobile people, it was an effective pressure tactic. The airport was in plain view of Dahieh, the southern suburbs and Hezbollah's stronghold—part of the reason U.S. planes, and by extension Canadian ones, wouldn't land there. Those same suburbs were now the main target for Israeli fighter jets.

As West Beirut neighbourhoods go, Hamra was relatively safe in this conflict—notwithstanding the rockets that blew out the lighthouse on the Corniche a couple of hundred metres from my home the morning after I arrived. I was in the middle of a live telephone report at the time, and the percussive booms made my voice quaver and my hands shake. But this was ostensibly a war against Hezbollah, and so it was the south of the country and southern Beirut—both Hezbollah strongholds—and some parts of the Bekaa Valley that took the brunt of the bombs. Still, in tiny Beirut we were close enough that every morning around 4 a.m., the bombing shook our windows and rattled us out of bed. The Israeli warship docked off Beirut's coast was closer, lobbing shells that flew over us in Hamra on their way to Dahieh. Those were much louder and harder to ignore. But the whole country, even far up in the Christian heartland, felt the war's effects.

The most immediate concern was the blockade, which prevented most supplies from coming in or going out. I spent half a day visiting ATMs to take out whatever money I could, and then Zouheir and I went shopping for an emergency stash of food while Hussein stocked up on water and fuel. The electricity had also become more erratic, even in my new home on well-maintained Bliss Street, to which I had moved earlier that summer. My landlord slapped a hefty premium on our generator subscription as gasoline started to run out, at the same time giving us fewer hours of backup electricity because the generator had to be stopped to guard against overheating. So we moved to a hotel, where we were joined by several CBC colleagues who'd come to help cover the war.

Lebanese, too, settled in for the long haul, as usual anticipating the worst. In Ashrafieh we met George, who had just opened a bakery a few months earlier and was heavily in debt. He stayed open now, but the place sat empty while he stewed inside next to an idle kitchen. And though he was quick to blame Israel, he also articulated what many other Lebanese were thinking: that Hezbollah had brought the conflict on by kidnapping those soldiers, apparently to exchange for its own fighters in Israeli prisons, a decision, he said, that set Lebanon back thirty years. But he said he believed Hezbollah really did it to abort that summer's ongoing political negotiations about the fate of its controversial weapons.

With all of Lebanon suffering the consequences, few were yet saying that publicly. And with their country under attack, Hezbollah's critics could only watch, along with their fellow countrymen, as Hezbollah chief Hassan Nasrallah took their country into new uncertainty.

A few days into the conflict we joined the hordes of journalists watching the bombing from a hill overlooking Dahieh. The huge plumes of smoke reminded me of Tora Bora and a different "war on terror." It had been five years and many, many explosions since that war, and I felt somewhat detached and weary. I had never aspired to be a television reporter, never mind a war correspondent—at least not the type of war correspondent whose main task is to describe the minutiae of modern warfare. In the past, when ground movements were a bigger component of combat—when there was a front line ebbing and flowing on the ground—a live thing that shifted and morphed and created movement that you could follow, war reporting might have been more interesting. But in these F-16 wars—with no way of ascertaining independently how they were progressing—I could only throw most of my energy into the stories of the people affected instead.

You could hardly ignore the deluge of people into Beirut and all parts north. Hundreds of thousands of residents from the south of Lebanon, and especially from Dahieh, were forced to leave their homes behind. Hamra's streets were jam-packed with their cars. Some ended up at the homes of relatives, friends, even total strangers who had thrown open their doors. Others, meanwhile, sheltered in abandoned buildings. Cognizant that squatting during and after the civil war was a widespread and aggravating problem that took years to untangle, Hezbollah swiftly announced that it would pay rent to the owners of the empty buildings and promised that the refugees would leave as soon as the war was over.

Many of the displaced had lived through this before. A good proportion of them had settled in Dahieh and Haret Hreik—which used to be largely Christian—during the civil war, including Nasrallah himself. But their prior experience did little to lessen the impact of this latest upheaval. And while schools and charities opened their doors and allowed people to settle inside, it wasn't a smooth process. One day, while driving in Ain Mreisseh, we were stopped by a group of displaced people who were standing in the middle of the street with nowhere to go.

"Get out of the car, NOW," a lanky, scruffy man yelled through Hussein's open window. "I beg you. Bring out your camera. Please!" His finger pointed at us and his aggressive tone indicated that he was ordering, not begging. He then reached into the car, grabbing at Zouheir and his camera. "You're getting out HERE, HERE, HERE. We are closing the street."

Hussein closed his window as we discussed what to do. Zouheir, CBC producer Christine Crowther, and I were on our way to the Canadian embassy for a rare debriefing with the ambassador on the latest efforts to evacuate Canadians. As we talked, the man suddenly climbed up on the hood of our van. He said he wouldn't move until we got out. So I got out and asked Zouheir to bring out the camera, just as the man wanted.

In the course of doing our job in this region, sometimes we had to beg people for interviews. We had to cajole, negotiate, and persuade, giving compelling reasons for people to "waste" their time with us and "tell the world" their story. On many other occasions, people really wanted to be interviewed. They begged us, and sometimes *we* were the ones who would say no. Other times, we had no choice *but* to interview or to film a scene—such was the desperation of the subjects for attention. This was one of those times.

Zouheir hoisted the camera onto his shoulder and started rolling. The sight of the large, professional camera at work seemed to soothe the angry man. His hands fell to his sides, and he put on the face of someone having his portrait taken. Other men with unruly hair and stubble looked on, arms crossed over their chests. Most of the children and women stood aside, except for one woman in black, who took on the role of spokesperson. She said they had lived under bombardment in the south until the day before. Unable to stand it any longer, they fled together and had arrived that morning, after many hours of dangerous travel. They hadn't eaten, washed, or rested for days, and they were desperate for a place to stay. At that particular spot, there was a private school that had refused to let them in. That incensed our man and his companions. But this was no mob. They were families desperate for dignity in displacement.

Eventually, they let us pass. I don't know where they slept that night.

In schools we visited that did open their doors, they were several families to a classroom, pressed up against the stacked desks and chalkboards of absent students who were far more fortunate, even in peacetime. In the underground parking lot of a brand-new supermarket in the neighbourhood of Shiyah—a stone's throw from Dahieh—we found hundreds more people. They gathered in clusters, each family anchoring itself to a pillar, breathing in the gasoline fumes, yet seemingly comforted by the proximity to such thick concrete walls. Leaflets dropped from Israeli aircraft had warned of an imminent attack and instructed residents to leave their homes, and the parking lot was the closest refuge. Some were now huddled around a large-screen television from which Nasrallah's face looked down, reassuring them in his latest of several wartime speeches. Their children tumbled around a small play structure around the corner. Everything was provided by Hezbollah. One family gathered around a young girl, not more than fourteen, who had just given birth to a tiny baby. The girl said that when her daughter grew up, she would regale her with stories of Hezbollah's victory. In another corner, another mother, much older, told me her sons were on the front line. By withstanding all this, she said, they were just doing their part.

We found yet more of them living out in the open in a small park nestled in a well-preserved, older quarter of West Beirut. With temperatures and humidity soaring, Sanayeh Garden had become one of the most popular destinations for those with nowhere to go. The garden people took refuge under large trees, resting on rare green grass, setting their children free to roam in safety among their plastic bags of belongings. Many of them had already been slumbering for days under the stars. Some were among Lebanon's poorest and most disenfranchised people. So they remained in the garden, watching and listening as jet after fighter jet flew over, delivered its payload, and went back for more.

The resilience, the total faith in the Party of God, astounded me. Not a single one of the garden people would say a negative word about Hezbollah. In interview after interview, they claimed they would be back at their homes eventually. They claimed their victory would come from god. *Allah ma biyinsa hada.*

☙

It had been a record-breaking summer for visiting Lebanese expatriates, and they, too, were caught in the middle of the conflict. One of them was Ali, an older gentleman who was in from Germany to visit family. When the conflict started he had one more week of vacation before returning to work, and he couldn't afford a delay. With the airport closed, he was forced to take a nerve-racking and costly taxi ride through Tarik Tarshish to Syria, where he spent three days scrambling to find a flight before making it home on time.

The experience revived painful memories of another escape almost exactly two decades earlier.

Ali was a god-fearing man. He had few vices but for the sweet taste of double apple tobacco, lit up with coals, the resulting smoke cooled by water before he drew on it deeply. In the early days of the civil war, Ali had moved into a rented apartment in Hamra, near his wife's family. Shortly afterwards, a pro-Syrian militia moved in right across the street and terrorized everyone in the neighbourhood. Among other things, they barred Ali's family from opening their windows, and their siege soon became unbearable. Ali found an answer when he ran into a relative who was escaping to Germany and pleaded for instruction on how to do the same.

Eventually, with his wife and three children, Ali headed to the airport. Their destination was East Germany. It was 1986. At the time, Ali explained, the communist government recruited refugees, placing newspaper ads for cheap flights, taking their money, and then spiriting them to refugee-friendly West Germany.

There were dozens of them on that journey. They paid about two hundred marks each, a significant sum for the time, and were dropped off at a bus station, where facilitators were waiting. They told them to walk through a narrow tunnel for about a kilometre. Police would be nearby, but they would turn their backs. Once on the other side, the refugees were free to go wherever they wished. Ali's family spent a weekend in a West German train station, tired, hungry, and cold, sleeping on newspapers. The two-year-old was ill and shivering. "She was going to die," recalled Ali. "We wrapped her and put her to sleep on top of our suitcases."

They eventually took a train to a village about a hundred kilometres away. Police then picked them up and fed them. He said residents donated clothes, food, a heater. The family was even given a bank account with money in it to get by. "We lived in comfort, where people were worth something," said Ali. "I felt secure—not like in my country."

It was such a traumatic experience, he vowed never to uproot his children again. A few years later, they all became German citizens, and for the lion's share of the rest of his life, he would only be a visitor in his country of origin. "You have to accept your fate," he said. "It is *maktoob* [written]."

He was among tens of thousands of other expats with as many stories of escape who found themselves reliving in 2006 what had been written and lived at least once before.

Foreign governments had started making plans to evacuate their citizens, and the most common mode was by ship from the Beirut port to Cyprus, Lebanon's old, reliable departure lounge. One early morning a handful of us journalists met in the lobby of the famed Commodore Hotel for a briefing on the start of Canada's long-awaited evacuation. The embassy contact and our guide was Claudie Senay, a bright, engaging diplomat who had organized the briefing and would lead us to the site of the seaside evacuation. "You have to make sure you stay with me at all times," she instructed.

Claudie was always extremely organized, meticulous in her planning, and ready for any contingency. She was hyper-vigilant, in the way a professional diplomat should be, especially when based in Lebanon. She was also courteous with journalists, in a way diplomats often are not. So we readily agreed to her rules.

The plan fell apart the moment we saw the huge throng of people massed at the Beirut port, pressed up against the fence at the start of what was already an exceptionally hot and humid day. Children were crying, and adults, too, were shedding tears. Someone passed out from dehydration. There were too many bags, too many people, too much dust. Tempers were flaring: women screamed at the security guards, begging to be let in with the indelicacy of the desperate. They screamed at each other for cutting into line. Canadians had been advised to stay home until they were contacted for evacuation. Many hadn't received the call but came anyway, and the embassy hadn't expected it. They were shorthanded, and Claudie abandoned us to pitch in.

It was several hours in the port's humid air before they started to bring people through the gates, and many were in tears as the first bus kicked off towards the main building. Nearby, Bassam, a Montrealer, was walking hand in hand with his little son. Bassam himself was only seven when the civil war broke out. The very land he walked on didn't exist back when he left—it was civil war rubble, pounded down to expand Beirut's girth. "My kids are young, and I wanted to show them Lebanon," he said, not quite strong enough to fight the emotions that surfaced. "And this is what they saw."

Hours later, only one boat showed up; the others were delayed, according to the embassy, because their security had not yet been guaranteed by Israel. Dockside, the chaos started anew. People's passports were missing, carried off in the hands of some official, but no officials were in sight. The *Blue Dawn* finally appeared on the horizon. But dusk settled in and no one had yet boarded. A commotion broke out, and in a final farewell, several explosions shook Dahieh and echoed ominously on the dock, silencing all of us. Only about three hundred Canadians left that night. One thousand slept at the port. Thousands more huddled in their homes, waiting their turn. Once it got under way, it was the largest international evacuation in Canada's history.

All foreign evacuations received extensive coverage on local networks, and conspiracy-minded Lebanese were convinced it was all proof that the worst was yet to come. Maybe Israeli ground forces would come as far as Beirut, as they had in the past. Many Lebanese were certain those foreign countries knew something they didn't.

୧

Shortly afterwards I finally drove south in the company of three people I trusted most in times like these: Kasem, Hussein, and Sat, the CBC cameraman with whom I had travelled to Iraq. As we passed Dahieh and entered a tunnel near the airport, I sighed heavily. Hussein, charged by the excitement of chasing danger, laughed almost maniacally and said what he always said when trouble loomed: "Whatever falls from the sky, the earth shall receive." I was never sure if it was an optimistic or fatalistic saying, or both.

We took another old war route to avoid the bombed-out main highways, meandering up into the breathtaking mountainside village of Jezzine and its waterfalls, almost touching the wreaths of fog at the summit before descending back to the sullen humid coast at the eastern tip of Sidon. It, too, had been targeted early in the conflict, but Sidon also took the brunt of the displacement from the south, gaining fifty thousand new residents. They'd come in convoys, many of them madly waving white sheets or rags out of their windows, a refugee's surrender. We stopped to talk to one car full of women who'd just arrived. "The planes were right over our heads, but god saved us," said one passenger.

Spotting our camera, another family stopped to talk to us. One of the men gestured at a tiny baby in her mother's arms. "She was born two months ago, and she's been fasting for days," he said. "No food reached us, no one looked in on us," he continued. "When we saw our children dying from hunger, we had to leave for their sake, or else we would have stayed steadfast. We don't know where we're going."

There were thousands of homeless mulling the same question, sitting on Sidon's sidewalks, loitering near school entrances and the roundabout in the middle of town, curiously pointing at buildings that had been destroyed in some of the early bombing. Their needs were enormous, but none of it seemed to faze the city's mayor, who allowed us an interview, even though several people trailing him needed his attention. We, too, followed him around from room to room inside city hall before we could finally speak.

"We've had a 35 percent increase in our population, and there's pressure on our infrastructure. But as long as we can help people, we are doing fine," said Abd al-Rahman al-Bizri. It was what would come after the war that worried him. "At night, when I'm alone, I try to think of what's going to be the future of the country, what's going to happen in the aftermath—the very severe political rift. The political map of the country is going to change."

At a private Sidon hospital we met a harried Canadian-Lebanese surgeon who'd made the decision to see his country through war. In those optimistic years before Hariri's death, he'd left a decent life in Hamilton, Ontario, to return to the country of his birth. He talked about living through the civil war, and about what this latest war was doing to the minds of Lebanese—including his son's and his own.

"It's unreal. You live through this once, and you think it's over and done with, and then you're going through it again. It's unbelievable," he said. "My son was very frustrated. Normally he's a very peaceful person. He said the other day to my wife that 'If something happens to my family, I'm going to go fight the Israelis!' Why would I want my child to think that way? Why would someone who grew up his whole life in Canada think this way?

"It's because of what he's seen," he concluded.

They had seen a lot—and if it wasn't in the flesh, they'd witnessed it all in the non-stop coverage on Arab television, where nothing was too gruesome to broadcast. The doctor decided to send his family home to Canada through Syria.

The farther south we got towards the city of Tyre and the surrounding area, the more visible the destruction. The main roads had been cut off by bombardment, forcing us to detour onto a dusty track through a banana grove that traversed the Litani River and added hours to the trip. We veered around cavernous holes made by falling bombs, into which cars had fallen along with their passengers. On the way, we could occasionally see bombed-out bridges dangling their metal innards, chunks of concrete scattered on the highways below.

Tyre was a ghost town, and at night drones and helicopter gunships filled the sky. The sound of aircraft swooping down towards the ground in what appeared to be pretend air raids regularly pierced the silence, as they had occasionally in Beirut. Throughout the towns nearer the border, the destruction in some stretches was total. It was the same in some parts of the village of Qana, where, believers say, Jesus performed his first miracle, turning water into wine.

Qana knew the cost of war. More than one hundred people who had sheltered in a UN compound there were killed in one episode of Israeli shelling during a brief 1996 skirmish between Hezbollah and Israel. In this latest war, the Qana area was struck again. Airstrikes flattened an apartment building perched atop a cliff overlooking a deep valley, where several families had taken shelter. Israeli forces said that Hezbollah fighters had been launching attacks nearby, and that it was using civilians as human shields. Hezbollah denied it. It mattered little to the civilians who were killed as a result of the strikes, among them more than a dozen children. Images of their bloodied bodies held up for the cameras were broadcast repeatedly throughout the Arab world.

One morning we drove gingerly towards Qana, and when we arrived, we could still hear explosions in the distance, despite Israel's announced forty-eight-hour cessation of air strikes while the incident was being investigated. The families' belongings were strewn about the area, a melange of tattered toys, clothing, kitchenware, and paper. There were few people around.

The incident marked a turning point in the war. Furious Lebanese erupted in protest in downtown Beirut, demanding an end to the bombing, while the gruesome images continued to be broadcast, riling most of the Middle East. But at the UN, there was still no agreement on stopping the fighting—partly due to a desire for the conflict to continue until Hezbollah, considered a terrorist group by most of the West, was neutralized. Many Lebanese were shocked at the reasoning. I wondered how many children and adults—in Lebanon and beyond—made a lifelong vow to seek revenge against anyone they felt was responsible for the continuing bloodshed.

⚳

In Beirut everything was running out, patience included. Bank machines were no longer spitting out money, and stores were running out of food. Gasoline was more expensive and in short supply, and the lineups to get it were long. Everyone was slipping into a state of hopelessness. Hospitals were urgently appealing for more supplies; some warned they would be forced to close within days if none materialized. The people were at a breaking point. At an emergency Arab League meeting held in the city, even Prime Minister Fouad Siniora broke down in tears.

Admittedly it was difficult for anyone to remain composed under such circumstances, including those who, like us, chose to remain even though they could have left. We were barely sleeping, and each day's demands and deadlines blurred into one another and the immense pressure toyed with our nerves. We of course had concerns about our own personal safety. Add to that the rigours of filing daily for three weeks, and I was becoming worn out and edgy. But I couldn't break down and surrender to the mental and physical exhaustion. Not now.

Meanwhile, the strikes inched closer to downtown Beirut, and even north into the Christian heartland. The neighbourhood of Shiyah, whose residents had sheltered in that underground parking lot, was targeted the very night after Siniora broke down in tears, collapsing a trio of buildings a short distance from the Grand Serail, the prime minister's office. We arrived to find people all over the site, heaving rubble aside to get at the dead bodies, perhaps find survivors. I watched little children look on as one body was carried away and wondered who would debrief *them*.

In a hospital nearby, I met a distraught elderly woman who'd actually survived the Shiyah strike. Her husband had been missing since and she presumed him dead. While we spoke, her husband finally called the mobile phone she'd been clutching; he had been taken to another hospital, alive but badly hurt. She burst into sobs of painful relief. It was hard to watch, and I was forced to walk away.

For the Lebanese who remained home, there was little to do but watch their televisions. To really get a handle on what was happening in the country, even in normal times, you had to watch several channels at once. The main evening newscasts were conveniently staggered in fifteen-minute increments to make that possible. LBC would bring you the latest from the war zone and tell you what the Christian Lebanese Forces leader Samir Geagea had to say, in veiled, judgmental references to Hezbollah's decision to abduct the Israeli soldiers. Future Television was Saad Hariri's mouthpiece, and it would tell you how the war was affecting Beirut and what the Sunni Muslim prime minister was up to. And so on. Meanwhile, Hezbollah's television network, Al-Manar, had gone into war mode. Normally, only die-hard Hezbollah supporters watched Al-Manar's mix of religious and political programming. But now, as its owners engaged in combat, it became both a propaganda machine and the source of choice for the latest on the fighting. Naturally, its viewership soared.

Israeli targeted strikes attempted to get Al-Manar off the air more than once—destroying its headquarters in Dahieh, which I'd once visited to interview its staff—but somehow it clung to the airwaves. It regularly showed threatening messages to the Israelis—knowing full well that they were watching, just as Hezbollah itself constantly monitored Israeli television, even when there was no fighting. In between news bulletins, it also played extended advertisements aimed at ordinary Lebanese, complete with military music and what appeared to be real combat footage from the ongoing conflict. Theirs was as much a war for the hearts and minds of Lebanese as it was one against Israel. Hezbollah could not afford to lose either.

I tried to watch all the networks at one point or other on each day, but there was hardly time for that, never mind for staying in touch with friends and family abroad. Occasionally I touched base with Leena, a prominent local journalist and a friend, and Weeda to compare notes, but I barely saw them. Work had always dominated my life, but in war it was all consuming, fuelled only by adrenaline and deadlines. But it was another thing to live in a war zone.

I did drop by to see Habib late one afternoon when we passed his place and saw that it was open. He was transfixed by a report on Al-Manar, a drink already in his hand. "Did you see it? They reported that Hezbollah destroyed another Merkava [tank]," he said, wiping his finger under one side of his wide moustache, as he always did when he was deep in thought. Then he launched into a tirade about how the war was destroying his business.

Despite the fighting—and because of it—Habib opened his pub in the daytime as usual to air it out, and by mid-afternoon he was already sitting with a drink and a remote control to watch the tiny television that hung in the corner. Habib had dispensed with his staff and the music—he wasn't getting anywhere near his usual crowds. But he said a handful of his die-hard customers didn't miss a beat and bellied up for their fix in the evenings to escape, or to try in a halo of inebriation to make sense of it all.

Habib was mostly alone, though. He confessed that he missed the camaraderie and the consoling presence of his customers in difficult times like these. "Bring your friends!" he repeated, as he poured himself another.

The tougher the war, the harder Lebanon's drinkers drank, the higher the smokers got, and the more fervently the faithful prayed. Lebanese people excelled at many things, one of which was self-medication, and many headed in droves to local pharmacies for relief. Despite Lebanon's renowned revelry, recent studies indicated that it had long been a depressed nation, a mood exacerbated by the recent resurgence of violence. Even before this war, many Lebanese exhibited some of the signs of post-traumatic stress disorder: excessive anxiety, hyper-vigilance, fatalism, depression, and jumpiness. This war would only magnify those problems.

Still, I was surprised to learn how many Lebanese friends were regularly self-medicating with pills better left for doctors to prescribe. Sales of Prozac, Lexotanil, and Valium had started mounting the moment Hariri died. Now with the war in full swing, the sales of such pills went through the roof. Lexotanil is supposed to be prescribed for anxiety and panic attacks. For the six months at the beginning of 2006, drugstores were selling an average of 30,777.5 units a month. By July, when the war started, that had shot up to 50,663 units—a 64.6 percent increase over the monthly average. Those left behind were still trying to escape—to cope—by any means available.

But then the war ended as suddenly as it had started. Both sides immediately respected a UN resolution that called for a halt in the fighting beginning on August 14, and ordered the deployment of thousands of UN and Lebanese troops to the south to act as a buffer. We headed there immediately, along with tens of thousands of others. It was only now possible to see the extent of the damage the war had wrought.

⚓

If cars could tiptoe they most certainly did on that day, barely slinking left to miss an obscenely large unexploded bomb lying at the entrance to Bint Jbeil. Seeing such a device up close stirred panic inside me. There was a real possibility it might still go off, but I was also disquieted that such a colossal weapon could fail in its mission, its only reason for being.

Still, Lebanese colleagues accustomed to war and bombs leaned over it and poked it, in a state of half curiosity and half bravado. They told me not to worry: it was inert, no longer capable of detonating the way it was intended. I knew better and, in vain, screamed at them to stay away. *Stop being so curious!*

The sun shone as if nothing had happened, bright and all-knowing, hastening the decomposition of bodies and filling the air with the sickly odour of death. Corinne Seminoff, the producer who'd come to help out in 2005 and had now returned to help again, pointed out a sinewy, severed arm that lay on the tiny island splitting the main street in two; it was pointing in the direction of an annihilated neighbourhood just below the road, where there were more bodies and the reek grew worse. In the other direction, young Lebanese Red Cross workers dressed in red bodysuits packaged an old man's remains into a clear plastic bag. He had been dead under the broken concrete for so long it was no effort at all to lift what was left of him.

The dead made their statement just by being dead, and throughout Lebanon's latest war and its aftermath, they were the centre of attention, celebrated stars in this macabre theatre well known for its repeated shows of violent drama. But it was the living who could speak, whose story was still capable of propagation, of development, of action. They—not the Hezbollah fighters or Israeli soldiers who had waged fierce battles here—were the story now, and the displaced were eager to tell it, even though many no longer cared to listen.

The occasional car full of returning residents silently swept past. Some of them came only to look, then drove right back out on winding roads laced with cluster bombs. Others stayed and picked at the remnants of their homes. One couple swept their front stoop, as if they had yet to notice that the house was gone. Others clambered over upturned concrete, grabbing at worthless objects—some destroyed, others miraculously intact—just because they could. They shook hands with their neighbours, congratulating them for remaining among the living. One woman looked over a cliff to where there was once a house. She said she was searching for a friend. *I don't know where she is.*

It was only now—seeing their town the way it was—that many of them took off the masks of bravado they had worn throughout the war and broke down. They insisted they would rebuild, but there were tears and sorrow in their words. A young man we met at the entrance to town said he blamed everybody. For him, nothing and no one could justify this.

Shortly after we arrived, it was time for me to call in for a live report. I pulled out my satellite phone, leaned against the hood of Hussein's car, and started to dial, when I suddenly felt faint. Bint Jbeil swirled around me, the Red Cross workers and the unexploded shell on one end, the severed arm on another, before it all faded to black. I bent down and held on to the hood of the car for a moment until the episode passed. I called in my report, chalking the spell up to the unrelenting heat and the pungent stench of death. But later, it would happen again.

On the roads we traversed that day we came upon more unexploded shells, as well as cluster bombs, those burnished killing balls that in the coming months, even years, would claim many more civilian victims. Though he knew those roads, Hussein drove hesitantly for the first time since I'd known him, and at least once he stopped while we helped him navigate a particularly perilous section.

On the road heading to Tyre, we carried on with thousands of others going home. They wore wide smiles and waved at our camera: they were returning, and that, in their estimation, made them victorious, no matter what they'd lost. Hezbollah had also survived, and it too announced victory, *Nasr min Allah*—victory from god—a play on the Hezbollah leader's name and the group's newest slogan. In the months and years to come, Hezbollah would become more powerful than ever, thanks to Syria's and Iran's help.

The conflict might have ended, but our work didn't stop. After moving our operation back to my apartment in Beirut, we visited Dahieh to cover the aftermath and the return of the many displaced. The damage was like nothing I had ever seen—whole buildings crumpled into mountains of concrete, electrical wires dangling on the ground, cars flattened nearby. We spoke to many people there, including a car mechanic who was busy clearing the rubble of his destroyed business. Just as Zouheir set up for the interview, I once again nearly fainted. The darkness lasted longer than the first time, and my breathing was far more laboured. I knew I was exhausted, but this was new and disturbing.

Nasrallah immediately promised to rebuild every home, every neighbourhood, "better than it was before." Within days, Hezbollah was handing out thousands of crisp U.S. dollars for the displaced to use to rent temporarily while they waited for the rebuilding to finish. I'd never seen so much money up close, and the word was that it came directly from Iran. Yet it took months for the government to begin disbursing assistance that came mostly from abroad. Several other countries stepped in to rebuild and peddle their influence among a vulnerable population, among them Qatar, Kuwait, and Saudi Arabia. One of the most prominent and generous, though, was Iran, now a sponsor of whole destroyed villages—including Bint Jbeil—and scarred stretches of highway.

Few thought to do much for the scars that remained in the minds of adults and children alike. On a visit to a school soon after the war ended, I asked a class of the older kids how many thought the war would return. Most of them put up their hands. Everyone believed what had just ended was part one. Surely part two would eventually follow.

I finally left to finish the badly needed vacation I had started back in July, and to try to clear my head after what were the most stressful weeks of my life. I spent five days alone in a picturesque town on the outskirts of Toronto before joining my family for a visit. In my waking hours, I flinched at the sound of aircraft. In my dreams, I repeatedly found myself riding a boat away from Beirut's coast. In my heart I knew I needed help, but I wouldn't ask for it.

ॐ

I don't know when precisely I became desensitized to seeing guns on the streets, but it happened somewhere between Baghdad and Beirut, and I became aware of my nonchalance only when friends and family visited me in Beirut and expressed shock at the sight of them.

Even before the war—due to the string of assassinations and bombings that preceded it—army and police checkpoints had become commonplace in Lebanon. So had the armoured personnel carriers that now protected everything from Parliament and the prime minister's office, to the personal residences of chieftains like Walid Jumblatt, the eccentric Druze leader (and one of my favourite interviewees of all time because of his unpredictable repartee). Theirs were the guns of soldiers, carried publicly, slung over shoulders, barrels down but at the ready.

Then there were the hidden firearms, the ones that rang out in Dahieh at the first sight of Nasrallah speaking on television, or in Tarik Jdeideh at the conclusion of a speech read live on Future Television by Saad Hariri. Supporters would unleash a barrage of happy gunfire, like punctuation marks. They might have been celebrations of verbal victories, but they also contained veiled threats for the other side.

Other guns might be concealed in jackets and in the smalls of backs, like those of the private security guards who sat in front of my apartment building day and night, sheltered in the shade of a tree. They were the protectors of a lowly MP who lived around the corner. The protectors of Saad Hariri's residence, meanwhile, carried their guns out and up; somehow they'd also been given the authority to set up their own checkpoints and nose into the lives of ordinary passersby and local residents. The irony was that Hariri rarely spent much time there at all.

Lebanon's various militias had supposedly given up all their weaponry at the conclusion of the civil war in 1990, and some had been symbolically entombed in a strange, pyramid-shaped monument near the presidential palace to signify a chapter closed. Hezbollah, the one exception in the deal, was allowed to hold on to its vast arsenal as a deterrent against Israel. There were also the guns Palestinian militias were allowed to keep under an obscure agreement that gave their camps relative autonomy from the Lebanese state and its laws.

Before and after the war, Hezbollah's weapons were the most contentious. But now, everyone was accusing everyone else of arming, another sure sign that confrontation was imminent.

The "foreign aggression" over, it was time for the local one: accounts had to be settled. The war had exacerbated the schism between Lebanon's two main camps, and they had now hardened their positions. Hezbollah and its allies accused the government of unsteady support during the conflict; they even accused some members of treason, of quietly cheering the Israeli war against Hezbollah. For their part, the ruling majority and the anti-Syrian camp openly resented Hezbollah's unilateral move, which had sparked the war, and they still resented those weapons. Prime Minister Fouad Siniora all but admitted to me in an interview a week after the 2006 conflict ended that in Lebanon, Hezbollah wielded far more power than anyone else.

Another fundamental point of disagreement was a planned United Nations tribunal to investigate the murder of Rafic Hariri—a tribunal that Syria's allies in Lebanon felt infringed too much on Lebanon's sovereignty. The ruling party, headed by Hariri's son and staffed by his old loyalists, decided the government would approve funding for the tribunal anyway, without the opposition's consent. The Hezbollah-led opposition then demanded a national unity government in which they would have greater say. The government refused. Relations between the two sides deteriorated quickly. The standoff deepened the existing rift and threatened what was left of the country's fragile stability.

The two sides embarked on a war of words. Although it played out mostly on television, a TV war did as much to divide Lebanese as any real conflict—sectarian sentiment escalated with every inflammatory word uttered. You could now hear that language on the street, and it was as debased as it had been in Iraq after the 2006 Samarra bombing.

Lebanon has often been held up as a beacon of press freedom when compared to other countries in the region. It is true that for its size, the country boasts far more newspapers and television networks than any other Middle Eastern country and censorship was virtually unknown. But on closer examination, you realize that the journalism was still wanting. Virtually every paper or network is loyal to one side, one chieftain or another, and tends to mimic that side's rhetoric and refrain from criticism. Though there is always a vigorous debate—which you don't see in much of the rest of the Middle East's press—there is also a general fear of the power of the media, the same fear that has traditionally prevailed throughout the region, and that led to the murder of influential writers and journalists in the wake of the anti-Syrian protests after Hariri's death. Naturally outspoken and unabashedly partisan as most were—and even if they weren't—journalists and media outlets often got caught up in Lebanon's violence.

For now, it was still only a war of words fought by two-bit political actors who spewed biting remarks as swiftly as most of us can recite the alphabet.

But no one had as much power or hold over television audiences as Hassan Nasrallah did when he appeared on Lebanon's electronic hearth. Since the 2006 conflict, when his security compound and home were destroyed, Nasrallah no longer appeared in public, out of fear of assassination, so his new pulpit was the television screen. Though it had been months since his war with Israel ended, he could still clear the streets with his televised sermons.

Nasrallah normally delivered—sometimes yelled—his speeches in formal Arabic, beads of sweat trickling down his forehead. But he

would often intersperse his thundering passages with bits of colloquial Lebanese Arabic, using street language to explain his ideas
and connect with his supporters. It was in one of those speeches
that Nasrallah threatened the government with mass protests if it
didn't give Hezbollah more say in a unity administration—an effective veto. The government stonewalled. And he made good on his
promise.

Hundreds of thousands of Hezbollah supporters and their
Christian allies descended on Riad el-Solh Square on December
1, 2006, a euphoric throng waving flags and shouting anti-govern-
ment slogans. This was no impromptu uprising though—it had
been planned well ahead of time. And while the protesters may
have been supporters of a group considered a terrorist organization by much of the West, the Shia among them (and they weren't
only Shia) had real complaints, not least the marginalization they
had long endured. Hezbollah didn't come out of nowhere. It is
precisely that very real marginalization—in addition to Hezbollah's
self-appointed role as the "Resistance"—which made the group's
emergence and clout possible. It had stepped in where successive governments had failed, to provide Shia Muslims with badly
needed social services, protection, and most important, a voice that
could no longer be ignored.

As many analysts pointed out at the time, there was something
symbolic about the presence of so many Shia in the ritzy downtown,
which had been rebuilt by Hariri not for them but for wealthy
Gulf Arabs and Lebanese with means. Many (but not all) of the
demonstrators were poor, living in the densely populated Dahieh
area with unreliable electricity and scarcely any work. Many had
been displaced by the last war, and other wars before that. For
them, occupying downtown was both a protest of the political
wrangle of the day and the culmination of generations of ill treatment and victimization. Collective grievances in the Arab world,

and the resulting anxiety, fear, and alienation, can last generations. Everyone in the Middle East has a long memory—they never forget.

Like all Hezbollah protests, this one was orderly, clean, and well organized. The group's young disciples swiftly assembled tents, bathrooms, and water tanks to service the huge crowd. They put up a large stage and a huge screen, from which Nasrallah would address the people, live. They fanned out through the crowd, wearing baseball caps and vests that identified them as stewards, and seized Hezbollah flags from anyone who'd brought one—it was to be a Lebanese flag–only event. Hezbollah was a lot of things, and one of them was image-conscious. Nasrallah had decreed this would be an orderly show of Lebanese discontent, and that's precisely what his organizers delivered.

The sit-in shut down a major section of downtown and completely surrounded the entrance to the Grand Serail. Out of fear, Siniora and several of his ministers were actually sleeping there under the protection of the army and its guns. No one said it out loud, for fear of the consequences, but some in the government linked the assassinations of anti-Syrian figures directly to Hezbollah and its allies. Only a few days earlier, the string of killings of such figures had resumed after a hiatus—this time, taking the young life of Industry Minister Pierre Gemayel (nephew of President-elect Bashir Gemayel, murdered back during the civil war). Now hundreds of thousands of the group's supporters were camped out in front of the prime minister's office, occasionally calling government ministers "Israelis." That left government members uneasy and concerned about their safety.

In the wake of Gemayel's murder, the ruling majority decided to hold another protest of its own in Martyrs' Square, a block away from the opposition camp. The army was forced to split downtown into two, using fences and razor wire, a modern version of the

Green Line. On the border between the two camps, a tattered Lebanese flag barely hung on the fence. The downtown that Hariri had painstakingly rebuilt—the Lebanon he'd painstakingly tried to stitch back together—was unravelling once again.

Everyone in Lebanon was in favour of free speech—until the opposing side got its turn. Many Lebanese were resentful of Hezbollah's occupation of downtown. Traffic in the area was snarled for months. The opposition supporters were "heathens" and "Persians," "backward," and "dirty." When supporters of the government protested, they were "traitors" and "collaborators" and "pawns of America" and, inevitably, "Israelis." I heard such racist and hateful words from many acquaintances, and even from a close colleague, and now I finally believed, as I had repeatedly been told, that there were virtually no independents in Lebanon. When push came to shove, you had to be allied, part of a clan, a tribe, or a political grouping. There were only a few exceptions in my circle of Lebanese friends, including Weeda, Hussein, and Leena, all of whom somehow stayed above the fray.

Slogans and posters of chieftains, dead and alive, were now plastered on every street, marking out territory. In Ashrafieh, random posters of murdered Christian Phalangist leader Bashir Gemayel grew into a full-fledged campaign of remembrance. Stylized images of him proliferated, reminding loyalists to remain "steadfast, today and tomorrow." In the neighbourhoods of Hamra and Tarik Jdeideh, pictures of Hariri still demanded the Truth and promised a reckoning. In the Chouf District, images of Walid Jumblatt and his father looked down benevolently from their own perches, a reminder that the son followed in the footsteps of the father. In the south, billboards of Nabih Berri, head of the Shia Amal Movement, multiplied, as did, of course, those of Nasrallah, which had always been there. Farther north, images of Christian leaders like Michel Aoun battled with garish advertising billboards to make their presence known. All their names were familiar. New generations of Lebanese were born—millions—and whole cadres of them had moved abroad since the civil war, yet their leaders hadn't changed, and neither had their ability to divide their people.

Nothing and no one could stop the festering hate, and it inevitably erupted into clashes. Christians divided between government and opposition loyalists fought, killing three. Clashes between Sunni and Shia Muslims also became routine. They were not big brawls at first, just a few young hooligans skirmishing on the streets, throwing bottles and rocks. But by January 2007, they'd evolved into armed clashes complete with rooftop snipers and sectarian roadblocks that in one terrifying night killed nine people. The images—so familiar to those who'd survived the civil war—shocked the country and elicited a front-page curse from one of the newspapers. Lebanese were flirting with the edges of the harrowing experiences of the past, and many feared that meant they would soon be revisiting them.

A month later and just a day shy of the second anniversary of Hariri's murder, there were more bombs to add to the agony of uncertainty. A pair of buses full of civilian passengers were blown up, minutes apart, in the Christian heartland. I went to see the smouldering, twisted metal, which was lying limply in the middle of a mountain road as the rain poured down. I was sick of it. How many bombs had it been? I had been living in the country for just over two years, and I had had enough. The Lebanese, who'd seen all of this before, were coping badly.

In the wake of more bombs and assassinations and political instability—and an intense conflict between the Lebanese army and extremists in the Palestinian refugee camp of Nahr al-Bared—I watched many leave. In waves that matched the spikes of violence, they pressed the panic button and scrambled for a way out. They dusted off foreign passports that they'd kept tucked away for just such an emergency. They booked tickets, filled planes, and rented out their apartments or shuttered them up. They headed to the sweltering and wealthy Gulf region, or reacquainted themselves with their civil war shelters in Paris, Detroit, and Montreal, their safe havens in Brazil, Italy, Spain, and even nearby Cyprus. They had abandoned, finally, their dream of reinstalling themselves in their land of plenty, explaining it all away as temporary madness.

It was like watching a film roll backwards. Lebanon had seemed on the way to better days. But then slowly it fell *back* towards all that came before, back from hope and promise all the way to the more familiar dread and despair—people leaving, more clashes, more guns, more deaths—the certainty of war.

༄

I had done little more than work for the better part of five years—my job was my entire life, my sole purpose. Between the bombs and civil war of Iraq, the troubles of Syria, the elections of Egypt, and the turmoil and war of Lebanon, I was constantly immersed, neck-deep in the violence and anguish that shrouded the Mideast.

I had some friends with whom I occasionally socialized, but in Lebanon I generally kept to myself, holed up in my apartment reading, watching, or writing the news, unless I was out gathering it. By early 2008, my dizzy spells had become pretty much routine. There seemed to be no pattern to them, no particular trigger, though I suspected stress was the culprit. So despite the tense situation, I made the unusual decision to take a month-long vacation—the longest I had taken since arriving in the region. Almost instantly the spells subsided. I returned to Beirut refreshed and ready for whatever came next.

Soon after I returned, I decided to host a handful of friends for dinner. It was a beautiful winter day, and I had nothing to occupy me but a morning workout, some reading, and preparations for that evening's meal. But halfway through my round of the local newspapers, I suddenly felt as though I was about to lose consciousness. It was the worst spell yet—the darkness shielded my eyes like blinders, and all I could hear was the thumping in the back of my head, the flutter in my chest. I doubled over but managed to find my phone. I called Hussein, but he was too far away and couldn't get to me, so he sent a driver. Somehow I got on the phone with Annia—did she call, or did I?—a neighbour, a foodie, and a friend who was coming over early to help me prepare for dinner. I told her what was happening and she said she'd be right over. I dragged myself to the elevator, half blind, and stumbled out to the street, where I found Jihad, Hussein's friend, and Annia, who had sprinted over. We rushed to the hospital. Leena and Hussein met us there.

Hours and many tests later, I was given a clean bill of health, sick only with embarassment. We returned to my apartment to have that dinner. For the next several weeks, I had every test imaginable. There was nothing seriously wrong with me. I eventually had no choice but to accept the ER doctor's explanation of a probable cause—overwhelming stress.

♌

Nasrallah was on television again, and it was not good news.

The government had taken an unprecedented swipe at Hezbollah and its formidable apparatus when, in May 2008, it fired the head of airport security because they considered him too close to the group. It also said the militant organization's private communications network threatened Lebanon's national security, and vowed to shut it down. It was a potentially incendiary challenge, even if it didn't address the core of the matter—Hezbollah's arsenal.

Still, it was done and Nasrallah was apoplectic. "A war was declared against us," he thundered. "A war that's being fought on behalf of the United States and Israel. Anyone who is going to target us will be targeted by us. Whoever is going to shoot at us will be shot by us." Nasrallah's long-standing promise never to turn his weapons against other Lebanese was about to be broken.

First the airport was forced to close, again. Hezbollah supporters burned tires and dumped rubble on the roads leading to and from it. Later, in retaliation, pro-government protesters blocked roads in the Bekaa Valley, choking off the route to the Syrian border. Lebanon was once again under siege—this time, by its own people.

It got worse. The night after Nasrallah spoke, Hezbollah-led opposition gunmen overran Hamra and Ras Beirut—my neighbourhood—and took it by force. It wasn't much of a contest, since the opposition supporters were better fighters and had the element of surprise on their side, but the death toll was rising.

I was out of town on assignment again, and our Mideast producer, Stephanie Jenzer, and I were forced to rush back that night, riding early in the morning with yet another unknown Jordanian driver through Syria and this time, on to Lebanon's northern border. We had to take a meandering mountain route, one of the most beautiful and treacherous I had ever seen in Lebanon, to get back to Beirut. Up in the heights of the mountain it was barely a road at all, and I cursed under my breath with every hairpin turn. Upon descent, we found the northern capital's roads on fire—lit up by Sunni Muslims protesting the opposition's takeover of Beirut—and we had to head back up again. Hours later we were finally just south of Tripoli, in northern Lebanon, exhausted from a trip that would have normally taken less than an hour from the border.

Later, as we drove towards Hamra and our office, young masked men stopped us just metres away from the spot where Hariri had died and asked our business. They were flanked by a couple of burning tires, and the acrid smoke billowed in our direction.

"We are journalists. We're going to our office," I said.

They checked our IDs. "Journalists! Let them through." Wars and elections. It worked every time.

The recently installed Hariri monument had been abandoned by the uniformed security guards who'd watched it day and night since it was inaugurated; they'd been replaced by heavily armed fighters in fatigues. I glanced over as we sped past and saw two of the masked fighters posing in front of the monument while another snapped their picture. We turned on to the beautiful Avenue des Français, the Corniche; it had taken on an ashen pallor. Smoke hung once again over Beirut's skyline, like thunderclouds heralding an impending storm. There was no one seaside, not even the fishermen who normally braved anything to throw in their bait. A few masked and armed youth kicked around bits of burning tires. A tall, bearded gunman stood at the base of the road leading up the hill to my apartment, seemingly unbothered by the weight of the ammunition on his chest or the passing of our lone car. When I finally saw the damage, I was stunned—burnt-out cars, bullet holes, blackened roads—all in a neighbourhood I had come to know street by street, the place I now called home. The heavy men protecting the MP around the corner were nowhere to be seen—all that remained were opposition men with guns. Residents quivered with anger and humiliation. The government called it a shameless coup. A few blocks away, Future Television, Hariri's network, was on fire.

Hariri's supporters were especially outraged that his television headquarters had been sacked, also his newspaper and radio station targeted. It was a direct assault on the younger Hariri, and an acknowledgment of the role of television in what was by then a bitter, eighteen-month impasse. The opposition didn't like what they heard on Future, so they silenced it. It was inevitable that the mounting outrage would eventually explode onto the streets, though no one imagined it would happen in quite this organized military way. The schism between the people, as well as their leaders, was now total.

The fighting spread to the mountains, and there, too, the government's supporters were handily trounced. The government had no choice but to capitulate, to agree to sit down with the opposition to work out a power-sharing deal that would end the fighting. Hezbollah's cynical tactic cost lives and did untold damage to its already tattered relationships in Lebanon, but its leaders took the gamble knowing it would pay political dividends for them and for their patrons in Syria and Iran.

While the leaders negotiated in Qatar, the airport remained under siege and the opposition remained in control of West Beirut's streets—as Stephanie called it, "the new normal." Not far from one of the main opposition barricades, a handful of brave Lebanese, mostly older women, gathered on the Corniche for yet another protest.

It was one of the tiniest demonstrations I'd ever witnessed, yet also one of the most profound. Their message to their leaders was simple and handwritten clearly in thick marker on small white placards: "If you don't agree, don't come home."

Only the wisdom of Lebanese mothers could manage to come up with a protest against both sides.

It took a few days, but the leaders did agree and Hezbollah would get the say that it wanted. And magically, the moment the deal was announced on May 21, 2008, all the debris and remains of burning tires on the airport highway were wiped away as several of us journalists watched. Just as magically, the sit-in camp downtown was swiftly dismantled. Stephanie, Zouheir, and I rushed to Riad el-Solh to watch as the garbage was collected, the slogans were cleaned off the walls, and streets that hadn't been traversed by cars in eighteen months were brisquely reopened to traffic. Hezbollah even replanted the flowers in Riad el-Solh Square.

What had been untenable just a couple of years earlier was once again reality—the exasperating status quo had been restored with the very tools that have protected despots around the region for decades: intimidation and violence.

ELEVEN

Disillusion

☙❧

*"Hammer water,
and it's still water."*
—ARAB PROVERB

I should have left after the war. My body and my mind were saying I'd had enough. But I insisted I wasn't "done" yet. So I stayed.

The truth was that I could no longer live without the next crisis hovering around the corner. I needed to pore over every bloody word written about Lebanon's—the region's—condition. Like the Lebanese, I now thrived on analyzing the present to predict a dire future, and I was getting pretty good at it. I also needed the loneliness of my office and the urgency of life's rhythm in a place like Beirut. There was an impunity to living life on a knife's edge, in the throes of a low-level war—and the occasional full-fledged one—that seemed to me, then, to trump all of life's other mundane trials and excuse me from most of its responsibilities. My emails and calls back to Canada had a familiar refrain. *Rob, I'm sorry I haven't written—I've been busy. You know, the fucking war. Daph, I'm sorry I haven't called as I said I would. I am sorry I wasn't there for you when you needed me, again, Sue. I am so very sorry our dear, precious Dennis has suddenly died—at his own hands—and I couldn't come to the funeral. I'm so sorry, dear Alex, I forgot to write back. I'm so sorry, Mom and Dad. I won't be visiting anytime soon.*

Normally, my phone conversations with Dad were brief and uncomplicated, not the kind of meandering chats that my mother and I shared, punctuated as they were by songs, jokes, and teary laughter. Dad usually wanted to know only two things: how I was doing, and what the weather was like. If he was chatty that day, he might also comment on the news. But his top headline was always the weather. It was as if knowing the climate conditions in Amman kept him in touch with his remaining family there. Tracking the precipitation in Toronto, where my sister lived, and in Beirut was a way of gaining some knowledge about how his daughters were. Telling me the wind speed and direction in Winnipeg was his way of reassuring me that all was fine. When it wasn't, I knew, because Dad would veer beyond the day's expected highs and lows.

"Remember So-and-so?" he asked once out of the blue.

Of course I remembered him. He was one of the few distant relatives who regularly dropped by with his wife to see us when we lived without Dad in Amman. So-and-so was the one with a sense of humour, a warm smile, and a thick moustache.

Well, Dad said, So-and-so's niece—whom I'd never met—was dead. I offered my condolences. But he wasn't finished.

"She was murdered," Dad said succinctly, like a wire alert. By her own family.

The details had come third- or fourth-hand, so they were sketchy. She had apparently been living on her own after a couple of failed marriages. A rumour circulated that she had been "dishonourable"—in other words, that she'd had relations with men outside marriage. It seems the family believed these rumours. Their "honour" had been compromised. So they "cleansed" it.

Dad was disgusted, said so as clearly as he would report a winter day's wind chill. I was shaken to hear that someone whose bloodline I shared, whose great-grandfather had been mine, too, was the victim of a so-called honour killing.

I had read extensively about honour killings. I grew up hearing about honour beatings, honour slaps in the face, and a variety of other honour-related punishments, which also included honour tongue-lashings and honour groundings. I'd even seen some of them meted out. Never an honour killing, of course, but those always loomed large at the far end of my fear horizon like a fat, growling Winnipeg thundercloud. The fact is that most of the murders committed in the name of honour are carried out on mere suspicion—the very whiff of an inappropriate liaison between a man and a woman—and so they were always theoretically possible, even if you were perfectly well behaved. Imagine constantly living with that fear, and how profoundly it would affect your every move. Think of that the next time you wonder why so many Arab women often fail to assert themselves.

Honour killings of women are erroneously believed—by the Western world that condemns them, and sometimes even by those who commit them—to be prescribed by religion. They are not. But they are certainly part of the same tradition that puts nearly the entire weight of a family's honour on the shoulders of its women, young and old. The same year that my distant cousin was killed, several other women in Jordan were murdered for the same reason, and more often than not, the killers got away with a light sentence handed down by a male-dominated legal system that all but excuses such murders.

Human Rights Watch says the vast majority of women killed under such circumstances are later found to be innocent of the accusations against them. There are indications that in some cases, honour wasn't at stake at all—that inheritance squabbles or family problems were actually the motive—but the killers exploit the legal precedent to get away with murder.

Though I was infuriated, I had to fight the urge to judge the entirety of the Middle East through this one lens. The truth was that women had made great strides in Arab countries, including Jordan, since I was a child; they were significantly more liberated and far less constrained than I remembered. Here was a country where an entire generation of educated, intelligent young women were entering the workforce, defying tradition, and taking their place in a society that had long shunted them aside. And yet every such killing—and every lenient sentence that absolved the murderers behind them—flew in the face of all their advancement, setting it back years.

My father's news weighed heavily on me, and I thought of how fortunate I had been, raised by open-minded parents and in Canada. There was never any doubt that I would attend university. I eventually moved away and lived on my own to further my education, working several part-time jobs to make it happen. I then travelled the world, free and unhindered. I now lived alone in the Middle East, made all my decisions for myself, and was free to leave at the time of my choosing. The vast majority who lived here—my cousins included—could not.

When I hung up after Dad's call, I wanted nothing more than to pack my bags and return permanently to the tolerant arms of Canada's coming winter. But I wanted to see my wars through.

⚥

In the U.S. president's vision, the liberation of Iraq was supposed to promote the spread of democracy throughout the Middle East, starting in Baghdad. Bush maintained that Iraq's example would inspire the rest to follow, just as, he said, Lebanon had begun to in 2005.

Years later, even Arab advocates of a democratic Middle East were despondent, adamant that the U.S. push for democracy had actually set back their efforts.

Many commentators agreed that while Bush might have been right about the desire for freedom among Arab people, he chose the wrong way of trying to bring it about, demonstrating a deep misunderstanding of their character. The modern Arab world largely views itself as both product and victim of Western meddling—even the borders were determined by colonial rulers seemingly blind to the complexities they introduced by drawing them the way they did. To a people long suspicious of the West, already scarred by war, and sensitive to anything that looked like occupation, Bush's Freedom Agenda looked a lot more like a self-serving crusade.

The pre-existing resentment against the U.S. didn't help. Arabs could not trust a superpower that had so consistently thrown its support behind Israel, to their constant chagrin. They also couldn't get their heads around a country claiming to bring freedom to a region ruled by despots it had steadfastly helped prop up.

There were other recent major missteps. Activists said the worst blow to their quest for democracy came with the Abu Ghraib scandal, which surfaced in 2004 when lurid photos revealed Iraqi prisoner abuse at the hands of rogue U.S. soldiers. The photos were damning—at exceptional odds with the rhetoric on encouraging democracy and human rights—and to many Arabs they were little different from the kind of torture some of them had suffered at the hands of their own regimes.

Then there was Iraq's civil war, its daily explosions as certain as the sunrise. There were the thousands upon thousands of deaths, the millions displaced, and Saddam's execution on the first day of an important religious holiday.

The remaining Mideast despots, whom the U.S. showed no interest in deposing, also showed no interest in changing themselves.

By 2009 the promised sea change in the rest of the region looked more and more remote and unattainable. With the exception of

Saddam's ouster, the political landscape remained ossified, seemingly with Washington's blessing. In Egypt in 2005, a cosmetic multi-party election gave President Hosni Mubarak both a landslide win and virtually a free hand to imprison and torture his critics. The much-hailed Saudi reform initiative was simply forgotten, and that nation's people were still kept down by two unelected authorities, one political and the other deeply religious. The Jordan First campaign withered along with the flags and slogans that rotted on the lampposts where they had been posted. Lebanon drifted back into Syria's orbit, and Syria hovered in Iran's—and both continued to actively stifle their people's demands for freedom.

There were some promising signposts. Iraqis did eventually hold that first free election in modern times in a former Arab dictatorship. Those images of ballot boxes and purple fingers we witnessed in person were beamed to Arab living rooms by the Arab networks. Iraqi society spawned independent newspapers, and its television news industry evolved at lightning speed. Former regime strongmen were tried in televised proceedings aimed at displaying the kind of transparency and fairness unknown in the region. But all those images paled in the face of the daily carnage, which suggested to many that the price of democracy was too high. Their own leaders did little to dissuade them from thinking so. They went further, painting reformists as pawns of the U.S. at every opportunity.

Pro-democracy activists despaired. If Iraq's free elections and Saddam's execution weren't enough to kick off the spread of democracy in the region, they reasoned, then nothing would. A costly opportunity for change had been squandered, their high hopes destroyed. Many of the ones I met in Saudi Arabia, Syria, Lebanon, and Jordan felt that decades of their work to promote freedom had been undone. In their view, the U.S.-led freedom campaign had been an utter failure.

Nitham, a middle-aged Jordanian reformist who ran an institute providing training sessions on human rights and democracy, was adamant that Arabs wanted freedom. But he acknowledged that making it reality under the current circumstances was a task akin to "hammering water"—in other words, utterly futile. This, he said, was not only because of the active stonewalling by Arab regimes, but also because of the perception of many Arab people that democracy was a Western—even American—concept, and therefore suspect. He told me that with every perceived U.S. misstep, like its position on the Lebanon conflict, getting Arabs to dissociate the idea of democracy from the Americans became next to impossible, keeping the region stuck in political backwardness.

Activists said repeatedly that to be legitimate and sustained, change in the Mideast could not be imposed from outside as Bush attempted to do. It *had* to come from within, tailor-made to each nation. And it had to come soon.

᯽

In Lebanon, anti-Syrian reform advocates had hoped that with the world seemingly in their corner, their country wouldn't again fall into the same maddening stasis. It seemed to many Lebanese and Syrians that after Syria's departure from Lebanon, the established and protected order might be crumbling at last.

That changed with the 2006 conflict between Hezbollah and Israel. Many Lebanese, even those opposed to Hezbollah and its weapons, were resentful of the U.S.'s continued support of the conflict despite the mounting civilian casualties. Secretary of State Condoleezza Rice said at the time that "a cessation of violence is crucial, but if that cessation of violence is hostage to Hezbollah's next decision to launch missiles into Israel ... then we will have gotten nowhere." The comment was widely criticized, and perceived by Lebanese and Arabs as a green light for Israel to continue bombing

Lebanon in the name of destroying Hezbollah—but at the expense of the entire country.

Asmaa, a young, articulate representative of the anti-Syrian voice and once a leading organizer of the March 14 protests, was one of those people. After the 2006 war ended, I met her in an empty Martyrs' Square, where just a year earlier, she had joined hundreds of thousands in bringing down the pro-Syrian government and forcing Syrian troops out.

"I think somehow we might have been taken for a ride," she said candidly. "There was a wave of support [in 2005], and it fitted their policy at the time. We were asking for words that ring well in the West: democracy and freedom and sovereignty," she said. "We were under the illusion that we were supported by the U.S. at the time, and I think that the round of war we've just been through proves that we weren't really, and we still aren't. The U.S. said they didn't want a ceasefire for a month, at which time we had one thousand people dead."

"I think in the ranks of the Arab liberals, there's been a lot of disappointment," Habib Malik, a Lebanese American University professor and my favourite analyst, explained in his sprawling Rabieh garden shortly after the Hezbollah–Israel conflict ended. "The rhetoric about democracy and freedom brought a lot of hope to liberal quarters of the Arab world, and then to see some of these setbacks happen is shocking. But I think this is where the United States can rectify the picture with some shrewd and prudent diplomacy now to actually push for peace."

It seemed too late, however, and certainly no one among those who were suspicious of the U.S. to begin with held out any hope. The Iraq and Lebanon conflicts had only reinforced their views, and groups that actively defied the West, like Hezbollah, only grew stronger and more popular throughout the region. In their view, the U.S. position on the conflict in Lebanon was evidence enough that there was nothing noble in its intentions, or in the so-called U.S. Greater Middle East Initiative, which was supposed to remake the Arab world. Much of the Mideast now tended to agree. Ask any man on the street why he thought Iraq had been invaded, and without blinking he'd say, "Oil." Few could be persuaded otherwise.

The lesson many took away was that Middle Eastern history always repeated itself, and that nothing could be had without violence—that (once again) change has proven dangerous, even fatal. That to hope was to bring on disaster.

The "Arab Spring" so many in the West had written about in the wake of Iraq's liberation in 2003 and Syria's departure from Lebanon in 2005 seemed already over. It was no surprise. If the Middle East excelled at anything, it was stagnation.

☥

There was, once, a so-called Damascus Spring. It came just after Syria's strongman president, Hafez al-Assad, died in 2000, before I'd arrived in the Middle East to work. With Hafez's U.K.–educated son Bashar as the new president, dissidents and intellectuals suddenly felt free from the usual, tyrannical constraints imposed by his father, and in a flurry of open gatherings, they brainstormed on how to lift the country out of its moribund state. But the spring was short-lived. Within just a few months, the regime restored the status quo and shut it all down, throwing many dissidents back in prison.

Syria's long winter began under the elder Assad, who'd built a police state par excellence starting with his "Corrective Revolution" coup in 1970. Assad was almost deified, his image kept Syrians company wherever they turned. Assad's Ba'ath Party was the ruling—and only—party, and you had to belong to get anywhere. The country was rife with intelligence agents who kept an ear out for dissident activity, and its prisons were fearsome and deadly.

Like pre-war Iraq, Syria was stuck in its own bizarre, outdated world, the country resistant to change and disdainful of foreign opinions on its internal matters. Perhaps one of the most staunchly Arab of all the countries of the region, Syria under the Assads was still a champion of the old nationalist project and a fierce—if purely rhetorical—advocate of "resisting" Israel and the West. The regime, even under the young Assad, blamed everything on the U.S. and Israel: Hariri's killing, the uprising in Lebanon, the dissident activity inside its own borders—they were all, apparently, the result of foreign meddling. The younger Assad tried to maintain his father's carefully constructed regional balance, which allied the country to the even more intransigent Iran while keeping cordial relations with other Arab countries. Damascus also supported groups like Hamas and Hezbollah, yet occasionally quietly negotiated peace with Israel over the Golan Heights.

And yet the threat of renewed hostilities with Israel was used to justify the endless state of emergency that had allowed Syrian authorities to violate people's most basic rights since 1963.

Officially, Syria was a united nation, its people madly loyal to their leader and believers in his vision. In reality, it was always divided, both politically and along class and sectarian lines. Its citizens include Catholic and Orthodox Christians, Kurds, and Druze. The vast majority of the population, though, are increasingly religious Sunni Muslims. The Assads, meanwhile, are Alawites, a minority sect with some similarities to Shia Islam. Among its people are some of the poorest in the region, yet also some of the richest—glaring evidence of the wide gap between its classes. Unsurprisingly, Syria was then home to a corruption problem among its low-level, poorly paid officials. Just one other reason behind the people's deep hatred of the Assads and anyone in their service, one of an infinite number of reasons why millions of Syrians have left to live abroad.

Damascus was only a couple of hours by road from Beirut, and I travelled there several times a year throughout my time in the Mideast. Every time I was struck by the yawning gulf between the Ba'ath Party's reality and that of ordinary people. In the middle were Syria's reformists—the unofficial, unsanctioned opposition— some of the most sophisticated I had met anywhere. Now here was hope, in the form of intelligent, articulate, and courageous critics. At the time I thought that with such able help, Syria would be among the first in the region to modernize, reform, move forward.

Over the years, I met dozens of reformers, but some of the first were members of the al-Bunni family. By 2005 the al-Bunnis had served, between them, some sixty years in prison (though I suspect that number is higher now, as two of the brothers have been imprisoned again). I met Akram al-Bunni, a writer and reformist, that year. By then, he had spent a total of seventeen years in Assad's prisons, and had permanent back problems because of the torture he'd endured for the crime of belonging to a communist party. Even his wife had been arrested. We met at his home just days after he, along with 139 other intellectuals, boldly signed a public letter advising Bashar al-Assad to withdraw from Lebanon. It was just a week after Hariri was killed.

"It is futile to insist upon outdated political means of dealing with crises," said the letter. "If this initiative is implemented today ... the excuses of external [elements] will be overcome."

It was a risky undertaking, but at al-Bunni's house that night, the gathered reformists were upbeat. For years they had worked behind the scenes for change, and they felt that the increased international pressure on Syria in light of Hariri's murder had presented the opportunity they'd been waiting for. "Syria has no more cards to play," al-Bunni told me. "If Syria stays [in Lebanon], it will mean increasing violence and sanctions. It means the road to democracy is obstructed and change is postponed."

But the regime didn't want change, and instead it sanctioned protests in Damascus that week blaming the same old bogeymen. We came upon two such demos—one mounted by state "journalists" and the other by members of the public, predictably wiping their shoes on American and Israeli flags. "Resistance is the only choice," one of the protesters told me. "War is written for the U.S., and resistance is written for us."

Shortly after Hariri was killed, I interviewed then information minister Buthaina Shaaban, who said demands for Syria's withdrawal from Lebanon harboured a hidden agenda. "The issue is neither the presence of the Syrian troops nor intelligence," she said. "The issue is to extend the chaos in the region to Syria and Lebanon, and to forget about the Israeli occupation of our lands."

In June 2005, the regime began to show some willingness to change. Zouheir and I travelled to Damascus to cover a major Ba'ath Party conference to review its policies, and, apparently, to introduce much-needed reforms. Bashar al-Assad claimed the conference would mark a great leap forward for his country, and would even introduce freedoms for political parties to develop and participate in elections. None of those promises materialized. Syrians were not surprised.

The reformists persisted, and later that year an even larger group of them signed what they called the Damascus Declaration. This was even bolder: it was a scathing rebuke of the human rights situation in Syria, of the lack of freedom, of the absence of a free press. It labelled the regime authoritarian, totalitarian, and cliquish. The signatories called for the establishment of a democratic national regime and set out a plan for making it a reality. They also demanded the release of all political prisoners. Akram al-Bunni was both one of the signatories and a member of the council that conceived it. He and eleven others were arrested and eventually imprisoned for "weakening national sentiment" and "damaging the state."

In 2006 came yet another declaration on the Lebanon situation—this one much more damning than the first polite letter, and co-signed by the Syrian Muslim Brotherhood, a group reviled by the regime. That landed Akram's brother, Anwar, a five-year sentence. Anwar was a well-known human rights lawyer who'd already caught the regime's unkindly attention many times before.

The al-Bunni family had taken the brunt of the regime's allergy to criticism, but there were many more prisoners of conscience, some of Syria's brightest languishing in the country's most notorious prisons. Akram al-Bunni and many others served time at Tadmor (or Palmyra in English), a feared institution that reportedly couldn't be more at odds with the sleepy little town it was named after. I once visited the ancient city of Palmyra, whose breathtaking, tourist-friendly ruins are its modern claim to fame. But there was no way I could ever see the prison—short of getting arrested and sentenced to serve time there.

The best insight I would have into the conditions in Syria's prisons was actually from former Lebanese inmates who'd served time in Tadmor, as well as Sidnaya, another infamous slammer. It was in Beirut that we actually got a small glimpse into the kind of torture they liked to administer. In the seaside West Beirut neighbourhood of Jnah, the Beau Rivage, originally a hotel, was the headquarters of Syrian intelligence in Lebanon, and it was opened for visitors shortly after the Syrians withdrew in 2005. A nearby building with a sea view housed a basement holding centre where Lebanese were routinely tortured. We saw for ourselves the grimy holding cells and the iron bars from which to hang prisoners from the ceiling—little different from Saddam's torture houses back in Baghdad.

I met Munir al-Masri at a small protest near a UN building in

downtown Beirut shortly after the Syrians left. Until then, disappeared Lebanese who'd been shipped to Syrian prisons had been a
sensitive and taboo subject. Now protests demanding their return
had become regular, and the number of those reported missing
was rising. Activists organized an open-ended sit-in in downtown
Beirut, demanding to know their fate. They hung pictures of the
missing around a tent on the grounds of the UN building.

In 1987, al-Masri was arrested in Lebanon, accused he said, of
bombing Syrian positions, a charge he denies. He was first taken
to the Ottoman city of Anjar, where he was hung upside down and
whipped with electrical wires to "confess." He was then transferred
to Syria. There he was moved from prison to prison for eleven
months. At every stop, he said he received a welcome beating. At
his final destination, Sidnaya, he received five hundred lashes on
admission. In the end he served four and a half years, with one
stint in solitary that lasted forty-five days. When he finally returned
home, no one could believe he was still alive.

Though only in his forties, al-Masri moved like an old man
because of repeated injury. He refused to take off his sunglasses,
which served to hide the scars and bloodshot eyes. "Every day you
had to have a beating, until you say yes, just to stop the torture,"
he said. "That's in addition to the illnesses, the lice, the smell—
and the psychological torture you had to endure." Another man we
met, Nader Suleiman, spent ten years in a Syrian jail. He said that
as a result of years of torture, he still has nightmares. He sleeps in a
room alone so he can spare his family his screaming at night.

A few days after meeting them, I attended a Maronite church
service in Al Hadath, where hundreds of people had gathered for
an annual remembrance of another man who'd gone missing—
only this one had yet to return, fifteen years after he was snatched.
Albert Cherfane was a priest, and no one knew why the Syrians
took him. His niece Thérèse was certain he was still alive. If so, he

would be seventy years old. "He's like our father, and we will never let him stay there. Even if he will live just one more day, he will live it with us."

In Syria, families who'd lost members in much the same way couldn't contemplate having such conversations, let alone with foreign journalists. Criticism of the state was forbidden, period. And if your son was lifted by the authorities and stowed away in some godforsaken prison, you'd be lucky just to know which one it was.

On every visit, I tried to reflect those challenges in one way or another in our pieces. It wasn't easy. Notwithstanding the coldly cordial bureaucrats at the Information Ministry, the authorities were generally disdainful of and even hostile to the foreign press, especially television networks. Most of the time we could not work without minders, and if we did, we risked getting thrown out or worse. Zouheir and I were once detained, roughly handled, and loudly dressed down by a police official as if we were criminals. Thanks to Hussein's quick action, the Information Ministry intervened and got us out. I had interviewed the minister the day before, and that probably saved us from hours of unpleasant interrogation. Still, our tape was confiscated. Our offence? Filming a poster of the Assads that happened to be hanging on the outside of a police station.

Despite the restrictions, over the years I did meet many young, educated Syrians who walked in the dangerous footsteps of the al-Bunnis and others who had sacrificed so much in the name of freedom—among them bloggers, citizen journalists, human rights activists, and democracy advocates. One memorable evening on one of our trips, I had the privilege of sitting among a large group of them, and these young people were unafraid to tell me precisely what they thought. They said they were tired of having to look abroad for opportunities and freedoms they should have at home. They were weary of having every book sold to them vetted by the state. They'd had enough of slow, restricted Internet services, and of having to pay bribes to get things done. They also told me that without change, Syria risked turmoil—that the simmering anger could explode anytime. Most of all, they said they'd had enough of the past haunting their future.

Many of those brave enough to speak the truth to me in Syria agreed that the regime relied on historical grudges for its survival. In modern Syria, it meant change was elusive. It meant fifteen million Syrians lived abroad, having escaped the inertia or been exiled because they challenged it. It meant citizens who remained were forever imprisoned by lack of advancement, lack of openness, lack of opportunity, lack of a voice. Religion, I was repeatedly told, was an increasingly popular antidote for the masses. The growing number of niqabs and gloves among women in the Hamidiah souk in old Damascus was, too, a silent form of protest.

In Syria that past simply wouldn't recede or fade, so long as its haunting losses remained unresolved, so long as those most affected weren't given the means to move on, and especially, so long as a tyrannical regime used that history to control the lives of Syrians today.

⚘

Just before the fortieth anniversary of the 1967 war, I travelled to the Golan Heights to try to capture the magnitude of what had happened during those crucial six days. It wasn't easy to visit what remained of the Golan under Syrian control. You had to apply for permission, and generally, as a journalist, you could go only on Fridays, when Syrian Golanis often went to picnic and recall better days. Armed with my reading on the war and a few chats with prominent experts on its impact, we made our way southwest.

It was a fine, sunny spring day, and it was easy to see why both Syrians and Israelis laid claim to the Heights. The air is exceptionally clear, like that of Vancouver Island after a sprinkling of rain. The horizon is vast, the green rolling hills almost devout in their silence. Across the border, the only structures visible for miles were a couple of buildings that kept watch, each with a different flag. The two countries that straddled this border were, despite the ceasefires and the occasional secret negotiations, still substantively at war.

Syrians who had once called the Golan Heights home still came to visit the truncated area. They came just to breathe the air they grew up breathing—balm for their souls, they said—and to teach their children to yearn for it, too.

In the city of Quneitra we came upon the Youssef family in a lovely spot under the shade of a large tree in the midst of a blanket of green grass, where they were just starting to prepare lunch. The children roamed freely nearby. Some of the older ones played a game of pickup soccer, while the younger ones amused themselves with horseplay. "For them it's just a trip," one mother said, gesturing at the children. "But for the older ones, we know the history."

The family came from Mughair, a village a mere three kilometres from where they sat. The oldest woman, Um Abdo, remembers how families escaped the fighting by running away on foot. Many of them ended up sheltering in schools in Damascus, lost in the big city, hoping to get back to their villages in a couple of weeks. But eventually they settled into a life in exile, never quite getting used to the city. That's why they still come back to the Golan. "We never forget. We can die and come back and we will still not forget," she said, gesturing with henna-inscribed hands. "We tell the children how we lived, and how it was. They remember it as if they were living with us." *Like a family heirloom passed from one generation to the next.*

One of the men, Ali, spoke up next. "The Golan is my life, my home, my everything," he said. "What was our mistake? What did all these people do to lose their homes, to lose everything?"

I asked if he'd heard about the possibility of Turkey brokering negotiations between Syria and Israel over the Golan's fate. "I watch the news always, hoping we get good news. We don't know exactly when, but we are sure we will go back to our village."

The war had long been over, but the disappointment lingered in thousands of homes all over Syria—and Egypt, Jordan, Lebanon, and beyond. It pervaded every facet of life, freezing many Arabs and their regimes in time, in a constant lament for the past and a paralyzing fear of the future.

On the Syrian side of the Golan Heights, it meant that forty years later, the city of Quneitra was still exactly as it looked when it was destroyed in the fighting with Israeli forces in 1967. A city of remembrance permanently frozen in the past.

It was among its flattened buildings that the children now played. The broken roofs made a perfect slide. The overgrown crevices inside a collapsed house were perfect for a game of hide-and-seek. The children were just playing. But ultimately, their horseplay here during some of the most impressionable years of their lives was anything but a game. It was another lesson in displacement, and in the consequences of war.

☙

In this region, conflicts always overshadow all else; they alone make the headlines. And only the parties to such conflict can have the spotlight—the fighters, the extremists, the politicians, and occasionally, the liberals or the reformists. Everyone else is largely ignored—by the media, by peace brokers, by their own governments. They appeared in our stories when they became caught up in or displaced by one of the conflicts—otherwise they played a minor role as members of that vast sea of people we called ordinary civilians. During the seven years I spent in the Middle East, I sometimes managed to fleetingly reflect their presence in the news pieces that drove my mandate or the occasional feature. But they were not "the story" very often. Their mundane, daily struggle of simply living in today's Middle East was always overshadowed by the region's spikes of violence, which got all the attention.

My final year in the Mideast was consumed instead with election campaigns, and there were a few coming up—in Israel, Lebanon, and Iran—any of which could determine the direction of the region for the next few years. In the meantime, I was also busy planning my exit.

The original plan had been to spend two or maybe three years in the Middle East. It was so temporary in my mind that I did the bare minimum to facilitate my life there, even when my stay became longer. I made few friends—never wanting to get too close—and put down few roots. I also repeatedly put off taking care of my health. For years I had ignored the nightmares, the near-daily replay of that violent day in Baghdad, my ongoing disbelief that I actually survived. I acted as though I was only role-playing. It was all temporary. None of it was real.

In the intervening years, real life had leaped ahead back home. Friends married, had children, and moved on. My parents became grandparents. Two cherished colleagues and friends died. Early in 2009, I was starting my seventh year in the region, and I suddenly realized this had been no interlude. Those years were a significant part of my life.

Belatedly, I scrambled to make the best of my final few weeks in Beirut. I spent time at the beach under the sun, walked along the Corniche, went out at night—things I had done only occasionally in the years I spent there. I attended the summer music festivals for the first time. I even saw Fairouz live and watched thousands of people revelling in the moment. Though they knew their peace was temporary, they made the best of it. And that made them much better at living than I had been.

In those last few weeks, I also took a farewell journey to Syria. Despite my affinity to Beirut and Baghdad for all the memories I had made in those places, Damascus was ultimately my favourite Arab city, and though I never lived there, it felt like a third home after all my visits. For the first time since I had arrived in the region in 2002, I wandered for hours in Souk Al Hamidiyah—the souk that sold everything—unencumbered by deadlines or the news. It was Ramadan, and the warm, conversational evenings stretched late into the night, the atmosphere kept alive by the old city's whirling dervishes and singers who exulted in the holy month's return. Damascus was a city of long history, the oldest continually inhabited city in the world. Somehow, its winding, ancient alleys, its ornate, Ottoman-era Christian quarter homes, the splendid mosaic and inlaid wood works of art, always helped me put things in perspective.

For all the time I'd spent predicting the next misfortune, I'd spent a greater amount of time looking for any indication that all the despair I had witnessed would somehow be washed away or given some meaning. In those last few months, I'd also spent a great deal of time trying to persuade the CBC to keep the Beirut bureau open. The modern Arab world story was just beginning, I argued. But the decision was made, mostly for financial reasons. I spent days packing up my library of hundreds of tapes to ship abroad. Seven years' worth packed up in boxes then suddenly gone.

In Israel, the right-wing Likud government eventually prevailed. In Lebanon, unsurprisingly, the March 14 coalition, now led by Saad Hariri, defeated Hezbollah and its allies in the 2009 election. Months later, over more discord, the Hezbollah ministers resigned, bringing down Hariri's government. The opposition took over. The status quo had once again been restored. And not only in Lebanon.

ᛉ

Near the end of my time in the region, I realized a longstanding dream: visiting Iran for the first time. Stephanie, Margaret, Pascal (our cameraman), and I arrived in Tehran a week before the presidential election in June 2009. It appeared that Iran was on the verge of astounding change.

Like the rest of the region, Iran had a population dominated by young people, most of whom had known the country only as an Islamic, authoritarian state closed to the rest of the world and plagued by religious and political restrictions that were among the most draconian. The young Iranians were, perhaps, some of the most politically active in the region. Protests, often originating at the universities, were certainly not unknown in Iran, but they were usually quickly shut down and, as a result, mostly unknown to the rest of the world.

Yet the opposition rallies we witnessed contradicted all that. In the pre-election gatherings, we saw echoes of the protests I'd witnessed in Beirut just after Hariri died. Hopeful young men and women organized themselves through Facebook and SMS messages, adamant it was time for Iran to break President Mahmoud Ahmadinejad's hold, and perhaps, even that of the clerics who controlled every aspect of their lives. They held nightly rallies, chanting for change, while good-naturedly jostling with the pro-Ahmadinejad supporters who'd come out to make their voices heard, too.

Mir-Hossein Mousavi, an artist and once part of the establishment, seemed to be the front-runner among the opposition, and his supporters adopted green as their colour. At one of the rallies, a young woman presented each of us with a green ribbon and a smile, both symbols of the optimism she and so many other women felt.

"It appears that an earthquake, a flood, an avalanche is coming,"

Sadegh Zibakalam, a Tehran university professor, told me. "We are surprised, we are baffled, but it is coming."

The opposition candidates also experienced a modicum of freedom that they didn't enjoy in non-election periods, when the world's media were gone and no one could be held publicly accountable for shutting down dissent. Mousavi and his wife were generous with their criticism of Ahmadinejad and his erratic leadership. They, along with so many of the young men and women we met, told us they were tired of being isolated, tired of Iran being the world's pariah. They believed the upcoming vote was their chance to begin to change that.

Zahra Rahnavard, Mousavi's wife, a sculptor and a professor, was playing a prominent role in her husband's campaign. She granted us an interview in which she, too, said it was time for "a great change." "It's time to improve Iran's image abroad, and fix all that's wrong on the homefront," she said. "We'll work on the economy and unemployment across the country, and freedom of speech."

Voting day came on June 12, and hopes remained high among the opposition—until the results started coming in. Almost immediately after polls closed, it was clear Ahmadinejad had a decisive advantage. The opposition insisted the polls had been tampered with. It was all so familiar. Only in Iran, in 2009, the streets came alive with fury as a result.

Over the next two days, we witnessed some of the protests and the disproportionate response from the state. Protesters marched where they could, setting garbage bins alight and cursing Ahmadinejad's name. The regime's backers came out in force, including the feared Basij, armed volunteer goons in civilian clothes and on motorcycles fiercely loyal to the regime. We were witnessing the start of what was perhaps the most serious challenge to Ahmadinejad's rule since he first became president in 2005.

But with the election over, there was no more patience for criticism, or for the presence of foreign journalists. We were denied an extension to our visa, and I regretfully made my way back to Beirut to cover the protests from a distance as they gained strength.

Yet as the number of foreign journalists in Tehran dwindled, information about the growing protests still kept flowing. Savvy youth captured video on their cellphones and uploaded it on the Internet for the whole world to watch. Twitter and Facebook lit up with minute-by-minute updates on the protesters, their whereabouts, the numbers, the viciously fierce response by the authorities. It wasn't ideal, but with such access, the news cycle kept making room for the story, and I kept filing, tethered to my computer in Beirut, as Stephanie was to hers in London, conversing with people from the opposition whom we had met while in Tehran. In the region, it was a first—and the Arab world kept a close watch.

Who would have imagined that day after day, young men and women would keep coming back to face down one of the most repressive regimes in the world, even when it started accusing them of being mobilized by "foreign hands," and even when its security apparatus started using live ammunition against them? Who in the region could have imagined anyone caring much for a bunch of youth trying to bring attention to the oppression in which they lived? They, now, were the kind of underdogs the people of this region loved cheering for. The Arab media lauded them as brave and steadfast. Arab youth, especially, took notes.

The protests went on for weeks. But in the end, the youthful uprising was no match for the determined security forces, and after several months, the Green Revolution was snuffed out. Mousavi was put under house arrest. Ahmadinejad was confirmed as president on August 5. It was the last story I filed before moving back to Canada.

So much had happened over seven years, yet so little had actually changed.

Just days before I left Lebanon for good, I dropped in with some friends to see Habib one more time. It was a good night, and nearly every table was full. Habib looked satisfied, came around the bar as he always did, and gave me the usual big hug.

"Habibti inti," he said, beaming. *You're a dear. Don't leave!*

He also revealed that he was closing the place and moving. I was happy for him but sad that this place, where I had spent some of my best and worst nights, just trying to understand, would no longer exist. I told him I would always visit. I knew that although I was leaving a city that had broken my heart, I could never leave it for good.

Abbas warmed up his oud, and the crowd fell silent as they waited for the nostalgia to ooze from its strings. He launched the evening with a rendition of "Wadah Hawak," a melancholy classic by Egyptian singer Mohammed Abd Al Muttalib. *Wadah hawak.* Say goodbye to your love. What has gone will never return.

Close to 3 a.m., only a handful of us were left and Abbas packed up and left. Habib put on his retro CD and his reading glasses, and happily tallied his earnings behind the bar, drink at the ready. His television was on, tuned once again to Fashion TV.

A few days later, Hussein drove me to the airport, and I bade him farewell. On the Middle East airlines jet, an instrumental version of a Fairouz song played in the background. *"Nihna wil amar Jeeran,"*—we and the moon are neighbours. I sat back, closed my eyes, and left Beirut and its moonlit nights behind.

TWELVE

Watch Egypt

Nothing wipes your tear
but your hand.
—ARAB PROVERB

LONDON, DECEMBER 31, 2010

It had been just over a year since I left the Middle East, and my transition back to Canada had, once again, been a difficult one. The truth was that much as I was relieved to finally be out of the Middle East, I missed it terribly. I barely changed my habit of reading all I could about the latest twists and turns—yet no longer were there many around as eager as I still was to discuss it all. Worse, there was no manual on "reintegration," no guide to re-teach you how to navigate life in Canada after nearly a decade of absence. In the first few weeks I was taken aback by the slightest obstacle. I, who had made a living out of traversing difficult borders, at covering conflicts of all kinds, at cutting through the thickest layers of Arab bureaucracy, was stymied getting a driver's licence, reduced to tears over problems with the health insurance company. Most of all I missed the sense of purpose that working in the Mideast gave me. I felt lost and aimless, not quite depressed but far, very far, from happy. Admittedly, coming home was what I needed—I was grounded again and the symptoms of the stresses of living in a troubled zone subsided completely. But I often felt stifled and imprisoned, even though I travelled enough to keep at bay the feeling I had given up one big world for a much smaller one.

Watching the midnight fireworks with friends in central London on New Year's Eve brought much-needed relief. That Christmas, I had been asked at the last minute to cover for a colleague, and I could never say no to London, where the whole world is compressed into one gargantuan city, happily nestled within reach of two of my worlds, Canada and the Middle East. The painful reality of cost-cutting in journalism had meant the closure of foreign bureaus and less frequent travel. Although it was far from ideal, we often had to make do with covering a large portion of the planet from London. Within a few days of arriving, I had reported on events in the Ivory Coast, Egypt, and Iran without taking a single flight.

But Tunisia, a country I'd never visited, was dominating the news. Large protests were racking several of its towns and villages, and from thousands of miles away we struggled to understand precisely why. When the story of a one-man protest in the poor Tunisian village of Sidi Bouzid surfaced, I understood instantly.

Mohamed Bouazizi was twenty-six years old, and he had apparently just started trying to make a living selling produce out of a cart. He was one of the millions of the region's discouraged majority youth population who tried to make do despite little opportunity. On December 17, local police harassed him for not having a licence to sell on the street. They slapped him around, as local police do in those parts, and confiscated his produce. Humiliated and clearly at the end of his tether, he carried out a desperate one-man protest: he set himself on fire. And by so doing, he single-handedly ignited the tinderbox that was his generation.

Brisk protests and heavy clashes spread steadily throughout Tunisia, led by angry, unfocused young men and women who openly called for the regime's downfall. They were treated to tear gas, then rubber bullets, and eventually live ammunition—true to the traditions of Arab police states.

But a few days into the new year, the story began to deviate from the usual, tired plot. The protesters wouldn't be quelled and kept up their rebellion, despite the increasingly violent authoritarian response. The old formula was no longer working: the tougher the regime's tactics, the more people joined the protests and the more fervent their anger. They used Twitter and Facebook to mobilize more of the like-minded, and to stay a step ahead of the authorities. They captured the brutality on cellphone video and posted the footage online. The president, Zine al-Abidine Ben Ali, then appeared on television to address them, claiming, "I understood you." Brien Christie, our assignment editor, prescient as always, pushed us to pay more attention. Perhaps we should go?

Bouazizi then succumbed to his substantial injuries.

The youth who clashed with police chanted his name as though he were a freedom fighter or a war hero. I doubt any of them had ever heard Bouazizi speak, let alone seen him in the flesh. No one knew his political philosophy, if he even had one. No one was compelled to go to the streets by the way he carried himself. Nor did he impress them, like some of the region's leaders tried to, by wearing pseudo-military garb or brandishing a weapon for effect. But it didn't matter. Those agonizing days he survived, he was branded a living "martyr." In death he became a victim, the kind of underdog that Arabs loved cheering for, someone in whom they could see themselves. And with a single act of self-immolation, he'd done what no self-styled leader in the Middle East had managed in decades: he'd ignited the passions of young people and mobilized them into action.

That was seemingly beyond the capability of the likes of Ben Ali, the country's autocrat president of the past thirty years—despite the endless billboard-sized likenesses; the flowery rhetorical speeches designed to glorify, to deify, to command loyalty; the ribbon cuttings and visits to orphanages and girls' schools to show he cared for the common man. One of Ben Ali's most recent photo opportunities was of an ill-advised visit to the hospital to see Bouazizi—who was wrapped from head to toe with gauze—in an attempt to show he "understood." When Bouazizi eventually expired, the picture disappeared from Ben Ali's website, where it had been prominently placed. On television, he appeared with new concessions—all of which fell short of the protesters' demands—until he, too, disappeared from view as the protests glowed with anger.

As more and more pictures emerged of the country's enraged youth, Ben Ali, a long-time U.S. ally, suddenly looked ridiculous: the dyed hair, the forced smile, the flat speeches about his sacrifices for the country. Even seen from as far away as London, Ben Ali, like so many of the region's leaders, seemed entirely out of touch with his people.

The youth pressed on, and the crowds grew even bigger and reached the capital. They in turn inspired doctors, teachers, government workers of all ages to join in—they were all Bouazizi, and they, too, stood up to the increasingly baffled riot police. In clip after clip I viewed in the safety of our office in London, protesters repeatedly said that the "fear was gone."

In all my time in the Arab world, I'd never heard a single person say that.

I, too, began to feel that Tunisia's New Year protests signalled a rupture, a shift in a region better known for standing still.

In the face of such momentum, Ben Ali's belated concessions were simply not enough. Before we had managed to make a move, the president's regime crumbled and he stepped down, fleeing with his wife to Saudi Arabia. I filed the story from London.

It was January 14, 2011. Minutes after the news of his fall hit the wire, my mind was working a hundred miles a minute and I urgently called Brien.

"Watch Egypt," I said.

ℵ

If you take the right flight to Cairo, you might just spot that symbol of Arab independence glistening in the distance, in the distinctive shape of the Suez Canal, the narrow strait that was national-ized by former Egyptian president Gamal Abdel Nasser in 1956, feeding Arab pride and making him a national hero. A few minutes later—if you're sitting on the correct side of the plane—you might just glide over the pyramids, monuments to just one chapter of a glorious past. As the plane descends and approaches the edge of the city, you move along with the thousand-year march of Islam in Egypt: hundreds of mosques wave at you with their minarets, their domes stolid and unmoveable—symbols of a different kind of rebellion today. On the way to the final approach to the airport, the twenty-first century rushes beneath you in the form of tens of thousands of satellite dishes staring up from virtually every rooftop, beaming the world into living rooms where two out of every five women are still illiterate.

Cairo at once inspires and infuriates. It's a monstrous, polluted metropolis of an estimated seventeen million people crammed mostly into crumbling concrete tenements that always seem on the verge of collapse. They occasionally do collapse, claiming the lives of their wretchedly poor inhabitants. The buildings that remain standing defy gravity, despite age and poor construction, and despite the sheer weight of the huge families that inhabit them, even on the roofs. The city is as vast as it is oppressive, its streets a terrifying tidal wave of cars and pedestrians always at risk of injury or worse. Fat Mercedes sedans sporting tinted windows mingle perilously with the occasional donkey cart piled high with grain and vegetables; hundreds of mobile phone outlets stand elbow to elbow with *eish* bakeries—the ubiquitous purveyors of Egypt's most basic necessity—where in recent years people have been forced into long lineups just to get their daily bread.

Cairo's soul is embodied in the Nile's majestic shimmer in its midst, the palm trees that watch over it, the proudly poised pyramids, and its humble and boisterously humorous people. Still, it is a wasteland of sorts: dirty, dusty, and stupidly hot in the summer, and inexplicably poor given that Egypt is the second-largest recipient of U.S. aid after Israel. And if I had been under the illusion that Baghdad was the region's corruption capital, then Cairo was surely its epicentre and place of birth: little got done without *baksheesh*. Large-scale corruption was said to infect everyone, from the family of President Hosni Mubarak all the way down to the traffic police who manned the streets and guarded the airport (openly asking for a tip as they scanned your luggage). And like Baghdad, Cairo was ruled by an elaborate bureaucracy, gaudily festooned with red tape.

For decades Egypt was a significant exporter of cheap labour. Young and old sought work throughout the Middle East in construction, restaurants, and hotels, sending their money home to relatives or perhaps to be put aside for marriage (such an expensive proposition in modern Egypt that many young men have to delay it repeatedly until they can afford it). But Egypt had better-known exports. It had long been the trendsetter, the military and political beacon of the Arab region, the birthplace of most of its big ideas. It was the home of the Arab League. And it was a rich source of thinkers, writers, and scholars who helped shape the Middle East's modern psyche.

Egypt was also the region's long-time musical and cinematic hub. The early films my grandmother watched, shot in black and white, were surprisingly current and strikingly similar to Western films of the time in orchestral arrangements, feel, and fashion. Many were musicals, featuring the moment's hottest artists—Farid al-Atrash and sister Asmahan (originally Syrian), Abdel Wahab, Layla Murad—backed by a chorus of beautiful, provocatively dressed women and men who mingled and danced freely together. They lived in beautiful villas filled with ornate furniture, servants, horses, and automobiles; wine was drunk from crystal glasses under glimmering chandeliers. In those films, life was grand and unapologetically colonial in feel. The 1944 film *Gharam wa Intiqam* (Love and Revenge) could have easily been a British or French film: Asmahan sings and fans herself with feathers, while men in morning suits and women in debutante gowns waltz across a stage to the tune of an Arabic song incongruously titled "Merry Nights in Vienna." It is still considered a classic.

Later, when colour made its debut, Egyptian films took on a more Arab flavour, but they retained the irreverence and light-heartedness. The genius of Al-Atrash and Abdel Wahab at playing the oud overshadowed any roles they took on, and Abdel Halim Hafez's velvety voice made unrequited love a state for which to yearn.

But nothing that Egypt ever exported before or after would rival the influence of Oum Kolthoum's voice. During my mother's teenage years, Oum Kolthoum gave monthly concerts that were broadcast live on radio throughout the Middle East. Her physical and aural presence was overwhelming, looming large on screen, on stage, and on the airwaves. Her brassy voice was incomparable, so forceful it was too much for most microphones and she was forced to stand back from them when she sang. Her lamentations of love, borrowed from some of the best Arab poets, drove listeners to near hysteria. Grown men attending her concerts would get out of their seats and scream and whistle, sometimes interrupting the musicians, who would be forced to start over, if only for the benefit of the recording. Her singing moved people to tears, to *tarab*, a word that is so inadequately translated that it is impossible to give its proper significance in English. It is a state of exultation, glee, heightened enjoyment particular to listeners of Arab or Middle Eastern music; people close their eyes and swoon, moving to the lilt, raising their arms to sway with the flirtatious quarter tones that define Arabic music. Oum Kolthoum's concerts were huge, but her death brought millions to the streets. She is still revered as Kawkab al-Sharq, the Star of the East, her music sold, played, sung, and imitated around the Middle East as if she had just given her last live concert yesterday. You couldn't walk a block in Cairo's streets without hearing her soaring voice.

Oum Kolthoum was Egyptian, and Egypt was Oum el Kul— the Mother of All—the Arab world's star. It was the cradle of Arab nationalism and the carrier of its mantle, the centre of the Arab world's universe.

And yet Cairo is also the city of a thousand minarets, a religious hub, the birthplace of modern Islamist thinking. Only Cairo is capable of being all that at once. It is home to Al-Azhar, the Sunni Muslim world's highest authority, a mosque and university rolled into one. It is where many of the region's notable Muslim scholars trained, and from which much of the current thinking about Islam stems.

In modern Egypt, extremist Islamists were always present— Egypt is, after all, the home of Ayman al-Zawahiri, Osama bin Laden's deputy. It was also the birthplace of the Muslim Brotherhood, in 1928. While the rest of the region was still flirting with the idea of pan-Arabism, the Muslim Brotherhood espoused a more ambitious pan-Islamic world, in which god ruled supreme and the Koran was the sole legal, political, and spiritual foundation. Its founder, Hassan al-Banna, called on Egyptians to re-embrace their religion and reject Western influence. The group also founded a military arm that carried out attacks and assassinations to further their goals. As a result, the Brotherhood was outlawed as early as the 1940s, its members at risk of imprisonment or worse. Al-Banna himself was assassinated in 1949.

The Brotherhood's influence grew in the years after 1967—along with the influence of Islam as a whole—when the nationalist dream faltered. The group attracted a serious following among a people disillusioned with an entrenched secular leadership that ignored their needs and left them powerless. Though its military element continued to be linked to bombings and attacks—and an offshoot was blamed for the assassination of President Anwar Sadat in 1981—more recently, the Brotherhood's mainstream elements espoused non-violent means of achieving democracy. They were confident a free vote in Egypt would easily catapult them into power.

By 2005, when Mubarak ran in a multi-candidate election for the first time since he became president, Islam was a dominant force in Egyptian society, and the banned Muslim Brotherhood was, hands down, the country's most popular party—and his most feared enemy.

ℵ

In August 2005, cameraman Zouheir Bizri and I arrived to an Egypt in full election campaign swing. Mubarak, known to Egyptians as Baba (father) Hosni, appeared nightly on the state broadcaster to showcase all he had done for Egypt. Baba Hosni was reaching out to an electorate slightly baffled at being wooed by a man who'd never before given them a choice. For many citizens, that alone made the entire enterprise suspect.

Like many of Egypt's recent leaders, Mubarak started his career in the military, then later became a pilot who was noted in campaigns against Israel. He eventually became chief of the air force and vice president under his predecessor, Anwar Sadat, whose assassination Mubarak witnessed. As president, he distinguished

himself as a cunning, staunch ally of the U.S., and as a kind of
regional godfather, often mediating between Palestinians and Israel
and others. Little went on in the region without his input.

At home, Mubarak derived most of his power from the military,
which had also been the source and protector of the two presidents who preceded him. Egypt had also been in an official state of
emergency since 1981, the year Sadat was assassinated and Mubarak
assumed the presidency. He renewed martial law every three years
thereafter, arguing that terrorism continued to pose a threat.
Indeed, there were sporadic attacks attributed to Islamists within
Egypt, many of them against foreigners, especially in the 1990s
and mid-2000s. Mubarak had also survived no fewer than six assassination attempts himself. But the emergency law also made it easy
to arrest and indefinitely detain ordinary citizens without charge,
to deny individuals' basic human rights and curtail freedoms of
speech and the press. Egypt was a country where military courts
were the norm and critics were routinely and brutally silenced.
Mubarak's mantra was stability—at any cost.

It was normally infuriatingly difficult for us to work in Cairo.
If we weren't harassed at the airport by officials who panicked the
moment they saw our array of equipment, then policemen on the
streets would constantly stop us and ask our business. Thankfully,
Osama, our long-time fixer, knew his way around the irritating
obstacles of working in his country. Otherwise, I don't think I
would have filed a single story from Egypt.

But on the eve of elections, we worked relatively freely, even
dispensing with the usual visit to the Information Ministry,
that dingy office in the Radio and Television Building tasked
with tracking foreign journalists. Admittedly, this was no Iraqi
Information Ministry—the friendly staff were content simply to
know when you entered the country and when you left, and with
what equipment—but it was headache enough.

We stayed at the Ramses Hilton, a reasonably priced though outdated hotel popular with Gulf Arab tourists mostly because it housed a casino—many Arabs loved to gamble, though Islam prohibited it. It was also an occasional intelligence hangout, where burly men in black suits watched the foreigners, especially ones with big cameras. Police stationed at the main door were armed with sniffer dogs; others stood inside, ready to be deployed with journalists and foreigners. More than once they tried to join us on our various expeditions to cover the election campaign, but Osama handily dismissed them.

The campaign had an Eid-like feel: colourful, musical, and light-hearted, like the Egyptians themselves. A beaming, glossy Mubarak, looking far younger than his seventy-seven years, smiled at his people from building-wide posters and larger-than-life cardboard cutouts, waving and beckoning for their vote. He promised reforms, including an end of the reviled emergency law. His rivals, meanwhile, mounted tireless campaigns that took them daily from one event to another, yet lacking Mubarak's resources—his influence over the state broadcasters, for instance—their ads seemed diminished by comparison, their posters less polished than the incumbent's.

Perhaps the best known of the other candidates was Ayman Nour, a parliamentarian who was head of the Al-Ghad (Tomorrow) Party, one of the few to have official status as an opposition entity. I first met Nour at his house, where he held an informal chat with several foreign journalists just days before the vote. At first glance, he seemed a shy man, with a small smile, a pudgy yet short frame, and a round, bespectacled face. He spoke only in Arabic, with his glamorous wife, Gamila, doing the translating. Despite that, Nour was a Western journalist's dream: a convenient hero, a righteous dark horse who dared to challenge the establishment. He was a reformist who openly criticized Mubarak's regime, and though he spoke weak English, he still spoke "our" language, using words like "democracy," "human rights," and "freedom."

That Nour was also fresh out of prison for charges levelled by the very regime he sought to oust only added to his reformist credentials. He had been arrested in January for allegedly falsifying documents and signatures to enable his party to be registered. His arrest was condemned by the Western world—including Washington—leading, naturally, to accusations that he and his followers were American stooges. Two months later, he was released, claiming that he had been framed.

He seemed an unlikely leader for Egypt's dissatisfied poor as he chatted with us in his richly furnished home that sunny afternoon. Though known as an effective and at times loudly combative contrarian—even in Parliament—he was no match for Mubarak. Still, Nour was certain that if Mubarak played fair, he—Nour—would win. "Our real gain is that we broke the silence barrier in Egypt," he said. "This allowed Egyptians to ask, 'Why didn't we say no before?'"

Indeed, if anything came out of Egypt's nascent democratic exercise, it was exactly that—the ability of opponents to publicly criticize Mubarak's policies on a national platform. (Never mind the fact that the nine candidates running against him were first vetted by his regime.) Protests were still banned during the elections, but police seemed to tolerate the few dozen demonstrators who made it to Tahrir Square under the leadership of the group Kefaya. There was a limit, it seemed, to what Mubarak's administration was willing to do to stifle dissent in an exercise that was ultimately undertaken to mollify the West.

Kefaya (Enough)—or more formally, the Egyptian Movement for Change—the pro-democracy group that organized the failed protest, accused the police of breaking up their marches and hunting down dissidents before they even got to the square. Yet at the same time, Kefaya was now freely handing out printed booklets that outlined a detailed way forward for Egypt without Mubarak. Its motto was "No to Extension [of Mubarak's leadership], No to Inheritance," a reference to Mubarak's seeming intention to pass the mantle on to his son Gamal. In the thirty-two-page discussion paper, Kefaya advocated, among many other things, an end to the emergency laws and the introduction of freedom of the press and an independent judiciary. Notably, it said that the organizers were surprised at their own popularity, that they hadn't imagined the extent of the national desire for change, and that the "hopelessness that appeared to dominate ... did not kill hope among Egyptians."

The chief of the movement at the time was George Ishak, an affable older gentleman whose English was embossed with a cheerful Egyptian accent. I went to interview him in his dark, wood-panelled office. "We change very slowly, but deeply," he said, raising his eyebrows and finger at once. "The door of change is open and nobody can close it again. Look how the regime let us down ... They have to learn something called 'dialogue.' Not 'monologue.'"

There were many others eager to believe that the election, flawed as it might be, was a harbinger of change. But on election day, the turnout was low—as low as 15 percent—partly due to restrictions on voter registration, partly to prevailing cynicism that the election was rigged or orchestrated expressly for foreign consumption. The opposition complained that votes for Mubarak had been baldly bought, that ballot boxes were slyly stuffed, and that people were bused in to vote for him, sometimes when they were ineligible to do so. They also complained that their observers were harassed and prevented from entering polling stations—while dozens of pro-Mubarak lackeys were allowed in to greet voters with songs that praised the current president. I saw them myself at one of the polls, and they sang to us, too. Yet foreign observers were banned altogether.

Unsurprisingly, Mubarak won, with more than 88 percent of the vote. Nour managed just over 7 percent. The opposition demanded a new vote, but Mubarak would be sworn in for his fifth term as president. Any remaining foreign journalists were made to feel a little less welcome. The Information Ministry clamped down, its officials slipping applications under our hotel room doors to demand that we register at its offices. The free show was over. The world wanted an Egyptian election, and the world got one. End of story.

Washington, the chief advocate of the elections, proclaimed the result a historic departure for Egypt.

Shortly thereafter, Mubarak's regime embarked on a new campaign of arrests, imprisonment, and torture. Ayman Nour was sentenced to five years and thrown back into prison.

Neither Kefaya nor the Al-Ghad Party had been able to short-circuit Mubarak's decades-long "monologue." Nor could they, on the eve of the election, garner enough support to either launch a revolution or execute a coup. Egyptians—deeply resentful of the regime and eager for freedom as they might have been—didn't see *them* as the solution. Many saw their only hope in Islam and the Muslim Brotherhood, the only opposition group that, thanks largely to the mosques, still managed to organize and win the hearts and minds of the people despite Mubarak's efforts.

The Brotherhood was banned and did not officially exist as a party. It did, however, nominate candidates for parliamentary elections, and they always ran as independents (if they weren't arrested and thrown into prison first). They did relatively well in those elections. They were popular in Egypt (and in Jordan and Syria, where they had independent branches) because of their charity and organization, and because they were regarded as more honest and more in tune with their people than any current Arab leader. In Egypt they also had the sympathy of the common man because they had long challenged Mubarak, earning prison sentences and impressive credentials and clout as an opposition group.

But they were also seen by others as a sinister, power-hungry organization with violent, anti-Western tendencies and extremist designs. The latter view ensured that few Western promoters of democracy and human rights cared much for the thousands of the Brotherhood's members who languished in Egypt's prisons without trial or due process.

The Brotherhood and other Islamists have been a big part of the West's dilemma in dealing with authoritarian Arab leaders. The U.S. had encouraged those regimes to introduce reform and to allow more freedom as an alternative to the extreme types of Islam (to which some were turning in the absence of any other option). But the U.S. felt it could push only so far because, the argument went, the fall of some of those long-reigning leaders could lead to the formation of dreaded "Islamist" governments. The West, chiefly the U.S., supported those regimes ostensibly because they were preferable to the Islamist alternative. Unsurprisingly, the West's continued backing of existing Arab leaders only fuelled people's distrust of both the U.S. and those leaders, pushing many of them still closer to groups that were religiously inspired.

Later in 2005, Egypt held its parliamentary election (a separate election from the presidential one), and though it, too, was marred by arbitrary arrests, harassment of the opposition, and widespread fraud, Muslim Brotherhood candidates, running as independents, won an unprecedented 88 seats in a house of 454 members. Previously, they had held only 14.

I once visited the Brotherhood's offices to talk about Mubarak's re-election. I was surprised to hear them talk about democracy, human rights, and the rule of law—the same language used by

Nour and Kefaya. "We consider [the presidential election] only a small hole in the thick wall of dictatorship," the spokesman told me. "A small hole that could be closed easily at any time. But the truth remains that it's the people who have the real role in returning their rights of freedom and democracy.

"Freedom isn't awarded. Democracy isn't given—it is seized."

THIRTEEN

Revolution

✾✾✾

Enduring patience
brings down mountains.
—ARAB PROVERB

CAIRO, JANUARY 28, 2011

It was inevitable that Tunisia's successful youthful rebellion in late 2011 would stir up the latent discontent around the region. And the biggest, most vulnerable Middle Eastern tinderbox had always been Egypt.

On January 25, thousands of Egyptians gathered to put on a protest planned weeks earlier against police brutality. The large crowds surprised even the organizers. "We are all Khaled Said," they cried, chanting the name of a young man who had been brutally murdered by policemen the summer before. But within hours, their chants evolved into calls for the regime's downfall, inviting the unpleasant attention of riot police.

Three days later, we landed in Cairo on what the protesters had dubbed the Friday of Wrath. Despite a maddening delay at the airport as an Information Ministry official dragged us through the customary red tape, producer Erin Boudreau, cameraman Richard Devey, and I made it to the Ramses Hilton to join Margaret Evans and Samer Shalabi just before the Friday prayers had finished.

Shortly afterwards, as promised, protesters unleashed their wrath in several cities, and suddenly all mobile phones were cut off. The authorities had also pre-emptively disabled the Internet a day earlier. It was an extraordinary, unprecedented move aimed at stopping protesters from communicating—on Facebook and Twitter, as well as by text—but it was surely also a form of collective punishment. We had to get on the air, and after several failed attempts, Erin managed to get a landline out to Toronto. For a long time I sat on the floor of the hotel mezzanine, on the air, explaining the culmination of a generation's anger while a young, bemused bellman listened in.

Who are they? What motivates them? They're not protesting against the West, Israel? What do they want? The anchor was full of questions.

No one had ever asked me such questions before, but then again, there had rarely been an opportunity over the better part of the violent past decade. There had been little time for or interest in that huge segment of society: the dissatisfied, the disenchanted, ordinary citizens whose ambitions went beyond the meagre opportunities and humiliating existence they knew in the modern Middle East. Those who had no one speaking for them, whose voices had been lost, drowned out by the pronouncements of extremists, politicians, and their stale regimes.

Now the world wanted to know. I had witnessed the beginning and middle of it, and the words just flowed. Egyptians were saying out loud what so many young people throughout the Middle East, from Syria to Libya to Iraq to Jordan, had long been thinking.

Much had happened to deepen the chronic malaise since I was last in Egypt. Despite a marked increase in the number of those attaining higher education, it was getting harder to make a living— youth unemployment stood at about 25 percent. Rising inflation ate at what little money people could earn. The bread lineups had gotten longer. In 2008, thousands of Egyptians rioted, indignant at the humiliation they endured for a few loaves to get their families through one day. Despite his election promises, in May 2010, Mubarak again extended the state of emergency for another two years. In the fall of 2010, exceptionally fraudulent parliamentary elections raised the ire of the people. Furthermore, all trials were still presided over by the military, and they were especially swift when a member of the opposition was in the cage reserved for the accused. Prisons were still inhumane and torture routine. The regime seemed particularly obsessed in recent years with Internet bloggers and self-styled journalists who openly objected to the lack of freedom and broadcast their grievances to the world online. In the summer of 2010, Khaled Said, the young man whose name the protesters chanted in 2011, was tortured and murdered by two policemen after he filmed evidence of police corruption and posted it online. The circumstances of his death, the subject of more online activism, also fuelled the simmering discontent and led directly to that first protest on January 25.

As the protests started, Mubarak was also starting his thirtieth year as president.

♌

Our next, unexpected challenge after our arrival on January 28 was getting Richard's camera up to the room. The hotel staff forbade it, presumably so that we couldn't film the chaos in plain view of our balconies. Predictably, the employees had turned from gregarious tourist hosts to callous state enforcers. This was neither a war nor an election meant for foreign consumption. So the state was going to do whatever it could to hamper our efforts to document it.

As soon as the protests began that Friday, the inevitable crackdown materialized quickly and violently. Walls of riot police, clad in black and hell-bent on shutting it all down, struck savagely with batons, water cannons, and tear gas—the tried-and-true counter-rebellion arsenal in Mubarak's Egypt. Only this time, the numbers were too overwhelming and the protesters kept coming. They threw stones and sent tear gas canisters flying back from whence they came. They took on riot police and commandeered some of their personnel carriers and paddy wagons, rocking them back and forth and setting some on fire. They openly chanted for the regime's downfall. Across the country—in Suez, Alexandria, and Cairo—young men and women shouted for "Bread, freedom and justice." They kept it up even when the retort came in the form of bullets.

It was no accident that bread was at the head of that list. As much as this rebellion was about freedom and human rights, it was equally about the tattered economy, and about the millions of educated youth who could find no work and had poor prospects of marriage as a result. It was about demeaning wages and the dearth of opportunities, the indignity of living hand to mouth—just as it was in Bouazizi's protest. It was precisely why I had told Brien to "watch Egypt." These had been the conditions for Egypt's youth for some time, and it was inevitable that one day, when the right opportunity presented itself, their fury would find an outlet.

At times during our stay, the Ramses Hotel became an army and intelligence hideout, and a part of the battlefield; at others, it was a shelter for protesters, and a convenient prison for foreign journalists. Several times in those early days, the hotel manager, sweaty and relieved of his dark suit jacket, marched from room to room with burly security men, knocking on doors and then aggressively barging in to look for cameras surreptitiously recording off the balconies. They marched into my room uninvited at least twice, and into our workroom several other times.

Occasionally the hotel's state enforcers didn't have to do much to stop us from documenting the protests—the cloud of tear gas outside the hotel on one day was simply too much. Instead, throngs of protesters, mostly women, flooded into the lobby to escape the noxious fog, mixing freely with the terrified tourists and journalists stuck inside. In subsequent days, the hotel "staff"—now augmented by those burly men I remembered from 2005—guarded the elevators and the main entrances, which had been reinforced with wooden planks to prevent protesters from entering again. At one point they even disabled the elevators for our "safety," until those of us on the higher floors complained and they relented.

Yet at the same time, the staff promptly delivered a multi-page fax from Toronto full of the latest wire stories on the riots, packaged in crisp hotel stationery. They slipped letters under our doors asking us to be patient under the circumstances. I never liked staying at that hotel, but it was close to the action and to a satellite feed point, and in the end, that trumped all other considerations. Besides, at one stage, we'd tried the various other nearby hotels, and none of them would take us in. Upon learning we were journalists, the polite, foreign-trained staff of one major establishment first made a phone call, then unceremoniously kicked us out.

That first day we managed to get out of the Ramses for a short walk during a lull. Ahead on the street that led to the state broadcasting building, a woman dressed in black and trailing several children walked a gauntlet of expressionless policemen, lecturing them the entire way in a brave show of motherly disapproval. "How could you do this to your own brothers and sons? How could you strike your own countrymen?" she admonished them. We caught up with her and her children within view of the Nile. She said she'd brought them along so that they could be witness to history. "We will stay standing and say to them, 'NO,'" said her daughter, suddenly bursting into tears.

Across the street, in front of the Radio and Television Building, the black-clad riot police were immovable, dispassionate, and seemingly uninterested in anything but standing perfectly still.

State television had acknowledged that something was afoot in Egypt, but over the coming days, it repeatedly showed pictures of a quiet, empty downtown Cairo, a flagrant fabrication designed to delude the masses. It was the regime's dedicated mouthpiece; no wonder it needed such diligent protection.

Looking down from the balcony of our workroom, we could see that Cairo was in undeniable chaos. Despite the curfew announced that night, clashes continued in streets dotted with fires. Erin and I looked out at the very moment a police vehicle exploded just metres from the hotel. Dozens of people died that day, but it was just the beginning.

Early that evening I was working in my room when I heard the familiar rumble of heavily armoured tanks. I looked out the window, and sure enough, the army was moving in. Some soldiers had also stationed themselves by the Radio and Television Building around the corner, where we'd heard there'd been a clash after protesters tried to storm it. Mubarak finally addressed the nation on state television—late—to say the current government would step down, to be replaced by another that would address "the situation." By then, hundreds of youth had converged on Tahrir Square.

Late that night—in fact, early the next morning—we sprinted into the tear gas to get to the satellite point a couple of hundred metres away to file our report. As I started speaking to the camera, a building that belonged to Mubarak's National Democratic Party lit up with flames behind me. I realized then that Egypt had turned a corner, surpassing the 2005 experience and every other mini-rebellion before or since. Everything that came from now on was new to Egyptians—to the Middle East—and certainly to me.

I had long wondered when the ordinary people of the Middle East would address the injustices of their existence, and here, finally, was the answer. After all those years in the wilderness, the bottomless pit of seething anger had finally erupted. All the lies, the empty promises, the humiliating poverty and powerlessness that conspired to destroy any sense of belonging, any loyalty to flag or country, had finally ignited the people's wrath. All those decades of mediocrity, of dictators stringing a tripwire that arrested change of any kind, had been undone by the people. The fear was gone. And I was here to witness it. After all the time I'd spent in the region, hearing about and documenting its endless frustrations, living amid its violence, listening to its grievances, I felt incredibly lucky to see this. It was historic, and there was nowhere else I wanted to be but right in the middle of it.

If Mubarak had chosen a different path in 2005, he might have avoided some of this. He'd had twenty-nine years of chances. I woke up the next morning certain he would be swept away with the debris now littering Cairo's streets. It was just a matter of time.

𓏏

The protesters' goal from the start was to get to Tahrir Square. That Saturday, thousands converged there, watched over now by the army's tanks and personnel carriers, which largely stood by, unengaged. The riot police—all police—had disappeared. We walked over to that still-smouldering NDP building to see the damage for ourselves—it was surrounded by the curious, who pulled out their mobile phones and took pictures. The streets were littered with the remnants of yesterday's battle, and an unmistakable hint of euphoria was mixed with the inevitable unease among the crowd.

"The young people are [moving] in the right direction," said one middle-aged man. "The young people of Egypt have proven that they are the future." As he contemplated the burning building, he said he was the happiest he'd been since he finished his A-level exams.

Walking back, Osama, our fixer, was exhilarated. "I have never felt so free in my country."

But Egyptians were also experiencing an instability that was costing lives and fuelling rage on all sides, and they knew they were divided, for not everyone wanted to see Mubarak gone. Hundreds of protesters had died on the streets, and on a visit to Cairo's main morgue, we were told by the head of the forensic medicine authority that the majority had been killed by bullet wounds. But then he wandered into the politics of the situation, despite making me promise to avoid it. "How many are in the protests, half a million? A million?" he asked. "This does not represent the people of Egypt. We are eighty million. They don't want Hosni Mubarak? *I* want Hosni Mubarak."

In the foyer outside, a grieving family waited to retrieve the body of a man who had been a guard at the NDP building that had burnt down. They wouldn't talk to us and repeatedly blocked Richard's camera from capturing their mourning.

Across the street from the morgue, in a sign of another festering problem about to get worse, we came across a huge lineup of women and children, even angrier than they normally would be, waiting at the *eish* bakery. One woman told me she'd travelled an hour and a half to get here because the lines were shorter. "We are six," she said. "Will it be enough? It won't be enough. What shall we do?"

It was a question many more Egyptians were asking as the battle for Egypt intensified.

Mubarak's own battle to survive wasn't over.

One morning we heard the explosive sound of fighter jets. *Could it be?* We looked out our balcony and there they were, two of them circling over and over, breaking the sound barrier and thundering over Cairo as though in search of a target. At first, the protesters were incredulous, they later told us—what was this supposed to mean? The air force had been Mubarak's school, an institution of

which he was particularly proud. Then they were angry—infuriated that the regime would resort to such scare tactics. Never in
their memory had fighter jets been deployed in the middle of
Cairo. What were they going to do, bomb Tahrir Square? It was
ridiculous, an empty threat, the protesters said. Instead of scaring
them, the menacing air show seemed to galvanize them and bring
even more Egyptians to the square.

While Cairo convulsed, the exodus began. First it was the
tourists and students, then Egyptians with foreign passports
thronged to the airport as more journalists made their way in.
Samer and I went to the airport in search of a group of Canadians
who were about to be evacuated. The terminal was crammed with
people of various nationalities trying to make their way out. We
found the Canadians, many of them sleeping on the floor, near
a maple leaf flag that had been hastily draped over a counter as
their meeting point.

We followed them as they were loaded onto buses, then dropped
off on a grassy hill near the departure terminal. Samer valiantly
pushed to get permission for us to film—the airport was infested
with intelligence agents and was as dangerous as any government
building, and we stood a great chance of getting arrested if we didn't
ask. But it was out of the question, so we were reduced to capturing
it all surreptitiously with our phones. A generous young Canadian
couple later lent us their holiday camcorder and a tape, and that
improved our odds of getting some decent material. A Canadian
Egyptian colleague who arrived at the airport separately also filmed
secretly for the night's story. The officials were none the wiser.

After we left the airport, I got a phone call from one of the
evacuees: this was citizen journalism at its finest. The police had
refused to let them board without the payment of a $2,000 U.S.
"departure fee," a monstrous bribe. The diplomats were forced to
take up a collection from the passengers, promising to pay them

back once they got home. It reminded me of that obtuse official at the Baghdad airport. Like him, Egypt's airport guards knew the game was almost up, and they wanted to cash in while they still could. The plane took off only when the money was safely in their greedy hands.

It was dark and silent when we finally left, the curfew already in effect. By then the telephones were working again and I had been tweeting regularly. So I invited my followers to come along as we made the trip back. "Just came across out first checkpoint," I tweeted. "Two large tanks and four friendly soldiers."

That first stretch of road outside the airport was controlled by the army, with tanks and armoured personnel carriers blocking the way at several points and soldiers inspecting anyone coming in or out. At one of the checkpoints, the officers insisted we take a side road, off the main highway, which took us through dark neighbourhoods we probably would have been best to avoid. After a few minutes, the army checkpoints petered out, giving way to vigilante ones: three, four, or five groups would stop us in the span of one kilometre, each one protecting its patch. They were a disconcerting sight: young, swaggering men—boys, really—with axes, sticks, and knives of all manner, some as large as machetes, who menacingly approached our windows to look inside. Most of them were eventually satisfied by our Canadian passports and waved us through; others asked big questions and insisted on looking in the trunk of the car for anything suspicious.

In the darkness below one of the mammoth bridges downtown, we came across a particularly nasty group of stocky young men wielding machetes, their faces sweaty in the light of a huge bonfire. They had no authority, yet their knives and large knuckles were convincing enough for us to hand over our passports for an inspection that took far longer than it should have. They were less than friendly and began to roughly question the driver. They wouldn't give the passports back and started taunting us. My tweets had to stop, and I hid my phone under the seat. Finally, after a great deal of yelling and cursing and phone calls, they returned the passports and we were on our way back to the hotel and my looming deadline.

"We were sent in circles and through several dodgy neighbourhoods," I finally tweeted, the phone's keys soothing in my fingers. "Truly terrifying."

After that first day of looting, theft, assaults, and destruction of public property, vigilante groups had sprung up all over Cairo to replace the police, who had simply melted away. We'd interviewed a group of them near a hospital that looters had attempted to vandalize, and they were a courteous if emboldened group of kids. But at least they were overseen by the block's elders, who welcomed our questions. In a city as large and dangerous as Cairo could be, they said, there was really no other option. They would have to protect themselves while the regime was occupied with protecting *itself*.

Of all the tactics the authorities had employed to do so, none perhaps was more underhanded and cynical than pitting Egyptian against Egyptian to fight it out on the streets. It appeared that Mubarak supporters had been ordered to rally in a show of support for the leader, in a tactic used by despots all over the Middle East. I had seen such "spontaneous" rallies used repeatedly to bolster regimes under attack in Lebanon, Iraq, and Syria. Samer and I attended the first of them, at the state broadcasting building, and they were an aggressive crowd, complaining that the media had focused too much on a minority of dissidents and forgotten about "the majority" who loved Mubarak. It was a spirited defence of the status quo.

"He won't leave! He won't leave!" they countered in chants whose volume was directly proportional to the direction of Samer's lens. They grabbed at our camera, while others grabbed at the microphone in my hand. One of them snatched it and started a monologue before I snatched it back. Samer was getting increasingly irate as we were pushed around and swarmed by people, all wanting to talk at once and yet pointing fingers of blame in our faces. It took a while to extricate ourselves from their grip, and though they were pushy and rough, we were unharmed.

In what was clearly an orchestrated move, the pro-Mubarak protesters then began to march en masse towards Tahrir Square, which the opposition had by then claimed for itself. A clash was unavoidable. We were in the middle of the pro-Mubarak crowd when the first rocks were thrown, sending people—including me—stampeding in the opposite direction.

The brutality simmering just under the surface was unleashed shortly afterwards, in a way that only pro-regime Egyptian thugs— *baltagiya*—were capable of when given a chance. The two sides clashed, hurling pieces of pavement that caused serious injury among the crowd and invited a return torrent in kind. Bizarrely, an army of horses, camels, and chariots then charged into the anti-Mubarak crowd, their riders whipping their adversaries with clubs and canes and sending them running. A few of them were pulled to the ground and beaten mercilessly, while the rest eventually retreated as the army tried to separate the two sides. As night fell, more troublemakers arrived, flinging a new volley of rocks and insults from a bridge that overlooked the edge of Tahrir. That progressed to hand-to-hand battles, with the *baltagiya* occasionally administering their trademark gang beatings on an unfortunate member of the other side caught in their midst. Back at the hotel and well into editing, we watched and filmed as the two sides went at each other in several running street battles. We had a perfect view of the extraordinary melee, a mini civil war fought out with sticks, Molotov cocktails, and bare fists. We could see men standing on top of a building and throwing down Molotovs at regular intervals, and in one corner we suddenly saw a man on fire, a human flame running at speed. It was unlike any war I'd ever witnessed: we could see them viciously beating or stoning one another from our seventeenth-floor room, though we could hear almost nothing but the occasional burst of gunfire in the army's half-hearted attempts to stop a battle that pitted the desire for freedom against the desire for stability.

Over the next few days, egged on by the state broadcasters, some of Mubarak's supporters also targeted foreign journalists. Several were swarmed and beaten up or had cameras and tape recorders confiscated or smashed; others were detained for hours or days in prison. Almost every one of our crews had an incident. It was clear this, too, was orchestrated, and it almost always happened near a pro-Mubarak protest. So some of us decided to temporarily stop offering ourselves up as convenient targets for irrational, orchestrated rage. On one outing together, Samer, Margaret, Osama, and I did our best to avoid them—even taking a boat taxi ride on the Nile, a walk through the Zamalek district, and then a winding taxi trip that, inadvertently, took us straight into a crowd of pro-Mubaraks gathered under a bridge.

The driver, whom we'd met only a few minutes earlier, froze, unsure whether to listen to us, screaming for him to back up, or to the men on a motorcycle and the thugs surrounding the car, who were demanding we drive toward a dead end. They swarmed our little taxi, staring at us through the windows, hurling insults and a variety of ominous threats. "Should we cut their throats now or later?" asked one of them.

Thankfully, a policeman showed up. He took my passport and disappeared, leaving us to the angry Mubarak supporters, who were undecided on how to proceed now that authority had intervened. I walked out after him and saw he'd gone straight to a high-ranking army officer. I went over to explain, but he refused to allow us to walk to our hotel, which was just a few hundred metres past the crowd, beyond the dozens of army tanks parked in between. He admonished me for endangering the lives of my colleagues and being out on "a day like this." Indignant, I fought hard against the temptation to hurl the blame right back at him. Eventually, after consulting with a superior, he let us pass through the impressive honour guard of tanks and soldiers protecting the state broadcaster, leaving the angry crowd behind. Still, some of them lurked wherever they thought they could find us. Late at night at the satellite feed point, they gathered behind the line of army tanks and heaved insults and stones at the dozens of us journalists who were forced to go there at all hours of the day and night. The language they used made you feel as though you were frequenting a brothel. The soldiers did nothing to stop them.

Other soldiers were eventually installed near the entrance to the Ramses Hotel, ostensibly to protect us, yet they, too, checked us for cameras and detained a number of our colleagues and their equipment. Once, late at night, they marched up to me and Samer and confiscated our tape just as we set up for a standup.

As the tension mounted, the army at one point offered journalists staying at the Ramses a ride to the Zamalek district—surely the result of intervention at a much higher level. Zamalek, an island in the Nile that was home to the diplomatic corps and many wealthy Egyptians, hadn't been touched by the violence. We were offered the ride, too, but we declined and stayed, reluctantly, at the Ramses. That night, I watched with a colleague as a group of journalists were loaded up into two armoured personnel carriers with their belongings. I couldn't blame them—they were with the English arm of Al Jazeera, whose Arabic sister network had been shut down, blamed for inciting protesters and "telling lies." Clearly the regime was aware of the power of the pan-Arab networks—later polls found more than 80 percent of Egyptians followed the revolution on television.

But this was a twenty-first-century rebellion, and while television was central, Twitter, Facebook, and mobile phones were also key in this attempt at revolution. Mosques, too, were important sources of information and acted as gathering points, as did the metro stops. Good old brute force was also vital. In the end, after hundreds of injuries and many deaths, the anti-Mubarak side prevailed in the mini civil war, repelling the thugs and liberating Liberation Square. They enclosed themselves in Tahrir, and they called it the "New Egypt."

ℵ

The moment you stepped into Tahrir Square, you could see what Egyptians were capable of achieving when they found hope.

In its congested confines you encountered people of all ages and classes, a growing nation of like-minded citizens, each of whom pitched in to make it work in a way that Egyptians—Arabs—rarely did on ordinary days. Polite young people policed the entrances to check IDs and bags. Enthusiastic mothers and fathers and children acted as cheerleaders, a welcoming party, singing songs praising the returning injured revolutionaries, even the foreign journalists. Young doctors treated the injured in a nearby mosque and in lobbies of buildings surrounding the square. Young women in hijab and gloves were on sanitation duty, walking around picking up garbage. Volunteers handed out water and food—dates, loaves of bread, juice. *Here, take another one.* In one corner, older labourers in jalabiyas had chained themselves to the tanks that stood guard, in a more emphatic show of civil disobedience. In another across the square, a group of lawyers sat under a makeshift canopy discussing a future constitution. Nearby, a middle-aged man gave revolutionary haircuts and beard trims for free to whoever wanted one. Those who'd thought to bring a tablah led small groups of protesters in raucous song and dance. No Egyptian gathering is complete without song and dance.

If you'd lived in the Middle East and had known the rampant apathy like I did, you couldn't help being impressed by such efforts. These were people more accustomed to saying, *"Ma fish faydah,"*—there's no use. Now, it seemed, there was. As the gatherings grew, we returned daily to criss-cross the square over and over to tell its story. I had never before walked in the midst of so many people, never before imagined that such a huge gathering could be so peaceful and orderly. I hadn't imagined I could ever again walk through a crowd that large after what happened in Baghdad, and while I had a few weak moments, I was euphoric I did it, time and again—it was a significant personal victory. It helped that foreign journalists were welcomed unconditionally. The protesters courteously offered us places to rest, made way for our cameras, volunteered to be interviewed—they wanted us to be there. I had never been welcomed so warmly in Egypt or anywhere in the region while on the job.

In the heart of the square, young men and women organized a collection station for the hours of video and hundreds of photos captured by ordinary people over the past few days, an archive of the regime's misdeeds. All along, at all hours, someone was on the stage nearby, leading the masses with chants and speeches and songs aimed at keeping spirits high. Someone had also thought to put up enlarged pictures of the revolution's "martyrs" at one entrance. There was even a curbside museum of their bloodied clothing, souvenirs of the conflict and reminders of the cost of freedom and the obligation to keep going. Someone else had displayed a raft of ID cards they'd wrested from the pro-Mubaraks, proving that some of them were policemen, or at least in the employ of the state.

The citizens of the "New Egypt" were poignantly inclusive: Christians prayed in the open air while Muslims kept watch for threats. Muslims then prayed while Christians watched their backs. Given the violence of a few nights earlier, they kept piles of broken pavement nearby, primitive ammunition depots they could access in a moment should anyone think to attack again.

They chanted against violence, against destruction of public property. "He who loves Egypt won't destroy it," they sang. Every once in a while, they erupted in a "Peaceful, peaceful, peaceful," a reminder this was a people's uprising, civilian and unarmed, and would remain so despite what had come before. Even women felt comfortable there despite the presence of so many young men. On the streets, they were accustomed to constant harassment. In Tahrir, they told me they felt safe.

The younger, starry-eyed revolutionaries called it utopia. Indeed, it may have all been too good to be true. The biggest danger that this country faced now was having such high hopes deflated.

"We wanted to get to Tahrir Square. We had to get there at any price," one of the young protesters, Samir Saad, later told me. "I've been going to the street since the beginning, since Kefaya in 2005. We would go down, maybe twenty of us; we would get beaten up and then leave. I reached the point of political atheism and decided I wasn't leaving my house anymore.

"But when I saw the scene, the number was really huge. I said this looks like the beginning of a revolution. We felt some hope. And the behaviour of the stupid authorities, that is what made the ordinary Egyptian join us."

Indeed, the citizens of Tahrir were not natural rebels; many of them were ordinary, working-class citizens who were mobilized by the ferocity of the regime's response to the protests. It was a point that seemed lost on the authorities, not only in Egypt but also in Tunisia—that the harder they clamped down, the angrier the people became and the bigger the next protest.

Several times Mubarak tried to make amends, a replay of Ben

Ali's belated concessions. He initially appointed a vice president for the first time since he'd assumed power, then he promised he wouldn't stand for re-election. And in the same speech, he uttered the words "transfer of power." But he wasn't willing to offer anything more, as was made plain by that new vice president, Omar Suleiman, in an interview with ABC's Christiane Amanpour. Suleiman resorted to that old scare tactic, claiming the uprising was the work of the "Islamic camp."

Yet the Islamists—long considered the region's feared rebels—had been caught flat-footed by the uprising; they were a small, belated player in the upswell of youthful disenchantment. This was no Muslim Brotherhood event, no Islamist revolt. In fact, it seemed the beginnings of a third way, a peaceful alternative to the attractiveness of the violent Islamist movements—like al-Qaeda—which had long aimed to be the ones who deposed the Arab world's repressive regimes. The youthful rebellion seemed to supersede the Islamists' promises to liberate Arabs and Muslims from those despots.

No matter—the Brotherhood still believed that the fall of the regime would ultimately benefit them, however it came about. The fact remained, though, that religious slogans were largely absent in Tahrir, the crowd favouring instead chants about bread, freedom, and justice—chants that resonated around a region mesmerized by Egypt's revolt.

Suleiman's assertion about Islamist interference contradicted his "foreign hands" theory, which he also reiterated in that interview, saying the young people's ideas about democracy had come from abroad. In a statement that would seal Egyptians' disdain for the man, he then added that democracy would eventually come to Egypt, but only "when the people have the culture of democracy."

Many in the Tahrir crowd were highly educated, well-connected, Internet-savvy, and well-read Arabs who'd become accustomed to being largely invisible to the media and their own governments.

But they understood perfectly the concepts of democracy and an independent judiciary, and they yearned for an independent press. Even the least educated among them knew all too well the difference between their human rights and those of people fortunate enough to live abroad. They knew they had never enjoyed real freedom. And yet, they were not extremist and not necessarily anti-Western, and while many might have been religious, they had no interest in an Islamist state. They were people who had long been silent and now simply wanted dignity.

So the citizens of the New Egypt refused virtually all of Mubarak's overtures, as well as Suleiman's offers for national dialogue. Instead, they coalesced around one simple demand: Mubarak's resignation.

Even Egyptians living abroad were coming back to join in. We met Canadian, American, and British Egyptians in the square, people who'd left to escape the hopelessness and were now back to experience the hope. I'd rarely before seen expatriates returning to the Middle East for anything but weddings or funerals. Now they were returning to witness revolution.

⚢

A few days into what appeared to be the new status quo, our CBC bosses announced that they would scale back staffing, and that I would be going home the following weekend. One of them, Cathy Perry, gently inquired how I felt about the decision. I told her I would normally have been greatly upset, but I was convinced that events would overtake their decision, and that ultimately I would have to stay. I told her I was sure Egypt, in fact, was on the brink.

But you couldn't see that unless you were there, on the ground, listening and watching, reading the local press. On normal days, Egypt was an irrepressible, bustling country heaving with activity, bursting to the brim with people who lived hand to mouth. Now, it was at a complete standstill. If you took even a cursory look at the faces of its wretchedly poor—the majority—you knew there was only so long the country could survive without its bakeries and fresh supplies, only so long it could withstand the absence of police, the closure of its stock exchange and factories, the drying up of tourist dollars. If you could see all that and you'd witnessed Egypt's uncontainable energy in normal times, you could only conclude that within a couple of days, something would have to give.

Egypt had to go on, or its people would go hungry. And hunger, Arabs say, is *kaffer*—an infidel—meaning it could make you break all the rules. Either the protesters would have to be violently dragged out of Tahrir Square, to an international outcry, or Mubarak would have to walk.

Two days after my chat with Cathy, cameraman/producer Glen Kugelstadt, Margaret, Osama, and I drove for the better part of an hour, trying to locate rail workers who'd apparently gone on strike. We finally spotted them at the edge of a destitute neighbourhood, dozens of them blocking Cairo's main tracks, preventing any trains from coming in or going out. Egypt's rails and highways were its lifeline, and we'd heard that several highways had been cut off that day by truck drivers who'd also gone on strike, halting the movement of people and goods cold. The striking men probably couldn't have cared less whether Mubarak stayed or left, but they, like many others, wanted the stalemate choking the country and endangering their livelihoods to end, one way or another.

Glen filmed for a few short minutes before the men noticed us on the low bridge above them, and Osama, who normally liked skirting the edge of what is considered safe, ordered us back to the car, *now*. This was one of those "local" private moments that people here didn't like foreign journalists to document. Still, the angry sight of them standing there convinced me that Mubarak would step down within a day. Two at most.

In fact, there were rumours he would be stepping down *that* very day—an army officer with a megaphone all but said as much in Tahrir Square when he yelled, "Today you will get what you've been hoping for." We went down to the square that night to watch Mubarak's speech, along with tens of thousands of others who thought they were about to witness history. It was February 10.

If you listened closely, Mubarak *did* step down that night, but on his own terms. He said he was transferring power to his vice president and removing himself from the day-to-day operations of the regime. It was a classic face-saving Arab compromise, which he probably thought would appease the protesters while allowing him to retain some of his dignity. But for those in Tahrir, it was a huge letdown. In what is considered a grave insult in the Arab world, they lifted their shoes to face the large screen on which his image was projected and started chanting, "Leave, leave, leave." The world was astounded, not least Washington, which, like everyone else, had been assured he was leaving that night.

But as far as Mubarak was concerned, he had left. The following day, the Arab networks already had him relocating to the resort town of Sharm el-Sheikh as early as mid-afternoon. Then, further proof of a power shift, an army officer appeared on state television, promising that the military would end the emergency law, preside over reforms, and hold free and fair presidential elections. The army, Egypt's most important power broker, had sacrificed Mubarak to retain its privileged position and long-time hold on Egypt. It was over for Baba Hosni. But the protesters still wanted to hear that he was no longer president.

Finally, mid-evening, those words were uttered on state television by Mubarak's newly appointed vice president. "President Muhammad Hosni Mubarak has decided to step down from his post as president of the republic," he said, "and has empowered the supreme council of the armed forces to manage the affairs of the country."

Tahrir Square let out a euphoric cheer. In all the time I spent there, I'd never seen Egyptians prouder. "It is a beginning," said a young bearded man whom I'd met a night earlier. "It's the ultimate in hope and enthusiasm—I saw that in people's eyes."

Many pro-democracy activists immediately issued warnings. They said that the army could not be trusted, and that although Mubarak was gone, his spirit would live on with Egypt in the military's grasp. Many Egyptians knew there were more battles to fight, but they wanted to savour the moment.

They may not have been truly liberated, but they had overcome their self-hatred and powerlessness. With a future to look forward to, they had stopped lamenting a better past. Their crisis of faith in the existence of hope was over.

That night, the whole Arab world—or so it seemed—was suddenly trembling with excitement at the prospect of real change. Tunisia was one thing, but this was Egypt—the Mother of All—throwing off its dictator, and that dictator was Mubarak, the elder statesman of Arab leaders. That night and for many nights afterwards, I received texts and emails from Arab friends in Lebanon, Iraq, Jordan, and elsewhere around the world, offering salutations and congratulations, as if it were Eid. Across the region they wrote and blogged and cried about the Arab Spring. *Their* Arab Spring. The people became the heroes they themselves had long sought.

FOURTEEN

Victory or Death

If your ruler oppresses you,
complain to your creator.
—ARAB PROVERB

FEBRUARY 2011

The long-repressed cry of discontent, the abrupt shift that Egypt's revolution introduced to the Middle East's political landscape, reverberated and spread to many other countries throughout the Arab world. At various times it inspired dissenters to take to the streets in Jordan, Bahrain, the Palestinian territories, Yemen, Iraq, Saudi Arabia, and even Syria and Libya—that impenetrable and terrifyingly oppressive dictatorship, ruled by Muammar Qaddafi for four decades.

But then the city of Benghazi and the trail of smaller Mediterranean towns leading from there to Libya's eastern border have long been known for a streak of rebelliousness. Ask any kid—no Arab child graduates elementary school without learning the name of Omar al-Mukhtar, the elderly fighter who led Libyan mujahedeen in a war of attrition against the Italian occupiers from 1912 until his capture in 1931. He hailed from near Tobruk, the first real city you find as you cross the yellow desert from Egypt into Libya. The Italians eventually captured al-Mukhtar and hanged him. Inevitably he became an Arab Muslim hero, nicknamed the Lion of the Desert, and the subject of an epic film reportedly financed by Qaddafi. We were once taken on a school outing to see the film in Amman when I was about twelve. It was the first time I'd been in a movie theatre, and though I haven't seen the film since, I recall it with great clarity. Anthony Quinn played the old protagonist, and we were all shocked at the end when he was hanged.

Nearly eighty years after al-Mukhtar's death, I was on the phone from London with a nameless man in Benghazi; he was breathlessly running near the central courthouse, describing to me what he saw. Gunmen had opened fire near the *katiba*, Benghazi's military base and home to Qaddafi whenever he visited. And since it was also home to some of Benghazi's most feared men, it became the focus of insanely brave demonstrations marking the latest chapter of the Arab Spring. Eyewitnesses I spoke to kept saying that the authorities were shooting "14.5" directly at people. I had to look it up. It was the calibre of an oversized Russian cartridge normally used in anti-tank weaponry or heavy machine guns. In Egypt, the inevitable crackdown had been bloody. In Libya, it verged on psychopathic.

A couple of weeks later, I was on an Egyptian tour bus, along with cameraman Pascal Leblond and foreign correspondent Anthony Germain, on a bumpy highway making the long desert journey from Cairo to Benghazi. Someone decided we would sleep one night in Marsa Matrouh—an obscure, dusty oasis town a couple of hours from the border with Libya—so that we could meet up with the first CBC crew, led by reporters Carolyn Dunn and Tom Parry, that had been in Libya. I argued against staying in a remote, unknown town in a country that was still boiling with its own unfinished revolution, and also against travel on a Friday, still the preferred day for Egypt's continuing protests. After a day of epic travel, and with another looming, we needed rest in a secure place. But the decision was already made.

The town reeked of lawlessness, and within hours of our arrival, it erupted in disorder. A restive crowd gathered near a lone platoon of soldiers installed at a police building next to our hotel. A thick cloud of smoke hung in the air—something was on fire, something big. As the sun set, clashes erupted in the street and the stench of tear gas wafted over. By then, it seemed the entire angry town had shown up in front of our hotel. The familiar black-clad riot police—who hadn't been seen on Cairo's streets since February— started chasing people with batons. We spent the rest of the night listening to gunfire echo across town to the Mediterranean.

Egyptian tweeters informed me it was what they called their Bastille Day. Protesters had stormed the reviled state security forces buildings in Alexandria and Cairo—and in Marsa Matrouh someone had set it on fire. State security forces were responsible for the worst of the violence during the revolution, and were practised in the business of cracking heads both on the streets and in prisons. It couldn't have been a worse day for us to be "resting" in that town, or for our colleagues to be traversing the Egyptian desert.

The next morning we were finally at the border, and I slipped back into my other role as fixer and translator to get us through. I was momentarily transported to the Jordan–Iraq border, and the countless times I sprinted, several passports in hand, from one official to another to smooth our journeys across. Like every other land border I'd traversed in the Mideast over the past decade, the Egypt–Libya one was dusty, disorganized, and tiresome. This one had been overtaken by the displaced—thousands of people from several nationalities who had fled the hostilities in Libya, and now sat on the Egyptian side, suspended in a no-man's land, waiting for someone to get them home.

Shortly afterwards we were parked just inside Egypt's border, gently cajoling one of our young drivers to move the car forward, just a few hundred metres more, past the Egyptian side and just short of the Libyan one, so we could transfer our equipment to the cars that had come from Benghazi to meet us. He was terrified, and soon he was shedding tears, mostly out of humiliation (though the fear, I think, had also shaken him). I took him aside again and assured him that although there was war on the other side, it was very far away. He gritted his teeth and finally agreed to do it. Mohammed had never left his own country, and after seeing his reaction to the thought of crossing a border arbitrarily drawn in the desert long before he was born, I doubted he ever would.

The rebels of Libya's east welcomed us at the border, at every checkpoint, in every little town. The men we rode with (relatives of a Libyan contact back in Canada) were backers of the rebellion, proud and yet deferential, dressed smartly in suit jackets and polished shoes to meet us in our dirty jeans and boots. They instantly obliged when we asked them to remove the rebel flag from the dash of the vehicle, to ensure there was no question of our neutrality. The entire way we listened to Radio Free Libya, an upstart broadcaster speaking for, and to, the rebels, helping raise morale. For decades I'd heard much of the same nationalist rhetoric spouted on Arab airwaves, many of the same proud nationalist songs. Yet it all sounded different in the context of a real, ongoing revolution led by the people. It was genuine, exciting, and urgent. I wanted to visit the station at the earliest opportunity.

The vast, silent desert made way for the lush mountains of Jabal al-Akhdar, Omar al-Mukhtar's hideout and his base of operations for twenty years. His admirers in Benghazi had managed to brave the oversized 14.5 bullets and overwhelm the katiba—nearly miraculous given the fear those military bases instilled, and what punishment they had meted out on behalf of Qaddafi for forty years. Qaddafi's loyalists had mostly been forced out or silenced, and Benghazi and towns all the way east had been liberated. The rebels said al-Mukhtar had been their inspiration.

But they weren't entirely certain yet whether or not they would also meet his grim fate.

Libya was no Egypt or Tunisia, and Qaddafi was certainly no Mubarak. His forty-year "revolution"—launched in Benghazi, like this latest one—had quickly turned into a one-man occupation, a hostage taking of an entire nation. Qaddafi's brand of authoritarianism was uniquely his own—erratic, unforgiving, and exceptionally bloody. His prisons were as horrific as Saddam's or Assad's, if not worse: dissenters were treated to broken arms and cut-off fingers and ears. His state executions were broadcast on national television.

Behind the excesses of the privileged, who benefited from Libya's oil revenues, lay a population mired in poverty and unemployment, especially among young people, and especially in the east, an area Qaddafi was said to despise and purposefully neglect. He may have claimed to have no position, to be nothing more than an "adviser" to his people, but he was everything: leader, brother, judge and jury; author of the reviled *Green Book*, which guided the lives of Libyans; and even the architect of a calendar based on the death of the Muslim prophet Mohammed and used nowhere else but in Libya. His overwhelming, often eccentric presence stunted the development of any kind of institution and smothered even the idea of an independent press. Saddam may have been extraordinarily paranoid, but Qaddafi outdid even him: one day our Libyan staff counted from memory more than a dozen different security branches, tasked mostly with protecting Qaddafi and his hold on power. Like Saddam, Qaddafi had always planned for the day when his people would turn on him, for he, like Saddam, knew that day would eventually come.

Benghazi was a sun-drenched, quiet place overlooking the Mediterranean, a neglected, humble city now uncomfortably suspended between an ugly past and a promising future. We spent our first full reporting day at the *katiba* compound, which had been opened for citizens to inspect—entire families, with grandparents and children in tow, came to walk its grounds, tut-tutting and shaking their heads. A group of young men touring the place showed us the hole in the compound's wall where the rebels, aided by defecting elements of the army, had punched through to sack their oppressors. Others pointed out the underground prisons that had been pressed into the service of a regime that led through terror. Several people gathered around a hole in the ground told us that six men had been imprisoned there and were pulled out the day the *katiba* was overrun, though no one could point us in the direction of any of the former prisoners. It didn't matter to the people assembled there: they repeated the story as fact, and in any case, they knew enough first-hand stories of imprisonment and torture in that place and needed no further proof of their veracity.

I tried to reach some of the people I had spoken to over the phone from London. But the phones had been mostly cut off in Benghazi and I could never get through. I would never meet that breathless eyewitness who had taken me with him as he ran in the alleys near the courthouse. For all I know, he was cut down with the dozens of others who died liberating their city.

Benghazi seemed, then, a larger version of Tahrir Square at its finest hour, its people united by one purpose and fuelled by hope— as well as by the realization that failure was not an option. We met doctors who kept the hospitals running despite shortages of medicine and food, and volunteers who made it their business to bring wreaths of flowers and baskets of fruit to the injured fighters. We talked to families who were cooking thousands of meals a week—an assembly line of brothers, wives, neighbours, and fathers packaging pasta for the fighters and prisoners of war. We found women who spent their days giving out parcels of dry food to the needy, and men who organized traffic—all without payment. One woman told me that even the known criminals in town were lending a hand, providing security and joining the rebels to fight Qaddafi's forces farther west.

The rebels allowed us to visit Radio Free Libya, even though it exposed the operators to significant risk. Qaddafi's fighter planes were still in the air, and a single rocket was all it would take to silence it. All we needed to be granted a visit to the station was a handwritten letter from Mustafa Abdul Jaleel, former justice minister under Qaddafi and now, after becoming the first to defect from the government, the head of the National Transitional Council (NTC), which represented the Libyan opposition. I first met him in the corridors of our hotel following one of his news conferences, a serene, quiet man who said little but smiled warmly. He penned the permission letter we needed by hand, and his assistant (and son) imprinted it with a green stamp to make it official.

Visiting that radio station was one of the most exhilarating moments for me since I'd arrived in Libya. Though it wasn't exactly journalism the way we know it—it was the long-silenced voices of the oppressed now amplified and heard by hundreds of thousands—what could be more inspiring? It was the same feeling I'd had back in Cairo one night shortly after Mubarak stepped down, when Glen and Margaret and I arrived at the offices of the *Al-Ahram* newspaper, only to hear the staff upstairs trying to argue their way to change. It was the same in another corner of Benghazi, while spending hours with the mostly young female journalists who debated how to transform their old newspaper into a free, independent one. Watching the revolution in action among the Libyan fighters, with their guns and souped-up pickup trucks, was one thing. But watching it unfold among the people themselves was something else entirely, stirring to behold.

Inside the station, we found a handful of men who were high

on their own revolutionary rhetoric—men who had also accepted that they might die doing what they were doing. When asked about this, they repeated the revolution's mantra, once an al-Mukhtar slogan: "Victory or death." It may have been an oft-repeated phrase in Benghazi, but with vindictive Qaddafi as their foe, these were truly the only two options possible now.

It was also the favoured slogan of the hapless, undisciplined young men who'd signed up to fight without ever having handled a gun in their lives, as well as the motto of the protesters who gathered daily at the courthouse to vent forty years' worth of indignity and repression. Every Friday the protests grew larger, and with every day the demonstrators survived, their ambitions multiplied and their expressions of dissent became more brazen. On one Friday, as we filmed the throngs marching towards the courthouse, a middle-aged man approached us and asked us to deliver a message to Qaddafi. Just as Pascal started filming, the man pulled out a pistol from the small of his back and waved it at our camera. "We are going to kill you, Qaddafi. It won't be the West, not Europe. We will kill you with our own hands."

Qaddafi was making his own threats. He blamed the unrest on Islamist terrorists, and then promised to crush the rebels in the east like the "rats" they were. A large military force began moving in Benghazi's direction. The closer they inched towards the city, the more pronounced the defiance among its citizens, who vowed to fight with their hands if they had to. Yet many also resigned themselves to a crackdown they were certain would wipe Benghazi off the map, just as Qaddafi had promised.

Abdul Jaleel and other members of the NTC travelled widely to lobby for an internationally enforced no-fly zone to protect the rebels and the gains they had made in the east. Benghazians were floored when their city was mentioned by name on the international stage; it was unprecedented and significant, and for many,

that alone helped raise morale. Perhaps they were not alone on the
suicidal road to toppling a homicidal dictator.

The UN passed a resolution to enforce the no-fly zone and also
to allow military intervention to protect the civilian population.
French aircraft dropped the first bombs, annihilating Qaddafi's
killing machine just kilometres short of the heart of Benghazi. On
my second trip there later that March, its citizens were buoyed and
more hopeful than ever. They were enamoured with the French and
their handiwork, which was still on display on the road between
Benghazi and Ajdabiya in the form of the mangled remains of a
military convoy. Their city had now truly been liberated, and they
waited for the rest of the country to follow.

Benghazi's imposing central courthouse overlooking the
Mediterranean had become the de facto rebel headquarters, and
it buzzed with activity twenty-four hours a day. Stephanie, Pascal,
and I spent a long time filming at one of its walls, which by then
had become a gallery for the fallen: hundreds of pictures of mostly
young Libyans who had been murdered in years past by Qaddafi's
cruel men, as well as those who had died in the recent uprising.

A mother and her daughter joined the small and contemplative
crowd, but they had come to add another picture. The woman's son
had perished near the *katiba*, his body, the mother stoically told
us, ripped in two by oversized bullets. A young boy was hoisted up
by the men to pin his picture to the wall, and there he was, staring
back at admirers he would never know. The family craved revenge;
they wanted Qaddafi to be tried for his crimes in Libya. Nothing
less would assuage their grief.

There was still dry, angry tinder beneath the growing optimism
in that city. Yet Benghazi also overflowed with compassion and
became a welcoming refuge to hundreds of displaced people
who had escaped the fighting in Ajdabiya, Brega, Ras Lanuf, and
other places west. So much to mourn and so much to fight for,

yet thousands of Benghazians took an afternoon to hold a huge funeral for an Al Jazeera cameraman who was killed by Qaddafi's men in an ambush just outside the city. Al Jazeera Arabic, of course, was especially favoured for its unreservedly glowing coverage of the rebels. It was as supportive of their revolution on air as its owners (Qatar's rulers) were off air. Its disdain for Qaddafi—evidenced, not least, by advertisements that ran dozens of times a day that made him look ridiculous—was obvious.

Even I, as a journalist, was offered many tender condolences that day, for the loss of a colleague I didn't even know. Many rebels and ordinary people also approached us to thank us—the foreign journalists who had thronged to Benghazi—simply for being there, and for helping to shed light on their plight. They credited us with introducing the world to Benghazi, and with taking their city's name to the chambers of the UN. Rarely had we, as foreign journalists, been treated in such a way in an Arab country before. We were more accustomed to accusations of rubbernecking or espionage.

The fighting near Benghazi proceeded slowly. The rebels had neither the firepower nor the discipline or training required to progress. They failed to make any significant headway towards the west, or to hold any ground they did gain. They were "fighting"— a strong word for what they were up to—what some described as an "accordion war" that netted virtually nothing but casualties. It was clear to me early on that they certainly wouldn't get anywhere near Sirte, Qaddafi's hometown and also home, we were told, to many supporters and significant weapons caches. Like the more pragmatic among the Libyan rebels, I believed that for the uprising to succeed, Tripoli and other points west had to rise up, too. There were isolated reports of protests there, but with Qaddafi's propaganda machine at full tilt—his television station and spinners constantly churned out bald lies—it was challenging even for those journalists who eventually made it to Tripoli to determine the full extent of the support for Qaddafi's overthrow.

It would take many more months, but eventually that was precisely what happened: fighters in the west, aided by the NATO airstrikes, took Tripoli and finally tracked down Qaddafi.

In the aftermath of a well-aimed NATO strike on his convoy, Qaddafi was found on October 20, 2011, hiding in a sewer pipe in his hometown, much like Saddam was caught in an underground hole in his. Saddam was subsequently tried and then hanged by his people—some of whom mocked and ridiculed him as he fell at the gallows. Qaddafi's end wasn't much different, but it was much more abbreviated, and far more vindictive.

"Arab leaders don't learn from the experience of others," one Arab columnist wrote. "They haven't heeded the 'hole' lesson."

The images of Qaddafi's final moments, captured on mobile phone video, were gruesome: a bloodied and dazed colonel manhandled and then hoisted on the front of a vehicle by a frenzied mob. You could hear a voice or two on the recording demanding, "We need him alive! We need him alive!" But someone shot him anyway, and Qaddafi was dead. And though his capture would likely never have happened without NATO intervention, the mobile phone images provided enough proof that he ultimately died at the hands of Libyans, just as the pistol-wielding protester had predicted. It was what the Americans and their allies wanted from the start, to make their involvement palatable to their own people and especially to the Arab world.

The NATO intervention did have its critics, though, not least because it seemed, ultimately, a thinly veiled effort at regime change in the guise of protecting civilians. But it was an operation that still managed to break the mould for foreign intervention in the Arab world. Participating countries wanted it to be everything that the Iraq invasion was not: foreign intervention at the request of the people, with the cover of an Arab League decision and the participation (quiet or public) of a number of Arab countries. It involved no ground troops (notwithstanding the foreign special forces who helped direct air attacks). And while the U.S. played a large part in the early phase of the campaign to disable Qaddafi's war machine, it remained in the background and let others lead. Libya was no Iraq—it seemed a black-and-white case in comparison. Still, the operation looked refreshingly different to many Arab people—many of whom despised Qaddafi anyway. In Libya, the people were united in gratitude: they hoisted French, British, and even American flags, thanking the leaders by name. There was no better proof of that appreciation than the frenzied welcome given to French president Nicolas Sarkozy and British prime minister David Cameron when they visited Libya in September 2011.

Libya celebrated Qaddafi's end for days, impervious to charges that the circumstances of his death bode badly for the future of a new country that promised the kind of justice and humanity it had lacked under his leadership. Yet Qaddafi's fate also brought hope to those still in the throes of their own bloody revolutions that perhaps their turn, too, might eventually come.

ℵ

It was a dramatic departure from the narrative of revolution in Tunisia and Egypt. Yet with the summary execution of the third autocratic casualty of the Arab Spring, I couldn't help seeing glimpses of Saddam in what happened to Qaddafi. I could also detect traces of Iran's failed Green Revolution in 2009 and hints of Lebanon's Truth uprising in 2005 in every one of the Arab world's 2011 revolts. They had each been uniquely instructive to anyone in the region with revolutionary designs. Collectively, though, they provided a loose guide on how to transform such designs into reality.

Even though most of the uprisings borrowed the Arab Spring's now familiar chant, *Al-sha'ab, yureed, isqat al nitham!* (The people want the fall of the regime), it was inevitable that each country's revolt would unfold differently. While people across the region shared many of the same complaints, each country was troubled in its own way. None perhaps more troubled than Syria.

But how would the Syrians do it? In the first days of their uprising back in March 2011, the few voices that emerged on the international stage maintained the protesters did not want foreign intervention. But little did they know then how tenaciously the Assad regime would fight to cling to "the chair," the *kursee,* and how bloody their revolt would become. Syria's situation made foreign intervention exceptionally fraught and dangerous. The regime's staunch backing by Iran, Russia, and China ensured that there would be no repeat of the swift international action seen on the Libyan front.

Unsurprisingly, one of the first to revolt in Syria were the people of Hama, the city that had been razed once before, when its people rose up in 1982 under a different Assad. The Syrian government's retaliation was as swift this time as it was then. But the protests spread to other cities, to Homs, Palmyra, Latakia, and even Aleppo at times, and to several smaller towns and villages, including the suburbs of Damascus. The heart of the capital mostly remained sullenly quiet—partly out of fear, partly because its merchant class and religious minorities relied so heavily on the ruling Ba'athists and flinched at the thought of an Islamist alternative. Several months and many condemnations later, Assad clung to that chair, offering only vague promises of reform and dialogue.

But it seemed too late for dialogue, and the protests continued despite the death of at least six thousand people and the imprisonment of tens of thousands more. Demonstrators reported on their own peaceful protests and covered the sustained efforts to put them down—capturing it all on mobile phones and uploading it to the Internet.

But increasingly—with defecting soldiers now striking back— the situation in Syria edged towards a civil war. Thousands of Syrians had already fled and found refuge in Turkey and Lebanon—in the latter case, it was a reversal of roles the Lebanese found ironic. But in Lebanon there was also a sharpened anxiety, and renewed tensions between the pro- and anti-Syrian camps once again threatened that country's stability. There was a certainty that anything looking like a civil war in Syria would also bring out Lebanon's old sectarian demons.

After all the time I'd spent in Syria, it was hard to imagine its gentle people in internal conflict, its spacious boulevards besieged by tanks, or its ancient alleys haunted by fighters. And what would be the fate of the hundreds of thousands of Iraqis—and Palestinians—who had sheltered there for safety?

Though Lebanon had an extensive history of conflict, it was equally difficult to contemplate it once again being forced to pay the price for yet another fight that did not concern its people. Sadly, on every journey to Lebanon after the Syrian uprising erupted, I found it as usual uncomfortably suspended in the throes of regional instability, still cowering in dread of its future.

꙳

It had been an exceptional year. I had initially arrived in London to fill in for six days, and it became my base for nine months. In that time, I had been on assignment in Lebanon, Egypt, Libya, Toronto, New York, Los Angeles, Paris, and Oslo—the latter the scene of a tragic bombing and shooting attack by a madman opposed to the growing Muslim and immigrant presence in Norway. In between I filed from London, covering the summer riots there and a number of other stories. I lived out of a pile of suitcases stacked up in a tiny rented apartment across the street from the CBC office, in a state of near chaos that I was only barely able to contain. Even in the worst of the upheaval in the Mideast, I had never been so unsettled. And yet for the first time in a long time, I was at peace.

It occurred to me then that all that time I'd spent in the Middle East as a child and all those years working in difficult conditions there as an adult had been building up to this one singular year. The deflation I felt as I moved out of the Middle East in 2009 had vanished. Those seven exhausting years now made sense: they had been my preparation, my schooling in anticipation of what would eventually come.

Journalistically, the Arab Spring was a highlight for me—an event far more meaningful than witnessing the fall of Saddam's regime or watching the end of the war in Lebanon. It answered many lingering questions. Why were Arabs so silent? How could they withstand decades of authoritarianism? How would they eventually gain freedom? It seemed they had simply been waiting for the right moment. The apathy had existed so long as they hadn't found a way out of despondence. But now they had, and the apathy seemed to dissipate. The uprisings marked the end of one chapter and the beginning of a new one, and I hungrily read on, possessed, eager to find out what would happen next.

This one year also confirmed my long-held belief in the traditional model of foreign correspondence, in the benefit—the necessity—of living in a place, if only for a year or two, in order to really understand it. You cannot fully comprehend the reasons behind an eruption of violence, an uprising, without having understood its root causes. You must know every one of a country's opposing voices to truly reflect the tension between them. You must know something of the people's daily challenges before you could credibly speak to their frustrations.

You must also be able to put yourself in the shoes of anyone, anywhere, to truly tell their story. People are not quotes or clips, used to illustrate stories about war and conflict. People *are* the story, always. And you cannot know what people are thinking by reading wire reports. You must come to know them somehow. Speaking the language, as I did, helps tremendously, but it is not a prerequisite. Taking the time to speak to people *off* camera—at length—is.

But it is all consuming, and so for the better part of a decade, work had ruled my life. I did try, in the midst of it all, to find some semblance of normality, but my career always came first— whether I was in the Middle East, or on Parliament Hill in Ottawa. In the Mideast, it was much more emotionally challenging to be so remote from family and friends for so long. But work is second nature to me, a calling, as important as breathing—much like my father's work was for him. Looking back, there was no other possible outcome, no matter what I did for a living. My one but significant regret concerns the precious friends I lost in the process of gaining knowledge.

FIFTEEN

The Revolution Continues

*What falls from the sky
the earth shall receive.*
—ARAB PROVERB

I knew from the start that working in the Middle East meant total commitment. I had no choice but to immerse myself in every aspect, read every word, jump into every conflict. It is true that I overstayed, to the point of exhaustion, but choices always existed, and I could have left at any moment, with or without the CBC. I chose to stay, and while the unpredictability of life in the region partly determined how my life unfolded, I, too, was culpable, a willing participant whose only goal, always, was to deepen my understanding.

I did not initially understand the emotional toll of chasing the Middle East's endless crises. Admittedly, I was often surprised at the ease with which you could behold death, destruction, and bitter mourning—the ease with which you could then sleep that night and rise the next morning, like it was any other day. I did not expect that awful day in Baghdad, where I could have lost my life, to stay with me beyond the form of a terrible memory. I could not have predicted that it would have a profound effect, many months later, in the form of nightmares and daytime mind movies about what *could* have happened. And I didn't dare speak of it. I knew what happened to journalists who did. I'd seen the callous way in which others empathized and then wrote you off, limiting your career options before you were ready to call it quits yourself. We in the journalistic community talk a good game when the subject of stress and trauma among our own comes up. But in reality—with many exceptions—we can also be heartless and judgmental when we come upon it face to face. I know, I've seen and heard evidence of it at all levels of our business.

Thankfully, with the help of close friends and colleagues over a number of years, the worst of those stresses is over for me. It takes time, healing those parts of you that were the most vulnerable. But believe me—and I am living proof—that it's possible, one part at a time. You emerge stronger, far more resilient. A bruised spirit is only that, and bruises in time tend to heal.

The most healing experience for me was standing in Tahrir Square and watching the Arab world finally change. I had no role in bringing about that change, and no particular personal stake in the outcome. But it was the kind of payoff every one of us in this business craves. The euphoria gave some meaning to my years of witnessing uncontainable anger, unspeakable violence, and mind-numbing anguish. The physical and emotional dangers, the sleepless nights, the loneliness—it had all been worth it.

For a long time, the stagnant Arab world gave its people two choices: either live with it or leave—if you can. Faced with choosing between hopelessness and the possibility of a new start, many Arabs, including my own parents, opted to leave.

I often contemplated that small twist in our family's history, that hasty decision my father made to leave the Middle East back when he was a young man. Ultimately, it meant the difference between the relatively free, open lives we were afforded and the restricted, confining lives that so many in the Arab world still endure. It meant driving at sixteen, piano lessons, band and choir, and a graduation prom at eighteen. It meant the difference between a proper higher education, according to our wishes, and an education deemed "appropriate," especially for women, in a conservative society. It meant I could become a journalist and travel the world freely. I could decide to come back to the Middle East, and then leave it again, thanks to my father's decision. We knew about freedom and understood the definition of "human rights," and we could even choose to take them for granted, like so many others in the West. I never did, nor did I think myself better than my relatives. I considered myself incredibly lucky, that's all.

Of all the bizarre things people asked when I travelled in the Mideast, the most vexing was how I "got" my Canadian passport, as if it were a piece of jewellery. "How lovely. Where did you get it? Where can I get one?" "I was born with it," I'd always say. "Sheer luck." "Yes, but you're really Arab—you just have a foreign passport." *Well, not quite.* My being Canadian meant more than the mere possession of a passport. I tried to explain that it was a way of life, a way of thinking, of being, that began the day I was born in St-Boniface. But it was a difficult concept to grasp for those whose citizenship bestowed few benefits and meant little more than residence. It was hard for many of them to look past the notion that a foreign passport was anything more than a tool, a buoy that could solve all of life's problems, especially when they lived in a place with no future—or worse, when they had never had citizenship of any kind at all.

Yet the only time I felt I truly belonged anywhere were the first six years I lived in Canada after I was born and after our return from Amman, and it is those years in which my strong sense of attachment to Canada is rooted. I've often lived the life of an uneasy immigrant, the life of someone seeking refuge. Both times I arrived to live in the Middle East, it took years to adapt, to refine my language skills, to make friends and learn the mundane necessities of daily life. Both times I returned to Canada, it took time to reintegrate, to unlearn one way of life and reacquaint myself with another. In fact, for the better part of forty years, beyond the voices of my parents on the telephone, constants have been scarce. Yet it had become a way of life. Not ideal, not by a long shot. But comfortably familiar.

Growing up, I always knew my life would be defined less by a country or a city and more by a journey, one that I daydreamed about repeatedly before it ever happened. As a child I had often imagined that first farewell, when I would say goodbye to my family and leave them behind for some new place to call home, if only for a time. Isn't that what everyone did? When the moment came, I was distraught, but part of me was also happy the journey had finally begun. I knew I belonged in the airports that my parents had taught us to love and get excited about. I felt most at peace in a window seat, staring at the clouds rushing beneath me, aloft on mechanical wings and lost in thoughts about what I had left and where I was going. As long as I was going somewhere, I was fine.

While I was growing up, people were always leaving. It's what I knew. And I learned early on that it's far better to be the one leaving than the one left behind.

Having left so much behind, too, my parents taught us to always look forward. *Don't look back*, they said. *Carry on and move ahead. Walk on and walk fast, because if you don't, you might miss something.* Gibran Khalil Gibran, that prolific Lebanese American poet, counselled the same when he said, "March on. Do not tarry. To go forward is to move toward perfection. March on, and fear not the thorns, or the sharp stones on life's path."

I rushed headlong into everything, and yet I always looked back—even when bidding someone farewell. By doing so, I was breaking a spell not meant to be broken, the irresistible temptation to remember, for all time, the feel of that last embrace, the image of a regretful smile, the cheerlessness of that final meek wave and nothing else. Saying goodbye, I look back, and I look back again, waiting for acknowledgment, for the other person to look back, too. Sometimes they do; often they do not. But while I'm constantly propelled forward, I can't just walk away, carelessly strolling into the future. It isn't my nature.

When I look back now, the Middle East is often just a blur of guns and violence, of explosions and assassinations, of breaking news bulletins and conspiracy theories replaying endlessly in my mind. Those images from our grainy Amman television so long ago often came back to me as I watched another particularly violent period pass over the Middle East like an angry storm. I witnessed new losses magnify the old ones: the individual or inherited wounds of war, missing relatives, lost homes, separated families, and absent rights. The recent tragedies, the kind unique to lopsided conflicts, have been difficult to absorb: whole families obliterated by errant bombs, weddings turned into funerals, children left orphans. Then there are freeze-frames I simply cannot forget: the Hillah mourning queen in the throes of bereavement, the injured old Lebanese woman crying in her hospital bed, the first time you enter a refugee camp, in the dead of night.

It's harder to remember the happier images, but they, too, linger. I cannot forget the soothing sight of a Mount Lebanon stream, the brilliant green of the Golan Heights, the sun setting over the Mediterranean. I will always remember Fairouz singing live, the tens of thousands cheering in a traffic circle called Tahrir Square. I try to remember the people's generous spirit, and the friends who took me in, both literally and figuratively, when I needed it most.

Deeper into the folds of my memory are those daunting years we spent in Amman as children. Those years changed the course of our lives, setting me on a path that determined not only my lifestyle and temperament but also my career choice—they also taught me contentment with what you have is a treasure that never runs out. My father's own inner tug-of-war between tradition and modernity had forced us to become familiar with the Middle East—the good and the bad. Despite the difficulties—the sadness and hopelessness, the complicated politics, and the absence, always, of a straight answer to any question you posed—the culture intrigued me. My curiosity compelled me to try to understand, and so I returned, despite myself. I was always meant to. What is written, is written. There is no escaping it.

My mother's determination to ensure that we grew up speaking Arabic played an equally significant role. Those early, irritating lessons, neatly written by her on the back of the basement door, laid the foundations for my career and more than likely explains my focus on people—I could learn things about them no translator could ever help you learn. I would have probably hesitated to venture into the Middle East had I not spoken the language (mangled as it was by the time I arrived in Baghdad). Or if I had, I would never have been able to decipher the nuances, to learn that the word *watan* means more than the simplistic notion of "country," that the meaning of *musharradeen* is far deeper than the mere "displaced." I would never have been attuned to the outlandish embellishments of over-enthusiastic translators, or to the threats murmured on the edges of a seemingly friendly crowd listening to us conduct an interview. I would never have known the true meaning of *gorbah*, that one word that so aptly describes the alienation of separation and displacement that so many Arabs live daily.

Nearly three decades after I left Jordan as a teenager, angry at the inconsistency of our lives, at the separation, at the inequity and violence, I had yet to forgive the Middle East for what it had taught me, not once but twice: the elusiveness of contentment, and fear of the future. Having lived that reality, I finally understood, far more than I had ever wanted to, but not enough to forgive.

☧

Since the euphoria of revolution in February 2011, Egypt's ruling military council has managed to decelerate change dramatically. It still enforced the hated emergency law and put some twelve thousand more people on trial in military courts—an outrage, given that one of the council's first promises was to eliminate the laws that allowed this. It also oversaw one of the bloodiest crackdowns since the early days of the revolution, a ruthless shutdown of a Christian protest in October 2011, in which nearly thirty people died and more than two hundred were injured. It also imposed censorship on the media, and imprisoned and tortured bloggers, journalists, and protesters in a way that was little different from Mubarak's.

As one concession, the military council did put the president it had discarded on trial in August. The proceedings were televised to try to appease the roiling citizenry, but it wasn't long before the judge ordered the cameras out and continued the trial behind closed doors.

The day it began, I was standing outside the courthouse on the outskirts of Cairo with cameraman Richard Devey and producer Lindsay Isaac. Despite the heat and the early hour, and the fact that it was Ramadan, the month of fasting, dozens of people had come out to show their support or disdain for Mubarak. The early days of Tahrir Square replayed themselves in miniature: the anti-Mubaraks and the pro-Mubaraks, each trying to have their say, clashed several times in a shower of rocks and bottles, with walls of riot police occasionally intervening to stem the violence before it worsened.

At the entrance to the court, in the chaos of lawyers and journalists trying to get in, families of the revolution's victims screamed and pushed to try to get in, too. They had paid for the revolution with the blood of loved ones, and they wanted their rightful seat at the spectacle that could avenge their losses. A tiny woman head-to-toe in black hijab told us she wanted Mubarak executed in the street, just as her son had been. She was an echo of the mothers I'd heard in Baghdad, in Libya, and Lebanon. But nothing would bring their children back. Soon, Mubarak appeared on a gurney and pleaded not guilty to ordering the killing of some eight hundred protesters in the revolution. The sight was shocking to all Egyptians, and it unsettled the Arab world perhaps as much as his ouster had.

Yet just twenty minutes away, in downtown Cairo, Egypt had travelled back in time. The authorities were firmly in control of Tahrir Square, which was lined with motionless riot police who formed a human barrier against change in the midday Ramadan sun.

Dissatisfied with the progress since the revolution, protesters had returned to camp out there earlier in the summer, and a week before we arrived, police had forcibly turfed them out and seized the square, dismantling tents and imposing quiet. Late at night, after the daytime fast was broken, many of those protesters gathered at nearby cafes to smoke the *shisha*, drink coffee and tea, and discuss politics into the early hours of the morning. We went down one night to speak with some of them. Surprisingly, they were still upbeat.

"Did anyone imagine that we would see Mubarak in a cage?" Mohamed al-Naggar asked me. "It's a big deal. It's the first time in Egypt's history that it tries a pharaoh. We have made a lot of progress. The people are demanding their rights. Each knows how to speak up and say, 'I want my rights.' This didn't exist before. The negativity among all the Egyptian people was rampant."

His friend Amr Nasr said they would be patient, like so many revolutionaries before them. "I am ready to wait a year, even twenty years [for the revolution to succeed], but I won't be able to wait if we don't sanitize the country first," he said, referring to remnants of Mubarak's loyalists and the military. "And we may still go back to Tahrir, because we still have demands."

Al-Naggar nodded in agreement. "The revolution continues," he said.

Our conversation reminded me of an interview I once did with a prescient scholar at the Al-Ahram Centre for Strategic Studies after the presidential election in 2005. He said Egyptians—indeed all Arabs—needed to redefine "victory" in their discourse. That it need not be victory against a declared enemy, but "victory in education, in development, in the standard of life." That is the kind of victory these youth now desperately sought, that others sought around the region.

As the summer wore on, most of the revolution's demands were consistently ignored, and the revolutionaries' patience wore thin. They warned repeatedly that they would resort to street action again if the ruling military council failed to begin a transition to civilian authority soon.

Instead, the council attempted to enshrine the military's supremacy in law—a plan that would have put Egypt's military above any elected body, and its budget and inner workings well beyond the purview of any ruler. It was the last straw. Just days before the scheduled parliamentary elections in late November, the revolutionaries made good on their promise, and Tahrir Square suddenly came alive again with protests and then riot police. And once again, the more violent the crackdown, the more people arrived to vent their anger. Some forty people lost their lives, and scores were injured. I watched from faraway Toronto.

The military reacted by withdrawing the proposal and promising to move up the presidential elections to June 2012, a clear victory for the people and a proposal accepted by the Muslim

Brotherhood, now on the verge of real victory. But the military also vowed that the first round of scheduled parliamentary elections, just days away, would go ahead despite the chaos.

And as expected, Islamists—both the relatively moderate and well-organized Muslim Brotherhood and the more fundamentalist Salafists—did exceptionally well in those elections, raising alarm bells around the region and in the West. I, too, wondered how far the Islamists would go in restricting personal freedoms in the name of religion. How much would that religion influence the new constitution? And what of Egypt's women and Christians? And would the tourist dollars—which helped feed and clothe millions of Egyptians—ever return to an Islamist Egypt?

The post–Arab Spring emergence of Islamists (in Tunisia and Morocco and Libya as well), the violence of Egypt's renewed protests, the continuing bloodshed in Syria and Yemen—together they were declared by Western analysts and commentators as evidence of the end of the Arab Spring. Barely a year after the revolutions, they claimed the Arab Winter had begun.

The concerns were well founded. And yet it was too early to judge. Three dictators (Ben Ali, Mubarak, Qaddafi) had been deposed, a fourth (Assad) teetered, and subsequent protests demonstrated the people's realization that they now had a powerful role as active, vocal participants in their society.

There were other subtle but unmistakable advances. The conversation around the Middle East had shifted; people now spoke of freedom and democracy and human rights. Saudi's monarchy, while a long way from true reform, was forced to introduce a number of measures aimed at heading off unrest. But even in Saudi there were small uprisings. Saudi women, among the most oppressed of all people in the region, launched an ambitious campaign to defy the ban on female driving in the kingdom, a signal they were dissatisfied with the far more serious restrictions under which they lived. The Saudi king responded by announcing that women would have the right to vote and stand for municipal elections starting in 2015, and he agreed to include them in his next shura, or consultative council. These were embarrassingly small steps—especially given that women in Saudi aren't even allowed to move around without a male guardian—but even such small steps would have been delayed had it not been for the Arab Spring. It was clear that Saudi Arabia could no longer remain so firmly entrenched in the Dark Ages.

Jordan, too, introduced small changes, installing three different governments in the span of a year. The authorities even released political prisoners from among the Islamist camp as a rare gesture of goodwill. It was recognition that authoritarianism had not been the best antidote to the growing extremism, and in fact only encouraged it. Yemen and Bahrain erupted with the discontent that had long brewed under the surface, and while both uprisings sputtered, the desire for change could no longer be ignored. Even the mired Syrian uprising, probably the toughest of all, has realized some successes by isolating Assad's regime and highlighting to the world the brutality with which he and his father have ruled that nation for decades.

In Egypt, the people witnessed the birth of dozens of new political parties, as well as independent television networks and newspapers. People now openly question prevailing truths. They know that they have a say, and that the street is the pulpit of the masses. And there has been real debate about the country's future, about the role of women, about relations with Israel and the West, and about the role of Islam.

In all these places, debate has begun about the role of religion in politics—a conversation that has been waiting to happen. More than once, long before the revolutions, Arab analysts had told me that the only way to develop alternatives to the well-organized Islamists was to give people the chance to try them out—in democratic elections. Many Egyptians told me that the Brotherhood had four years to prove to voters that their Egypt was better than Mubarak's. If it wasn't, they believed they could simply vote them out the next time.

And yet major potential pitfalls lie ahead. With the arrival of hope, there is also the danger of dashing it.

Because the battle for and against change in the Arab world is just beginning. Beyond the deposed autocrats, there are institutions and powerful people—in the military, the merchant and wealthy classes, even at universities and among government officials—who will carry on that spirited defence of the status quo. There are also the region's remaining and powerful autocrats, whose own fears of instability will guide their policies in other countries. And there are the region's overarching battles—the long-simmering cold war between Sunni and Shia Muslims, and the intractable Israeli–Palestinian conflict—a convenient scapegoat in the Arab world for those attempting to protect the status quo, but like the former, a problem nevertheless that has long cried for a solution.

Real change does not happen in eighteen days of revolution, as in Egypt's case, or even in a year-long rebellion, as in Syria. It will take years, perhaps decades, and the danger is that it won't happen quickly enough to prevent despair settling back into the hearts of those desperate for renaissance. The region is still at great risk of returning to its dark, wintery past. Prospects are dim if the revolutions ultimately fail, if the Mideast is dragged into another controversial war, if thousands of people are once again displaced, if Islamists bring turmoil, if the hopes of the region's largest generation of young people are disappointed— or if, perhaps most important of all, the revolutions fail to bring economic improvements along with—even ahead of—political change. "*Bread*, freedom, and justice," they chanted. The gains of the Arab uprising are still extremely fragile, and even the smallest advance is precious because it was so hard won. But it wouldn't take much to undo the gains.

🏃

It was hard to believe a year had passed since Mohammed Bouazizi, that desperate Tunisian youth, set himself on fire, nearly a year since Mubarak was forced to step down. In December 2011, we were planning a return to Egypt to mark the first anniversary of the start of their uprising. Stephanie Jenzer and I, along with cameraman Ousama Farag, were assigned to travel there and try to look forward.

After a number of years in the region, I had once been able to read the tea leaves and predict the next turn in the Mideast's future—that's how predictable it was. But so much had happened in such a short time. So much had been out of the ordinary that anyone who told you they could foretell what would happen from here on in was almost certainly lying.

Cairo had erupted into protests again, and at that moment, the future seemed to be slowly unravelling. I couldn't be sure, though—not until I was back on the city's infuriating streets, to speak to people, to breathe the same air, and to watch the same networks and read the same papers.

I wanted to know to satisfy my own endless curiosity—about what happened in Egypt and everything else that happens in our world beyond our own borders. I wanted to know so I could explain to those of our viewers who cared enough to sit through a story about a people so very far away, and yet so very similar in ambitions, desires, and hopes. I wanted to know because it matters; because what happens there echoes here, loudly; because I wanted, above all, to tell their story and have it be heard.

I also wanted to know because I felt I needed, still, to earn my privileged existence away from all the turmoil that could very easily have been my whole life. Knowing and understanding it all reminds me of just how fortunate I have been.

With Christmas in the air and a new year around the corner, I had a sudden yearning to be home. I hadn't been to Winnipeg in more than a year. I called my mother. What I needed was more than her voice over the telephone. "Can I come home this weekend?" I asked.

She laughed. "The welder has no coal," she said, meaning she had nothing to do. "Of course you can come home. You can help me with my homework." My mother, who had been denied an education as an orphan, was, at age sixty-four, working on attaining her grade twelve certificate.

A few days later, the sun poured in through my window seat, keeping me warm the entire way, as if to atone for what would surely be a typically chilly Winnipeg afternoon. As the plane glided north and west, the blue of the Great Lakes made way for the familiar checkerboard of prairie farmland, now covered with a thin blanket of snow. Soon, the Red River was visible, snaking its way through perennial tree groves and the familiar rows of little bungalows on the edge of the city. It was a smooth descent in the crisp, light wind, ending with an almost perfect landing. I was happy to be home.

In between working out mathematical formulas, Mom and I kept an eye on the news, which Dad insisted on watching every hour on the hour. Iraq was in the headlines once more; the final convoy of combat soldiers had left overland to Kuwait, and suddenly that war was over. It was almost nine years to the day since I left for Amman, and from there for Iraq, on a journey that had dominated a quarter of my years. I couldn't help wondering how long it would be before Iraq's fragile quilt ripped apart again along sectarian lines.

Egypt and Syria, too, appeared in the hourly newscasts. More than six thousand Syrians were dead as an increasingly intransigent

Assad regime announced it would begin executing the "terror-ists" who were responsible for the unrest. In Egypt, meanwhile, the protests had escalated again, and the images were increasingly disturbing. As I watched, I wondered how long before Egypt's insurmountable economic woes overshadowed all else.

My mother, seemingly engrossed in her homework, suddenly looked up at the television, and then turned to stare at me.

"Are you staying somewhere safe when you go to Egypt?" Mom rarely enquired directly about such things, though I knew it preoc-cupied her daily.

"Yes," I said. "Don't worry. I will be fine."

AUTHOR'S NOTE

While writing this book, I have tried to focus on what I have witnessed and lived, the people to whom I spoke, their experiences and interpretations of events. Even then my accounts are often limited by the nature of the reporting I did at the time, my notes, and my memory, augmented by extensive reading and discussion with experts.

Inevitably, like all books, this one only provides snapshots of what is a vexingly complex story. I make no claim to being anywhere near comprehensive. This is one version of the story of the modern Arab world—mostly, the story of how its people are affected by a difficult past and a present and future fraught with uncertainty. It is not so much a political examination as a glimpse into the Arab condition, focused on how people become the product of their challenging environment—and on the civilians of the region who have long been mischaracterized and misunderstood.

Beyond the account of my early history as a Canadian of Arab descent, the book is anchored in my experiences in the Middle East as an Arab-world correspondent. It is based in large part on the stories that made news in the Arab world throughout that period— the conflicts, the violence, the political impasses.

There is so much more to the Arab world. Nonetheless, initially I wrote a book describing the stagnation, the violence and displacement, the moribund political scene, and the resulting widespread depression and inertia that plagued the Arab world. Those were the things that struck me most in the time that I spent there. In early 2011, though, I was forced to append new chapters to take into account where all those challenges had led: the Arab Spring. It was a perfect conclusion to what I had already written. But it is a story that has just begun, and will continue to write itself for years and decades to come. My cursory look at those events—my even more cursory analysis—will almost certainly be superseded.

On language: It is nearly impossible to find consistent English spellings of Arab names of people, places, and organizations. In some cases, I spelled names as they would sound in Arabic, in others I spelled them the way the individuals themselves preferred. That makes for many unavoidable inconsistencies.

An important final note: Many people I met in the Arab world over the years worked with us or spoke to us at great personal risk. It is for that reason that many names in this book have been changed.

ACKNOWLEDGMENTS

I must begin by thanking the CBC for permission to write this book based on my reporting and experiences while I worked as a foreign correspondent in the Middle East. It could not have happened without their blessings, and for that I am indebted to them.

Many thanks also to The Canadian Press for allowing me to draw on my reportage during my years with them.

My journey in the Middle East and beyond has always been about trying to understand, and I could not have done it alone. So my most sincere thanks go to all those who helped deepen my knowledge of a region that oftentimes defies comprehension.

I always marvelled that anyone would care to talk to us when in the midst of so much turmoil, and yet they did, the hundreds of people I met and interviewed over the years in Iraq, Jordan, Lebanon, Syria, Egypt, Saudi Arabia, Iran, Libya, Israel and the Palestinian Territories, the UAE, Qatar, Turkey, Afghanistan, Pakistan, and beyond. They often spoke courageously to me at great risk to themselves, so that I, and so many others, could comprehend. Thank you.

I could not have even begun understanding had it not been for the assistance and insights of colleagues and friends like Reem Kubba and Sadeq al Tai, Ahmad, "Waseem," "Jumana," and "Ammar" in Baghdad; Oraib al Rantawi and Ahmad Tayyoun and his wife, Areej, in Amman; Mazen Chouaib in Beirut and Ottawa; Samer Shalabi, Helen Hanna, and Nasser Atta in Ramallah and Jerusalem; Osama Fargly in Cairo; Lina Sinjab and many others in Syria; Ahmad Syed in Kandahar; and Kasem Durgham, Patricia Bou Nassif, and Habib Nehmeh in Beirut.

Special thanks to the cherished friends I found in Leena Saidi and Rana Nasser, and, of course, Zouheir Bizri and his wife, Rana, in Beirut. Weeda Hamza and Hussein Alameh in Beirut deserve special mention. Each in their own way taught me the nuances of Lebanese and Arab history and culture, while supporting me during the worst of times. Their patience and empathy carried me through five difficult years in Lebanon. That will never be forgotten.

At the CBC, many thanks are due to Jennifer McGuire, Jonathan Whitten, and Mark Harrison (and Jamie Purdon and Jack Nagler before them) for supporting not only my decision to write this book, but my work in general. Special thanks to Mark Harrison for also volunteering to take the time to read the manuscript, and to provide valuable feedback and insight.

Brien Christie, our long-time foreign editor, deserves unreserved thanks and admiration. For all my time in the Mideast—from the early days in Iraq right up to those incredible days in Tahrir—he was my lifeline, a comforting and curious voice over the telephone and later in person. He always asked the right questions, always pushed me to dig deeper, to "peel back the onion," as he often said. He also always reminded me that in a sea of negativity and turmoil there was always a glimmer of hope.

I was a distant and—at first—a reluctant member of the CBC family. Over the years I learned to appreciate the voices over the telephone and later got to know them in person. This space gives me a rare opportunity to thank the cameramen, editors, writers, producers, and assignment editors who helped me do my job— there are far too many to name individually, but they know who they are. I will single out Neil Macdonald, who was the first to suggest the insane idea of moving to the Middle East back when I was an ordinary political reporter in Ottawa. He then talked me into joining the CBC and introduced me to Tony Burman, who saw some potential and hired me. The staff of the London bureau deserve a big thank you, because from the start they adopted me as an itinerant daughter and always took care of me. Jim Hoffman, Margaret Evans, Stephanie Jenzer, Corinne Seminoff, Sat Nandlall, and Glen Kugelstadt shared many of my Mideast experiences and ably taught me so much, becoming friends in the process. They and many other colleagues, too numerous to count, shared their expertise and lent their friendships, unafraid to embrace a new, inexperienced colleague when it was so much easier not to.

Many, many thanks go to my friends and colleagues at The Canadian Press, also too numerous to mention by name, who taught me the value of teamwork and the importance of loyalty. Much gratitude to my many mentors on Parliament Hill and at the University of Manitoba (especially Dr. Robert O'Kell) and Carleton University for their encouragement and support.

This book would never have materialized had it not been for the idea initially planted by Eric Morrison, encouraged by Patrick Graham, then suggested (via her son Chris) by Dawne Kepron of Penguin, who eventually introduced me to Penguin editorial director Diane Turbide. Diane helped shape it from start to finish, patiently prodding me the entire way, and I owe her admiration and gratitude. My thanks also to editors Jonathan Webb and Alexander Shultz for their input, to Janice Weaver for copy editing, and Tara Tovell for fact-checking—and to Sandra Tooze and the rest of the Penguin team for helping get this book to the printers despite the time constraints and challenges. A big thanks also to Rihab al-Jawhari and Maria al-Masani for their valuable research, and to Sarah Hunter and Jet Belgraver for their photography.

There were also friends and colleagues along the way who lent their expertise on various aspects of the mysteries of writing a book, including Mark Mackinnon, Michel Cormier, Annia Ciezadlo, and Carol Off. Their advice was valuable and much appreciated.

Over the years, I have been lucky to continue to have the support and love of those who, despite my itinerancy, mostly remained friends, among them (in alphabetical order) Ayeda Ayed, Sue Bailey, Jean-Francois Belanger, Jet Belgraver, Mike Boyar, Mark Dunn, Daphne Enns, Brian Kelcey, Chris Kepron, Gord McIntosh, Farah Mohamed, Judy Pike, Rob Santos, Claudie Senay, and Alex Stephens. They all contributed support, encouragement, or insight (or all three) as I wrote this book; some took the time to read parts of the manuscript and give excellent feedback. They all deserve my undying gratitude. I especially thank Ayeda for (among so many other things) reading through my version of our family history and correcting the mistakes.

Finally, I'd like to thank my entire family for enduring not only the writing of this book—and helping jog my memory of days gone by—but for being there all along and putting up with what I did for a living. I could write another book and still not do my parents justice. Of all people, they were the most knowledgeable and most understanding. And without them I would have learned nothing at all.

Toronto, February 2012

INDEX